Guide to the CONNECTICUT SHORE

by Doe Boyle

The Globe Pequot Press

Old Saybrook, Connecticut

Cover photo: Jack McConnell/McConnell McNamara
Cover design: Sarayln D'Amato

Library of Congress Cataloging-in-Publication Data

Boyle, Doe.
    Guide to the Connecticut shore/by Doe Boyle. —1st ed.
        p.   cm.
    Includes index.
    ISBN 0-7627-0180-3
    1. Connecticut—Guidebooks.   2. Long Island Sound (N.Y. and Conn.)—Guidebooks. I. Title.
F92.3.B695   1999
917.4604'43—dc21   98-48022
                                                            CIP

Manufactured in the United States of America
First Edition/First Printing

Dedication

In loving memory of my father, Gerard Bertram McDonald
(1911–1997)

*As usual I finish the day before the sea, sumptuous this evening
beneath the moon, which writes Arab symbols with phosphorescent
streaks on the slow swells. There is no end to the sky and the
waters. How well they accompany sadness!*

—Albert Camus

The Connecticut Shore

Rhode Island

New York

Hartford

Pawcatuck
Stonington
Mystic
Noank
Groton
Waterford
East Lyme
New London
Niantic
Old Lyme
Old Saybrook
Westbrook
Clinton
Madison
Guilford
Branford
East Haven
West Haven
New Haven
Milford
Stratford
Bridgeport
Fairfield
Westport
Norwalk
Darien
Stamford
Greenwich

N E S W

Contents

Help Us Keep This Guide Up to Date

Every effort has been made by the author and editors to make this guide as accurate and useful as possible. However, many things can change after a guide is published—establishments close, phone numbers change, hiking trails are rerouted, facilities come under new management, etc.

We would love to hear from you concerning your experiences with this guide and how you feel it could be made better and be kept up to date. While we may not be able to respond to all comments and suggestions, we'll take them to heart and we'll also make certain to share them with the author. Please send your comments and suggestions to the following address:

The Globe Pequot Press
Reader Response/Editorial Department
P.O. Box 833
Old Saybrook, CT 06475

Or you may e-mail us at:

editorial@globe-pequot.com

Thanks for your input, and happy travels!

Acknowledgments

A simple travel guide crammed with as many details as sense and space will allow would not ordinarily be a work with unusual emotional importance. Whatever the depth of an author's affection for the places listed, the writing of their general descriptions and their hours and fees and phones does not typically tax the soul. Not so with this guide. Written in the months following the death of my beloved father, it tested my endurance time and time again as a million other memories vied for my attention and energy. If not for the love and support of my family, friends, and professional associates, I could not have completed the task. Now that I am finished and the enormous manuscript that eventually emerged has been pared to a reasonable weight, my patient editors would faint if I were to list the names of all the hundreds of guardian angels who offered their compassion and strength in a thousand different ways. I can only say that I give thanks every day that the darkest tunnels of my life have been lit by the candles of so many loving friends.

Buoyed by the comfort of my relatives, what seemed like all of the new and old friends I have ever had, every member of the SCBWI critique group led by the ever-positive Kay Kudlinski, and a special group of fellow master teaching artists of the Connecticut Commission on the Arts, I finally managed to pull from the well the restorative waters of writing. With the help of countless curators, docents, chambers of commerce, librarians, park rangers, publicity directors, and the staffs of the Connecticut Department of Environmental Protection, the UConn Connecticut Sea Grant program, and the Tourism Division of the Connecticut Department of Economic Development, this book was born.

In the process, I had some extra-special assistance I must acknowledge, with everlasting gratitude. Thanks are owed to: Nancy Wallace for the healing space of her window on the sea and for her gentle guidance to the hidden places in my heart as well as the best places to visit in Branford; Lorraine Jay for her confidence that the words would flow when I was ready and for her tender respect for the need to grieve—every bereaved soul should be blessed with a friend who loves a good cry; Beth Rowland for her incredible generosity of spirit, her sensitive insight, and also for her top-notch tour of Noank and environs; Loretta Krupinski, wise survivor who shared her ten-minute principle and her belief that challenge gives us strength; Lisa Silberstein and Michael Barrios for excellent hugs, real listening, and superior love and care for my children; Barbara Evans for her enduring vigil of faith and friendships throughout these painful months; Gillian Bowley for the inspiring example of her dazzling self and the sweetest of treasured gifts at a point I had neared exhaustion; Laura Strom, gifted Globe Pequot Press executive editor and special friend, for respectfully treading the waters with me and throwing out life ring after life ring as I rode the waves of grief; Mike Urban, editor-in-chief at Globe Pequot, for extraordinary patience and good cheer when he had every right to rip up my contract and write me off; Paula Brisco and Don Graydon for the skillful and sensitive editing of the huge tome I spilled on their desks; and, last and most of all, Tom Boyle and all of my precious daughters, whose unconditional love sustains me, whose admiration and devotion astounds me, and whose affection and companionship are my greatest joys.

Introduction

I was born by the sea, and I have noticed that all great events of my life have taken place by the sea.

—Isadora Duncan

Among my earliest memories are many closely linked to the sea—in particular, the pretty expanse of Long Island Sound just steps from the wide front porch of my grandparents' cottage in Fairfield County. I remember salt-stiffened hair and shell-stubbed toes, sandy bathing suits and outdoor showers, green wicker rockers and moonlit bonfires, Coca-Cola straight up from frosty sea-green bottles and pretzel rods taken outside to savor while nestled in the cool sand underneath the cottage itself. The rhythms of the tides and the winds predicted the movement of our days, and the sounds and aromas of the sea and the sand and the salt marshes aroused our appetites and our imaginations and finally, over time, our passion for life near the shore. A connection with the sea is not one easily denied or forgotten—perhaps then, if evolutionists are correct about humankind's origins in the seas, it is no surprise to learn that most of the world's population is crowded at the shores of nearly every continent. A love for the sea is in the blood, and there is no forsaking it.

The Connecticut shore is a unique and busy place—a far cry from isolation and wilderness but no less beautiful in parts than the edges of Maine or Cape Cod or Maryland. Long Island Sound is a mere 110 miles long, but the meanderings of its margins into coves and inlets results in a Connecticut coastline triple the length of the estuary. Its shape, its unusual east-west orientation, and its shallowness—an average of 65 feet in the center—contribute to the relatively gentle nature of its waters and thus its extreme popularity as a recreational resource. Sheltered from the high waves and winds of the ocean, it attracts an enormous fleet of pleasure boats, and the Connecticut shoreline is peppered with marinas, boatyards, launch ramps, sportfishing centers, ferry docks, and other sites specifically dedicated to marine recreation.

A mixture of salt water from the Atlantic and fresh water from the Housatonic, Thames, and Connecticut Rivers, the Sound is also a unique and fragile habitat. Its temperate waters and its barrier beaches, dunes, salt marshes, and tidal pools teem with life, collectively creating a diverse and valuable ecosystem that warrants protection. Programs and organizations such as the Long Island Sound Study, Connecticut Sea Grant, Save the Sound, and the Connecticut Department of Environmental Protection have ensured that the ecosystem is as well protected as possible from catastrophic misuse or overuse. Measures taken to preserve the habitat for its wild denizens also protect it for the continued success of its commercial fishing fleet and shellfish farmers and for the millions who merely swim and play at the beaches.

Tourism at the shore accounts for a significant portion of the state's economy, so the Connecticut coast is jam-packed with establishments that serve the visiting public. Connecticut's ancient history as a place of human habitation has left plenty of time for the development of parks, nature centers, amusement areas, boardwalks, campgrounds, museums, outdoor recreation sites, and other attractions catering to the pleasures of day-trippers and long-term vacationers alike. On the Connecticut shore, no shortage exists of hotels, motels, inns, and cottage rentals. Eateries ranging from ramshackle seafood shacks and charming tearooms to glamorous waterfront inns and urban rooftop restaurants keep the touring crowd well fed, and transportation systems of all kinds help keep the traffic moving (usually).

Guide to the Connecticut Shore will lead you to the best places to visit, to eat, and to stay at the northern fringe of Long Island Sound. I have spent the better part of a lifetime wandering the shoreline towns and cities, and this guide reveals the gems I have discovered. The crowded nature of this stretch of coastline prevents the inclusion of *every* minor attraction, performing arts venue, eatery and hotel, and so on, but the best are here and the rest you'll uncover as you explore. Don't be reluctant to wander further afield than the towns and cities covered in this book. If space had allowed, I would also have included information on towns located as little as ten miles from the sand. The towns along the Connecticut River, for instance, are also closely linked to the Sound and the maritime history of Connecticut, and the town of Ledyard, once a barely known rural community north of Groton and Stonington, is one of the most talked-about and visited tourist destinations in the Northeast. Its incredible Foxwoods casino and its fabulous new Mashantucket Pequot Museum and Research Center on the Mashantucket Reservation are bringing in tourists by the busload and ferry-load. Revenues from the casino in Ledyard and the Mohegan Sun casino just a bit farther inland in Montville have led to the development and improvement of all kinds of tourist-oriented facilities from highways to hotels at many points along the eastern shore.

Heavily urbanized and industrialized in some parts and still pristinely serene and rural in other parts, the Connecticut shore includes world-famous universities and state-of-the-art museums as well as fishing villages and lighthouses. You might tour a microbrewery that lies only yards from oyster beds and salt marshes, or go parasailing over a beautiful bay that has a nuclear power plant right at waterside. The fascinating inconsistencies you will encounter along the Connecticut seaside add to its vitality in all seasons. Put a good map on the car seat along with this guide, and enjoy the adventure of exploring both city hotspots and country niches. May the salt breezes draw you seaward, and the sounds of the waves and the gulls help you navigate.

Using This Book

This book includes twenty-six chapters devoted to the state's shoreline cities, towns, and villages. In order geographically from west to east, each chapter includes entries on major as well as little-known attractions and sidebars on everything from local lore to annual events. Each entry includes basic information such as addresses, telephone numbers, Web sites, admission fees, and hours, plus a review of what you might expect to see or experience at each site or event.

Following this detailed information are suggestions for places to eat and places to stay. Information on public launch sites for cartop or trailered boats is also listed after the main attractions entries. Ideas for obtaining further information are added last.

The Connecticut shore is one of the most densely populated sections of the entire Eastern seaboard, and Long Island Sound attracts more recreational boaters than any other body of water in North America. Space restraints prevented the author from compiling a comprehensive list of *all* charters, *all* seafood shacks, and so on. The selection was based on personal visits, recommendations, amenities, and services. For more information on topics of special interest to you, consider contacting the following agencies or consulting the following specialty publications:

Connecticut Department of Economic Development, Tourism Division 865 Brook Street, Rocky Hill CT 06067

(800–CT–BOUND or 860–258–4355). Ask for a free copy of the current *Connecticut Vacation Guide* or ask for information on specific areas or sites along the coast.

Connecticut Department of Environmental Protection, 79 Elm Street, Hartford CT 06106 (860–424–3200). Ask for a free copy of their guide to state parks and forests, the *Connecticut Angler's Guide,* or the *Connecticut Boater's Guide,* or ask for a list of other publications that may be useful to shoreline travelers. Call the DEP Fisheries Division (860–424–3474) for information on obtaining freshwater fishing licenses.

Embassy's *Complete Boating Guide and Chartbook to Long Island Sound,* published by Embassy Marine Publishing. Comprehensive listing of marinas, boat repair yards, and so on, with navigational directions and charts.

Rates

In the sections in each chapter that list *Places to Eat* and *Places to Stay,* dollar signs provide a sense of the price range at those establishments. For meals, the prices are per individual dinner entrees; for lodging, the rates are for a double room, European plan (no meals), unless otherwise noted. Keep in mind that meal prices generally do not change seasonally, but that lunch may be less expensive than dinner. Lodging rates usually *are* seasonal, with higher rates prevailing during the warm months or on and near major holidays. In Connecticut's coastal towns, the mild weather of spring and the foliage of fall can stretch the in-season from late April through Columbus Day, but rates are usually at their peak from mid-June through Labor Day. You may discover that weekend rates are higher in resort and top tourist destinations like Mystic and lower in cities where hotels usually cater to business travelers on weekdays. In any case, be sure to inquire about special packages and discounts.

Rates for Lodging		Rates for Restaurants	
$	up to $50	$	most entrees under $10
$$	$51 to $75	$$	most $10 to $15
$$$	$76 to $99	$$$	most $15 to $20
$$$$	$100 and up	$$$$	most over $20

If you would like to arrange lodging in an inn or bed-and-breakfast, call well in advance of your visit; relative to the total number of lodgings on the Connecticut shore, these types of hostelries are the rarest—and often the most popular. Be sure to ask about the number and size of the beds in each guest room; one double or queen-size bed is the norm. Roll-away cots and cribs (usually $10 to $15 extra) can be added to some inn or B&B rooms, but not all rooms are large enough to accommodate families. Some inns and B&BS do not, in fact, cater to children and may indeed turn families away in deference to an older or "romantic getaway" clientele. Others are small enough to welcome families one at a time and offer special amenities for their needs. These differences are not necessarily noted in this book, so be sure to inquire.

A Word to the Wise

While the hours and prices listed in this book were confirmed at press time, I recommend that you call ahead to obtain current information before traveling. Exhibits and facilities change—even locations shift, and unfortunately, some places close down altogether. Restaurants and lodgings are especially changeable, and beaches and parks are subject to the vagaries of the weather, pollution, funding, and other variables. Disappointment may be avoided by a simple phone call to each destination.

Safety Concerns

Each year on the Connecticut shore, local police and rescue squads as well as the Coast Guard and marine police respond to thousands of accidents and other emergencies. To ensure a safe and enjoyable exploration of the coast, in or out of the water, consider the following safety precautions:

• Take note of the marine forecast and pay close attention to the tides if you are boating, sailboarding, fishing, swimming, or even wading.
• Stay on trails and paths; stay off protected dunes and bluffs or cliffs (which may be unstable).
• Avoid unsafe activity on seawalls and jetties. Running and consumption of alcohol are the two top factors in accidents on such structures.
• Wear rubber-soled shoes or avoid wet, algae-covered rocks. As you explore, be aware of broken glass and shells, discarded fishhooks, and medical waste.

- Use life preservers when boating; all vessels must have one approved personal flotation device for each person aboard.
- Avoid the use of alcohol when boating. Alcohol is a significant factor in a large percentage of boating and drowning accidents.
- Wear sunscreen, a hat, and light-colored, long-sleeved coverings when in the sun for any period of time over fifteen minutes. Carry drinking water when hiking, biking, or boating. Use tick and insect repellent as necessary.
- Educate yourself about the symptoms of heatstroke and hypothermia. Both can develop rapidly and have potentially fatal or permanent consequences.
- Swim with extra care at unguarded beaches, avoid swimming alone, and stay away from culverts, storm drains, and other waste or water pipes.
- Riptides are strong but narrow bands of current flowing seaward. If you are caught in one, do not struggle toward the shore against the current. Swim *parallel* to the shore until you escape the narrow outflowing current.
- Pay attention to signage at shellfishing beds. Do not take shellfish from waters posted as unsafe.

The prices and rates listed in this guidebook were confirmed at press time. We recommend, however, that you call establishments before traveling to obtain current information.

Greenwich

Plush with green lawns and magnificent hardwood shade trees in the summertime, Greenwich presents one of the state's prettiest pictures of life along the Connecticut shore. One of the largest groups of islands on the Sound hugs closely to the town's coves and harbors, and sailboats and yachts cruising offshore add to the aura of wealth and leisure that is firmly anchored to this affluent suburb.

Located just 29 miles from Times Square with views of the New York City skyline from its beaches, Greenwich provides posh shelter for about 60,000 residents who take great pride in the rarefied ambiance of their coastal enclave. The varied interests and talents of its residents have enriched the prestigious town, which offers travelers perhaps the best dining options in the state, the most upscale shopping, and a state-of-the art natural history and art museum.

Best-known for these features and for its multimillion-dollar homes, Greenwich also offers much more than glitz. Adding to Greenwich's riches are its most beautiful assets: More than 1,500 acres of the town's 50 square miles are rolling hills and verdant woodlands preserved as parkland. In addition, counting the perimeters of its islands, the quirky twists of its coves, and the banks of its estuaries, the town claims 32 miles of shoreline. Although nearly all the coastal area and much of the woods is privately owned or reserved for the use of Greenwich residents, there is still much that visitors can share in this top-drawer community.

Originally home to the Siwanoy and Petuquapaen, subgroups of the Algonkians who came to the shore 10,000 years ago, Greenwich was "discovered" by Adriaen Block shortly after the turn of the seventeenth century. Although Dutch settlers were in the area because of its proximity to their colony at New Netherlands, the English seem to have laid out the first permanent European settlement in Greenwich in 1640.

The details of the next few years are not entirely clear, but before long, tensions arising from the culture clash between the natives and the newcomers resulted in the 1644 massacre of the entire native population by the combined forces of the Dutch and the English. A famed account of the incident recorded that "Nor was any outcry whatsoever heard"—a fact hardly surprising considering that every single native man, woman, and child was brutally murdered by the self-declared "saints" of the colony, who believed they were fulfilling the Lord's wish that the saints inhabit His Earth. Conveniently, this concept also left the English plenty of room to build their houses and lay out their extensive fields of potatoes and grain.

By the nineteenth century, grist mills, a woolen mill, a stone quarry, and other industries established Greenwich as a place where jobs could be found, and along with the railroad and trolleys came immigrant workers and their families. Soon Greenwich farms were subdivided into residential lots for a great variety of homeowners both rich and working class. Come to Greenwich to discover how its history has affected the growth of the town into one of the world's wealthiest suburbs—and one of the most sparkling communities on the Sound.

The Best of Greenwich

Downtown Greenwich

The commercial district of Greenwich centers largely on Greenwich Avenue between Railroad Avenue and Route 1, which in Greenwich is called West or East Putnam Avenue. Scores of shops ranging from the hometown jeweler to upscale chain stores to one-of-a-kind custom shops offering everything from couture evening-wear to hand-painted tiles and French textiles can keep even the most energetic shopper busy for days on end. Restaurants of every description ensure that no one faints from hunger in the process of consuming other goods. It is not unfair to exaggerate that there is not a bargain in sight anywhere, unless you consider 50 percent off a $600 duvet (or dress or place setting) a good deal. Come with a large credit line on your plastic or wads of cash in your pocket, or just window-shop until you drop. Parking is mostly metered street parking; bring plenty of quarters.

Exit 3 off I-95 (Arch Street) to Greenwich Avenue and surrounding streets.

Bruce Museum

One of the most sophisticated and definitively state-of-the-art museums in the region, the magnificently expanded and renovated Bruce houses more than 25,000 objects in three major categories: fine and decorative arts, cultural history, and environmental sciences. Pre-Columbian and Native American artifacts, nineteenth-century American paintings, prints, and sculpture, costumes, pottery, and

The Beaches of Greenwich

Unfortunately for the traveler, summertime shore access in Green-wich is closely guarded by the town ordinance against nonresident use of the beaches and shoreline parks. Stewardship of the land is most often stated as the reason for this protective restriction. Town officials fear that an open-door policy would bring in so many visitors that parking facilities would be inadequate and the ecology of the fragile shorelands would be compromised by overuse. They are probably cor-rect.

Travelers who want to enjoy the beauty of the Greenwich shore have to be content with waiting for the off-season to walk the trails at Greenwich Point Park (also known as Tod's Point). As is true through-out Connecticut, the edges of Long Island Sound are legally open to all people at any time as long as they remain seaward of the high-tide mark. The problem with exercising that right is finding access through private or even town-owned "public" property.

Generally, with Greenwich's town-owned properties, limited parking areas cause the restriction on out-of-town vehicles, although visitors with resident friends or relations can pay a $6 daily fee to go to the beaches with these pals. Creative travelers can circumvent the restric-tions by parking elsewhere in town and walking or bicycling into the beach parks. Even this loophole, however, is useful only at Greenwich Point.

If you can plan ahead, the beach at 149-acre Greenwich Point is a true gem. Officially, nonresidents can come only in the off-season from December 1 to April 1, but no attendant is here to check passes from shortly after Labor Day until shortly before Memorial Day. You may also find that walkers and bicyclists can enter without restriction even in summer. Connected to the mainland by a tiny strip of land called Tod's Driftway, Greenwich Point features ponds, a seaside gar-den, an arboretum, a swimming beach, and jogging paths. Anglers may enjoy the opportunity to fish here; bring green crabs along for bait and you'll be sure to go home with a bucketful of blackfish. Inquire too about shellfishing possibilities; delicious blue mussels hang out on the rocks here. Also a great bird-watching spot, the park offers beautiful views of the Sound, of course, and of Long Island's Oyster Bay area, only 7 miles across the water. On very clear days, views of New York City are possible. The park is generally open from dawn to sunset. Take Sound Beach Avenue south 1.8 miles from Route 1 to a right turn on Shore Road, and onward to the park entrance.

more are on view in the art galleries. The environmental science galleries focus on the past 500 years of local New England history and ecology, taking visitors from ancient to modern times with an environmental perspective. Within this wing, the cavelike minerals gallery preserves an extensive collection of ores, crystals, precious stones, and fluorescent minerals. An archaeological dig tucked in the Formation of Our Coast exhibit depicts the discovery of the Manakaway site on Greenwich Point and includes Native American artifacts unearthed during the excavation. Interactive exhibits allow visitors to experience the evolution and ecology of Long Island Sound. The environmental galleries also include a precisely re-created cross-section of a tidal marsh ecosystem, a 2,400-gallon marine touch tank, an Ecological Awareness gallery focusing on tree and water communities, and an interactive wall narrating the natural and human history of Long Island Sound.

The Bruce also offers a museum store and a continuous schedule of festivals, workshops, concerts, and lectures. Visitors with an interest in functional and decorative arts will appreciate the outdoor crafts festival in mid- to late May and the fine arts festival on Columbus Day weekend; both juried shows feature entertainment, activities for children, and free admission to the museum.

Adjacent to the museum is the Bruce Memorial Park and Playground, a great place to rest, run, or picnic. A playground and picnic tables make the park perfect for families, and views of a real tidal marsh and Long Island Sound provide the backdrop. Look for the herons that inhabit the area—they are beautiful. Leave your car at the museum or park on Museum Drive; the parking lot directly in front of the playground is reserved for Greenwich residents.

1 Museum Drive; follow signs from I-95 exit 3 or the Merritt exit 31 (203–869–0376). The museum is open year-round, Tuesday through Saturday 10:00 A.M. to 5:00 P.M.; Sunday 2:00 to 5:00 P.M. Closed Monday and major holidays. $3.50 adults, $2.50 seniors and children 5 through 12; under 5 are free. Free to all on Tuesday.

Audubon Center

Up in Greenwich's northern reaches, 8 miles of trails lead through 280 acres of open woodlands, meadows, ponds, and streams. The Center's Interpretive Building houses an exhibit gallery, a demonstration beehive, a bird observation window, a model backyard wildlife habitat, and the excellent Environmental Book and Gift Shop. Trail guides, maps, plant and bird lists, and a history of the area can be obtained at the shop with the price of admission.

Several loop trail options are available to fit schedules and hiking abilities. None of the trails are strenuous, but some are moderately demanding. The Discovery Trail leads past a great little pond replete in summer with bullfrogs, duckweed, and dragonflies. Stay on the trail long enough and you'll be able to walk right across the top of a very pretty waterfall at the edge of Mead Lake. The landscape here is extraordinarily restful. The trees are among the most awesome specimens in Connecticut. Return in the fall for the spectacular foliage and for the annual migration of hawks that can be observed from the Quaker Ridge Hawk Watch Site.

The Audubon Center offers outdoor walks, camps, and naturalist workshops for children, adults, and environmental science teachers. Every Saturday at 10:00 A.M. from June through August and on Sundays at 2:00 P.M. during the remainder of the year, you can join a guided trail walk at no extra charge, either here on this property or on other nearby Connecticut Audubon Society preserves. The Center asks that you leave pets at home and that you do not picnic on the grounds.

613 Riversville Road at the corner of John Street (Merritt Parkway exit 28) (203-869-5272). Open year-round Tuesday through Sunday 9:00 A.M. to 5:00 P.M. Closed Monday and major holidays. $3 adults, $1.50 seniors and children; members of National Audubon Society are free.

Fairchild Connecticut Wildflower Garden

Audubon Center visitors are also welcome to walk the trails of a second parcel just a mile away on North Porchuck Road. This 127-acre tract offers 8 miles of trails. Established by Benjamin Fairchild in the early 1900s as an example of naturalistic landscaping, the garden is lovely in the spring. On the two properties, more than 900 species of ferns and flowering plants, thirty-five species of mammals, and 160 species of birds have been recorded. The Fairchild Garden has no facilities for visitors except for a portable toilet, so bring drinking water if you intend to explore the whole area on a hot day. The mostly flat and easy trails lead through meadow, marsh, and woodlands. Picnicking and pets are prohibited.

North Porchuck Road. Open daily year-round from dawn to dusk. Free.

Bush-Holley House

If pre-Revolutionary American history or colonial architecture and lifestyles interest you, don't leave Greenwich until you've visited here. A National Historic Landmark and the home of the Greenwich Historical

Connecticut Impressionist Art Trail

The Connecticut Tourism Council has developed a guide to eleven
Connecticut museums that boast collections of American Impressionism artworks. The sites listed below are covered in this book. Check
the index for references to each site. For a free brochure on the entire
trail, call the Tourist Information Center (800–866–7925) or send a
business-size SASE to CIAT, P.O. Box 793, Old Lyme CT 06371.

Bruce Museum (Greenwich)
Bush-Holley House Museum (Greenwich)
Yale University Art Gallery (New Haven)
Florence Griswold Museum (Old Lyme)
Lyman Allyn Art Museum (New London)

Society, the 1732 structure is a classic central-chimney saltbox located
beside Strickland Brook in the historic district of Cos Cob. Multiple fireplaces, paneled walls, ornate woodwork, and a double veranda are
among its architectural features, but it is most famous as one of the
sites on the Connecticut Impressionist Art Trail.

Formerly the home of wealthy farmer and mill owner David Bush
and later a boardinghouse operated by the Holley family, the house
was once alive with the activities and creativities of one of the first
American Impressionist art colonies. Painters and sculptors, including Childe Hassam, J. Alden Weir, and Elmer Livingston MacRae,
worked here during the period from 1890 to 1925. A collection of
their works as well as an authentic re-creation of MacRae's studio are
on display here, along with a fine collection of household implements, tools, furniture, and textiles.

In the Impressionist works, visitors can see the artists' visions of
the warehouses, the tidal grist mill, the packet boats and fishing fleet,
and the shipyard that once were at the hub of the Lower Landing at
the small harbor of Cos Cob.

The latest addition to the Bush-Holley House is a visitor center that
traces the development of the Landing, the history of the original
families of Greenwich and the Bush-Holley house itself, as well as the
origins of the evolutionary art form that captured nuances of form,
light, and shadow and eventually became known as American
Impressionism. The visitor center is outstanding among its peers on
the historic home circuit; don't miss its wonderful light- and sound-
enhanced tableaus, its interactive displays, and its special changing

exhibitions emphasizing local history, art, and architectural and cultural movements.

Call to inquire about the ever-increasing activities of this museum. Children, for instance, may attend History Week annually during the month of July to learn about eighteenth-century colonial life and history. The annual Art-in-the-Yard Festival invites artists to paint on the grounds; visitors may reserve a spot in the yard for setting up their own easels, or they may watch as the empty canvases of other guests fill with their artistic impressions. At Christmastime (call for schedule) the house is decorated in a Victorian theme for candlelight tours.

39 Strickland Road in the Cos Cob section of town (203–869–6899). Open for tours from February through December; Tuesday to Friday, noon to 4:00 P.M.; Sunday 1:00 to 4:00 P.M. $4 adults, $3 students 12 and over, under 12 are free.

Putnam Cottage

Built circa 1692, the cottage was formerly known as Knapp Tavern and was used during the Revolution as a meeting place of military leaders, including former resident General Israel Putnam, second in command to George Washington during the war. Fully restored to appear as it might have in 1700, its unusual fish-scale shingles, its fieldstone fireplaces, and a pretty eighteenth-century herb garden are among its special features. The cottage's collection includes Israel Putnam's desk, Bible, glasses, the mirror through which he supposedly saw the British coming, and the uniform he wore during the war.

The grounds and outbuildings surrounding the house are as beautifully restored as the house itself. Come on the last Sunday in February to see the reenactment of Putnam's famous ride down the steep stone cliff to the east of the cottage. Redcoats and rebels in full regalia skirmish on the grounds as the actor portraying ol' Put re-creates the general's memorable flourish to Revolutionary history.

243 East Putnam Avenue, which is Route 1 (203–869–9697). Tours on Wednesday, Friday, and Sunday from 1:00 to 4:00 P.M. or by appointment. Admission $2; children under 12 are free.

Mianus River Park

This 215-acre park straddles the Greenwich-Stamford line and includes woodlands on both banks of the usually peaceful Mianus River. Several loop trails through highlands and gorge areas as well as lowland paths along the river help the visitor to customize a route that fits a day-tripping schedule. Rough maps are posted at some of the trail junctions, but you can also pick up a brochure with a complete map at the Greenwich Department of Parks and Recreation in the Greenwich Town Hall at 101 Field Point Road. Bring good hiking shoes because the terrain here varies from smooth dirt or gravel forest roads to knotty footpaths.

Mountain bikers are welcome on the wider gravel paths—as long as they obey the signs restricting them from the riverside trails. All of the trails are well maintained, but other than a picnic area, no facilities are offered for visitors so be sure to pack in your own water. Freshwater anglers may want to bring some tackle. A trout management area is located on the Merriebrook Lane side of the river near Dumpling Pond, where a colonial housewife once quickly dispatched a fresh batch of dumplings rather than feed them to the British who had invaded her space one eighteenth-century afternoon. The policy here is catch-and-release, and a license is needed for anyone over the age of 15.

From Route 1, take Valley Road north to Cognewaugh Road to the parking area at the main entrance between Hooker and Shannon Lanes. To reach the second entrance, take Valley Road across the Stamford line to Mianus Road, then take Westover Road north to Merriebrook Lane; a parking lot is at a dirt turnoff near the one-lane bridge over the Mianus River, marked by a small green sign. For information, call Eileen Schmeidel at the Greenwich Department of Parks and Trees (203–622–7824) or the Stamford Department of Parks and Natural Resources (203–977–4641). The park is open year-round at no charge from dawn to dusk.

For the Horsey Set

World-class polo players from around the globe hit the field at the **Greenwich Polo Club** for high-goal, high-excitement matches that thrill young, old, and in-between onlookers. Matches begin at 3:00 P.M. on selected Sundays in June, July, and September at the club at Conyers Farm on North Street. The public is welcome at a charge of $20 per vehicle, payable at the gates, which open at 1:00 P.M. Special events and displays are planned each week. Call (203) 661–1952 for match dates and to get details about such events as wildlife demonstrations, hat contests, clowns, fashion shows, and more. The people-watching is great, too, as members arrive for the charity luncheons they enjoy before match time. You can bring your own hamperful of picnic goodies or purchase lunch at the concession/bar. Halftime brings divot-stomping fun—come and join the festivities!

Places to Eat in Greenwich

Dome 253 Greenwich Avenue (203–661–3443). In a stunning landmark setting with a fabulous brick vaulted dome ceiling, this chic establishment is full of surprises, from its electric decor to its architectural presentations of an astonishing array of multicultural cuisines. Marvelous vegetarian choices, inventively garnished seafood, enormous steaks and chops. Open daily for lunch 11:30 A.M. to 3:00 P.M. and dinner 5:30 to 10:00 P.M. $$$–$$$$

The Ivy 554 Old Post Road No. 3 (203–661–3200). Rated excellent by the *New York Times* and tagged as one of the top six new restaurants in the state, this is a winner if you don't mind the din of the crowd that gathers for some of the finest food in the region. Outstanding breads, excellent salads, and extravagantly prepared entrees of seafood, poultry, and chops ensure that the Ivy is a favorite of sophisticated diners. Ask for the upstairs dining room if you'd like a quieter ambiance, and be sure to linger over the superb desserts. Open for lunch 11:30 A.M. to 2:30 P.M. and dinner 5:30 to 10:00 P.M. $$$–$$$$

Rebeccas 265 Glenville Road (203–532–9270). An excellent choice for aficionados of exquisitely presented food, this simply decorated establishment lets the food take center stage. Again, the noise of well-pleased diners may be off-putting to seekers of serenity, but the soul-satisfying cuisine may relieve any tension caused by the clamor. A top entree choice is the pan-seared duck in a raspberry sauce with a deliciously crispy potato pancake; among the desserts is the incomparable pear tart with house-made toasted almond ice cream. Open for lunch on Sunday and from Tuesday through Friday and for dinner Tuesday through Saturday from 5:30 P.M. $$$–$$$$

Restaurant Thomas Henkelmann at Homestead Inn 420 Field Point Road (203–869–7500). A diamond among Greenwich gems, the Homestead beats all in terms of the elegant ambiance of this rambling country inn. In keeping with its aura of refinement is its outstanding menu of French or French-influenced cuisine. Try the excellent seafood prepared to perfection or the unimprovable rack of lamb. The presentations of other supremely satisfying dishes make a meal here an extraordinary visual and gustatory treat. Dessert is a must. Open for lunch, noon to 2:30 P.M. Monday through Friday; Sunday brunch 11:30 A.M. to 2:30 P.M.; dinner daily from 6:00 P.M. $$$$

Sage 363 Greenwich Avenue (203–622–5138). Informal but charming for both adult diners and families, this friendly place offers the perfect setting for a delicious meal after (or during) a day of shopping or touring. Seafood lovers might try the excellent mussels or the perfectly done roast cod with a pesto crust. Carnivores will be pleased with unusual options like venison. Desserts are sublime; pray that the citrus cheesecake is on the menu when you visit. Open for lunch Monday through Friday from 11:30 A.M. to 2:30 P.M.; dinner Tuesday through Sunday from 6:00 P.M.; Sunday brunch from 9:00 A.M. to 2:30 P.M. $$$–$$$$

Thataway Cafe 409 Greenwich Avenue (203–662–0947). Perfect for taking a break during the formidable task of bargain-hunting in Greenwich, this informal eatery right at the heart of downtown offers burgers, sandwiches, grilled chicken, great salads, fresh-daily housemade soups, and great kids' choices like grilled cheese and chicken fingers. Cheerful service; great outdoor seating in season. Open daily for lunch and dinner. $–$$

Places to Stay in Greenwich

Greenwich Harbour Inn 500 Steamboat Road (203–661–9800). 96 rooms at water's edge, 2 suites, some balconies. Atlantis Restaurant, coffee shop, lounge. Boaters welcome at 530-foot dock. Senior citizen rates. Taxi and airport shuttle service. Open year-round. $$$–$$$$

Stanton House Inn 76 Maple Avenue (203–869–2110). 24 rooms in turn-of-the-twentieth-century mansion. Most rooms have private baths, some have fireplaces. A small suite has a claw-foot tub and a kitchenette. Outdoor pool, beach passes. Complimentary continental breakfast in mansion's dining room. Open year-round. $$$–$$$$

Homestead Inn 420 Field Point Road (203–869–7500). Handsome 1799 colonial bed and breakfast in beautiful Belle Haven neighborhood. In main inn and newer addition, 23 antiques-filled suites and double rooms, wicker on wraparound porches, flower beds along flagstone pathways, canopied beds, impeccable service, and complimentary continental breakfast in the award-winning restaurant. Open year-round. $$$–$$$$.

Harbor House Inn 165 Shore Road, Old Greenwich (203–637–0145). 23 rooms in Victorian mansion near the beaches. Seventeen private baths; others share baths. Coffeemakers and refrigerators in each room. Bicycles available. $$–$$$$

Cos Cob Inn 50 River Road (203–661–5845). 14 beautiful rooms, all with private bath, air conditioning, refrigerators, data ports, cable TV, voice mail, and much more in gracious Victorian home in historic Cos Cob. Queen-size bed in most rooms. One suite with Jacuzzi. High ceilings, lovely millwork, hand-painted floors, charming nautical touches. Complimentary continental breakfast, passes to beach. $$–$$$$

Hyatt Regency Greenwich 1800 East Putnam Avenue, Old Greenwich (203–637–1234 or 800–233–1234). Luxurious, tasteful, convenient to everything. Rooms and suites, restaurants, health club, indoor pool. Sunday brunch. $$$$

Howard Johnson Hotel 1114 Boston Post Road, in the Riverside section (203–637–3691). Standard best-bet for families. Restaurant, swimming pool. Continental breakfast. Kids stay free. $$$

For Further Information

State Welcome Center Merritt Parkway northbound between exits 27 and 28 in Greenwich (203–531–1902). Open daily from Memorial Day through Labor Day, 8:00 A.M. to 6:00 P.M. Restrooms, maps, brochures to attractions.

Metro North Commuter Rail Service (800–638–7646). Trains from New York to New Haven offering stations in Riverside, Old Greenwich, Cos Cob, Greenwich. Call for schedule of service.

Greenwich Commuter Connection (800–982–8420). Shuttle buses between the Greenwich train station and other parts of downtown and elsewhere in Greenwich. Runs every half-hour Monday through Friday during morning and evening rush hours. $1 fare.

 **Stamford**

Downtown Stamford is a busy hive of activity in all seasons, well established as a business center with a special focus on the financial and banking industries. Nearly thirty major corporations call Stamford home, and scores of restaurants, clubs, hotels, and a large mall cater to the needs of their employees. The museums, galleries, and performing arts centers sprinkled among the downtown office towers make the city's center sparkle with a vitality that draws travelers.

Down at the harbor, local sailboats are side by side with yachts from all parts of the globe, and the docks are awash with landlubbers as well as with old tars. Visitors should be sure to tarry awhile near the marinas and beaches or hop aboard a schooner to explore the water up close.

The hills north of downtown lure day-trippers to the hidden pleasures of Stamford's surprising woodlands. Settled in 1641 by families from Wethersfield, the city's farms and fields were once used as an important training ground for soldiers in the Revolutionary War. Today the training grounds and even the farms and fields themselves are overgrown with second-growth forest, cleared only to make room for the suburban homes that characterize the northern section of the city. A unique nature center and a noteworthy arboretum highlight the physical beauty that still remains in this otherwise urban metropolis. From nature center to nightclub, the city offers entertainment for all tastes and ages. Come to Stamford to discover the snappiest side of the Connecticut shore.

The Best of Stamford

Stamford Historical Society Museum

Visitors who would like to begin a city tour with a good sense of place may enjoy a walk through this historical museum. Chockful of furniture, toys, quilts, tools, and other permanent and changing exhibitions on local history, it highlights Stamford's famed citizens and inventions. Discover some interesting surprises on a visit here. Seasonal tours of the late seventeenth-century Hoyt-Barnum House (713 Bedford Street), once a blacksmith's residence, can also be arranged through the museum. Return in late summer for the beautiful Antique Quilt Show and Sale, which draws crowds every year.

1508 High Ridge Road (203–329–1183). Open year-round Tuesday through Saturday, noon to 4:00 P.M.; closed major holidays. Adults $2, children $1.

Whitney Museum of American Art at Champion

Visitors who'd like to jump right into the sense of modern big-city sophistication may want to start a tour of Stamford in the Whitney Museum. Fully funded by the Champion International Corporation, the Connecticut branch of the museum of the same name in New York City offers five or six changing exhibitions of American art each year. Its small size makes the Whitney wonderful for day-trippers hoping to visit a variety of sites in a short period of time, but its intriguing contemporary exhibitions have a big impact. Twentieth-century works form the backbone of the museum's permanent collection, and a full calendar of events contributes to the stimulating ambiance. Musical and dance performances, puppetry shows, short-story readings, art and craft workshops, and family tours are among the programs you may discover on a visit here.

Gallery tours are offered on Tuesday, Thursday, and Saturday at 12:30 P.M. In summer, an annual series of outdoor events (usually held at noon on each Wednesday in July on the Champion Plaza) adds to the creative, multicultural, and expansive spirit evident in every corner of this space. Bright and airy, the Whitney has an approachable nature for art lovers of all ages.

One Champion Plaza, at Atlantic Street and Tresser Boulevard (203–358–7630). Open year-round Tuesday through Saturday, 11:00 A.M. to 5:00 P.M. Admission is free, as are the gallery talks and parking in the Champion parking garage on Tresser Boulevard. Ages 5 and older.

Stamford Center for The Arts

The Rich Forum and the Palace Theatre have added more than a dash of panache to Stamford's cultural attractions. From September through June, the Truglia Theater and the Leonhardt Theater in the Rich Forum's lush performing arts complex host highly acclaimed theater productions featuring top performers from around the world. Many of these full-stage performances from Broadway and London are suitable for the whole family.

Designed in the 1920s by noted theater architect Thomas Lamb, the Palace Theatre is an architectural masterpiece with incredible acoustics. With seats for nearly 1,600 patrons, it provides a permanent home to the Stamford Symphony Orchestra, the Connecticut Grand Opera, the New England Lyric Operetta Company, the Stamford City Ballet, and the Connecticut Ballet. Here you might also enjoy short-run performances of music, dance, drama, and other entertainment such as circuses and musical comedies.

In all three theaters ticket prices vary widely, but costs can be cut by taking advantage of group rates, matinee performances, or seats in the upper tiers. Two children's productions are also usually offered at the Palace in the summer. Two performances, at 11:00 A.M. and 1:00 P.M., are given each Wednesday as long as the show runs.

Ticket prices start at $6.

The Rich Forum (307 Atlantic Street) and the Palace Theatre (61 Atlantic Street). Call the box office (203–325–4466) or the information number (203–358–2305).

Stamford Theater Works and the Purple Cow Children's Theatre

On the campus of Sacred Heart Academy, a private girls' high school run by the Sisters of Mercy, is a surprisingly contemporary Equity theater that stages not-for-profit and not-always-mainstream professional productions often lauded as innovative, experimental, and thought-provoking. New and socially relevant works are of primary interest, and a great variety of readings and youth theater programs are staged throughout the year.

The Purple Cow productions are wonderful performances for children ages 3 to 8. Affordable and fun, they are offered twice daily on selected late spring and early summer Saturdays. Reservations are required. Typical fare includes puppet shows, magic, fairy tales, and dramatizations of popular children's literature.

200 Strawberry Hill Avenue (203–359–4414). September through May on Tuesday through Saturday evenings and Saturday and Sunday matinees; tickets $17 to $25. Summer theater (May through July) for children.

Sterling Farms Theatre Complex

The two venues at this community golf/tennis/theater complex spe-

The Champion Greenhouse

High above the city streets on an upper terrace of the Champion paper company's headquarters building at One Champion Plaza at the corner of Tresser Boulevard and Atlantic Street, this urban garden focuses attention on Champion's commercial and environmental interests in studying and preserving forests. Changing exhibitions are great for nature enthusiasts who care about trees and their importance to our economy and health. A December exhibit explained the myths and folklore of Christmas trees and flowers; other seasonal exhibits are equally creative and educational. Stop here for a great view of the city and the Sound. Open year-round during business hours during the week, and on Saturdays from 11:00 A.M. to 5:00 P.M. Admission is free. (Call 203–358–6688.)

cialize in theater for the light-hearted, both at the Ethel Kweskin Theater, housed in a 250-year-old barn that apparently has its own ghost, and across the street at the cabaret-style proscenium stage of the Dressing Room Theatre.

The resident Curtain Call company does four comedy productions each year as well as musicals and dramas. The Players are the pros who produce the bulk of the terrific performances offered at off-Broadway bargain prices; the Half-Pint Players are an energetic company of talented teens with star qualities. Call for a calendar of this year's line-up and inquire as to the appropriateness of individual shows if you'd like to take the whole family. Many are just right for young audiences. Curtain Call also offers theater workshops for adults and youth.

1349 Newfield Avenue: information (203–329–8207) and box office (203–461–6358). Ticket prices are generally $20 adult, $10 students (all performances) and seniors (Sunday only). Open year-round.

Cove Island Park

Located on a small island at the eastern end of the city, Cove Island Park is an eighty-three-acre recreation area right on the Sound. The largest and most popular public park in the city, it is open year-round and offers a wide beach with a pavilion and concessions, picnic areas, horseshoe pits, tennis courts, basketball courts, a softball field, a playground, a path for walkers and joggers, a path for in-line skaters and bicyclists, a marina (no dedicated transient slips), and the Terry Connors Ice Rink.

Try to stay for one of the guided beach walks sponsored by Save the Sound, Inc., throughout the summer. Midday and evening walks offer a study of the animals and plants of the shoreline. Ask the park attendant for a schedule. If you can't take time for a walk, at least hop aboard the free tram that operates in season primarily to transport visitors and their beach gear to the sunny or shady spot of their choice. The tram can also be enjoyed just for the pleasure of touring the park; the full circuit takes about 15 minutes, depending on how many stops it makes. It takes visitors around the perimeter, pausing at picnic areas, the swimming beach and concession, the playground, and so on.

Cove Island Park is at the base of Weed Avenue at the corner of Cove Road. Open year-round from 5:30 A.M. to one hour after sunset. From Memorial Day weekend through Labor Day, nonresidents arriving by car can use the park Monday through Friday only, with the purchase of a one-day pass for $15 per vehicle; call the Stamford

*Parks and Recreation Department (203–977–4692 or 203–977–4641)
or the Terry Connors Ice Rink (203–977–4514) for details. Even in season, nonresident walkers or bikers can enter the park at any time at no
charge. Off-season, nonresident vehicles can enter daily and at no
charge.*

Stamford Museum and Nature Center

Up in the northern reaches of Stamford, this 118-acre park has features like no other nature center in the state. Heckscher Farm is a
working nineteenth-century New England farm re-creation that
includes a 1750 colonial barn on the rocky pastureland typical of the
self-sufficient farms of yesteryear. A garden sowed with heirloom
seeds yields a bountiful autumn harvest, and domesticated fowl and
livestock inhabit the enclosure. In the midst of the farm is a country
store and a tiny gem of an exhibit dedicated to eighteenth- and nineteenth-century farm life and tools.

In addition to 3 miles of woodland trails and a pond habitat with
an adjacent picnic area, a 300-foot streamside boardwalk with signs
in braille and sensory stations complements the Overbrook Natural
Science Center, which houses aquatic tanks that simulate natural
habitats of the small creatures that inhabit the woodland and its
streams. Outside the Center a beautiful brick walkway edges a garden
of native plants and flowers.

On the hillside nearest the parking area is the Stamford Museum,
which houses seven galleries of changing fine art exhibitions,
Americana, nature exhibits, and a permanent exhibit on Native
American life and history. Several beautiful dioramas are the highlight of the Native American gallery, which also includes fine artifacts
from four major North American Indian groups. The main building of
the museum also is home to a planetarium and an observatory, with
the largest telescope west of the Mississippi.

The museum has converted a wooded one-acre site to one of the
most unusual playgrounds anywhere. Up to 200 children at a time
can gain a bird's-eye or chipmunk's view of the surrounding habitat.
An 8-foot-high hollow log leading to a hollow branch opens onto a
sandpit where kids can dig for fossil replicas. A 6-foot-high hollow
stump features copies of insect galleries and honeycombs. Two 7-
foot-wide hawks' nests in which to climb, a large-scale chipmunk bur-
row in which to rest, and a 30-foot-long otters' slide on which, of
course, to slide are among other features. A large water environment
area includes play possibilities such as dam construction or boat rac-

Antiques and Home Wreckers

You might not plan an all-day excursion to **United House Wrecking** (203–348–5371), but it's such an unusual store that it appears frequently on lists of Stamford attractions. Five acres of land and more than 30,000 square feet of retail space make this a browser's dream-come-true. Architectural salvage—doors, stained glass windows, mantels, claw-foot bathtubs, and chandeliers—is the main seduction for renovators, but the fun only begins there. Furniture of every sort, pottery, jewelry, toys, china, books, and more fill the space to the brim. Mixed with this "normal" stuff is an ever-changing array of truly odd, absolutely fantastical, and downright weird stuff—gargoyles, dentists' chairs, a barbershop pole, jukeboxes, circus posters, subway straphangers—in short, everything under the sun including bells, whistles, and the kitchen sink.

Lovers of the sea and shore may have a special interest in the huge selection of nautical items. Ship wheels, sextants, telescopes, compasses, life rings, clocks, flags, and bridge glasses are just some of the treasures that may add to your collection for boat or home. The store is located at 535 Hope Street. It's open year-round Monday through Saturday from 9:30 A.M. to 5:30 P.M. and Sunday from noon to 5:00 P.M.

Shoppers who can't rest until they locate the perfect one-of-a-kind item might want to peruse the goods at the 22,000-square-foot **Antique and Artisan Center** (203–327–6022), a treasure chest of antiques and fine decorative arts. American furniture forms the core of the enormous selection offered by eighty-five dealers, but artworks, small collectibles, and functional and decorative pieces of every period, style, and description are among the thousands of collector-quality antiques available here. Located at 69 Jefferson Street (near Canal Street), it's open year-round Monday through Saturday from 10:30 A.M. to 5:30 P.M. and Sunday from noon to 5:00 P.M.

ing. A treehouse, a beaver lodge replica, and a rope spider's web complete the scene.

Among all of these areas the Stamford Museum and Nature Center staff conducts educational programs, workshops, lectures, festivals, and summer camps. Summer folk concerts, an autumn Harvest Fair, an Astronomy Day, and other annual events such as maple sugaring, ice harvesting, and apple cidering are all on the Nature Center's calendar.

39 Scofieldtown Road (203–322–1646). Open year-round Monday through Saturday and most holidays, 9:00 A.M. to 5:00 P.M.; Sunday 1:00 to 5:00 P.M. *Closed Thanksgiving, Christmas, New Year's Day. Planetarium shows on Sunday at 3:00 P.M.; adults $2 and children $1, plus museum entrance fee. Observatory hours, weather permitting, on Friday from 8:00 to 10:00 P.M.; adults $3, children $2 (no additional entrance fee). The fee to enter the Museum and Nature Center is adults $5, seniors and children 5 to 13 $4; no charge for children under 5.*

Bartlett Arboretum

Just down the road from the Stamford Nature Center is this ever-beautiful sanctuary of oak, maple, and hickory trees interspersed with evergreens, ash, birch, beech, and yellow poplar. Perennial borders, a conifer garden, a native wildflower garden, and a nut tree collection are among the major areas of this gorgeous property.

Five miles of trails lead visitors through the gardens, woodlands, and wetlands. A reflecting pond at the end of the Woodland Trail is a perfect destination for hikers, as is the boardwalk that leads through the Swamp Trail. The self-guided Ecology Trail combines portions of each of these trails. Pick up a guide book at the Visitor Center so you can enjoy the descriptions of twenty-seven marked stations.

If you are visiting with a child under twelve, borrow a nature activity backpack from the Visitor Center Shop before you set out on a walk. Crayons, scratch pads, a magnifying glass, and a wonderful set of cards with games, questions, activity suggestions, and educational information enhance the experience for the whole family.

Take a stroll through the greenhouse for a look at the incredible cacti and succulents among the other tropical and temperate plants in the collection. Lastly, stop by the Visitor Center, which houses an excellent shop of garden and nature books and gifts, an exhibition hall, an ecology research laboratory, and a lending library of horticultural materials.

The Arboretum offers a variety of classes and tours for adults throughout the year. Guided walks for the whole family are free to the public, as are Sunday concerts held approximately every other week in the month of July and August (call for schedule).

151 Brookdale Road (203–322–6971). Open daily year-round, 8:30 A.M. to sunset. The Visitor Center is open Monday through Friday, 8:30 A.M. to 4:00 P.M., except on holidays. The greenhouse is open every morning from about 9:30 to 11:00. Free.

Places to Eat in Stamford

Kathleen's 25 Bank Street (203–323–7785). A downtown favorite for delicious pastas, excellent seafood, and eclectic international specialties with Thai, Cajun, Italian, and French influences. Great appetizers and half-portions, innovative salads, and many choices for both vegetarians and red-meat lovers. Colorful sidewalk cafe in the warm season. Open year-round for lunch Monday through Friday 11:30 A.M. to 3:00 P.M. and dinner Monday through Saturday from 5:30 P.M. $$$–$$$$

Kujaku 84 West Park Place (203–357–0281). Step into Japan at this award-winning restaurant serving excellent sushi, tempura, and hibachi-style steaks and seafood. Traditional Japanese cuisine in private tatami rooms. Lovely ambiance and service. Open year-round for lunch Monday through Friday 11:30 A.M. to 2:30 P.M. and dinner Monday through Sunday from 5:30 P.M. $$$

Il Falco Ristorante 59 Broad Street (203–327–0002). A winner for authentic Northern Italian cuisine in a gracious and relaxing atmosphere. Soft peach walls are the perfect complement to regional specialties, homemade pastas, and seasonal game dishes. Excellent wine list. Open year-round for lunch Monday through Thursday 11:30 A.M. to 2:30 P.M. and dinner Monday through Saturday from 5:30 P.M. $$$

Amadeus 201 Summer Street (203–348–7775). This elegant

Eco-Cruises

If the smell of the salt breeze draws you away from downtown toward the water, try to catch a ride on the 80-foot *SoundWaters,* a replica of a three-masted sharpie schooner that offers two-hour public eco-cruises from June 1 to mid-October. Led by trained naturalists, the cruises focus on the ecology, history, culture, and future of Long Island Sound. You can help raise the sails, haul in the trawl net filled with creatures from the deep, and examine the catch in four stations that focus on aspects of marine ecology.

While the mission of this floating classroom is to reach as many schoolchildren and educators as possible, public sails are offered three to five times monthly during the warm season. Special sails, such as a Fireworks Sail in early July, are also open to the public. Call for a schedule or to reserve a place on these very popular cruises. All of the sails require advance reservation and payment.

You'll find *SoundWaters* at 4 Brewers Yacht Haven Marina, at the foot of Washington Boulevard (203–323–1978). Send e-mail to swaters@ clubnetct.com. Their Web site is at http://www.soundwaters.org. Adults $25, children 12 and under $15; sunset and fireworks cruises $30 per person. Private charters are also available.

restaurant is a stand-out, offering old-world charm as well as excellent continental cuisine with a Viennese flair. Come here for a special celebration and enjoy the pampering, the tinkle of the piano keys, and the exquisite taste sensations. Be sure to have dessert. Open year-round for lunch Monday through Thursday 11:30 A.M. to 2:30 P.M. and dinner daily (except Sundays in the summer) from 5:30 P.M. $$$$

La Hacienda 222 Summer Street (203–324–0577). An outstanding reputation for authentic Mexican cuisine is what keeps the crowds coming to this well-reviewed, award-winning eatery. Old-style traditional favorites, Tex-Mex American-style variations, and creatively contemporary twists on chicken, seafood, veal, chicken, and beef dishes are among the delights here. Open daily for lunch 11:00 A.M. to 2:30 P.M. and dinner from 4:45 P.M. $$$$

Crab Shell 46 Southfield Avenue at Stamford Landing (203–967–7229). Some say this is the best seafood restaurant on the Connecticut coast, with a huge menu of fish and shellfish including excellent lobster, calamari, tuna, swordfish, oysters, and much more. Nautical decor with beautiful saltwater tanks filled with tropical and exotic fish. Overlooking the marinas and water, with seasonal dockside bar. Open daily for lunch and dinner. $$$

Dagwood's 2326 Summer Street (203–323–5844). New York–style deli serving a wide variety of overstuffed specialty and traditional sandwiches, plus other deli favorites. Open Monday through Saturday 6:00 A.M. to 9:00 P.M. $

Places to Stay in Stamford

Budget Host Hospitality Inn 19 Clark's Hill Avenue (203–327–4300). 86 units, restaurant. $$

Stamford Suites 720 Bedford Street (203–359–7300). 42 suites with fully equipped galley kitchen, separate sleeping and living areas, and full bath with whirlpool tub. Walking distance to downtown. Lower weekend rates. $$$

Stamford Marriott 2 Stamford Forum (203–357–9555). 507 units, revolving rooftop restaurant, coffee shop, health club, sauna, jogging track, indoor and outdoor pools, sports court, game room. Lower weekend rates. $$$

Holiday Inn Select 700 Main Street (203–358–8400). 375 rooms, restaurant, health club, sauna, indoor pool. $$$

Sheraton Stamford Hotel One First Stamford Place (203–967–2222). 480 rooms, including 23 suites with one or two bedrooms. Full-service restaurant, tavern, health club, heated

Shore Points
Something Fishy

One of Stamford's most notable architectural attractions is its fish-shaped First Presbyterian Church, designed by Wallace K. Harrison, at 1101 Bedford Street (203–324–9522). Along with its unique silhouette, the church features the state's largest mechanical-action pipe organ and beautiful stained glass windows by artist Gabriel Loire of France. Visitors are welcome year-round, from 9:00 A.M. to 5:00 P.M. on Monday through Friday from September through June and from 9:00 A.M. to 3:00 P.M. on the same days in July and August. A donation is suggested. Free band and carillon concerts are offered on the green during July on Thursdays at 7:00 P.M.

indoor pool, Jacuzzi, tennis, room service. Shuttle to downtown. Lower weekend rates. $$$–$$$$

Tara Stamford Hotel 2701 Summer Street (203–359–1300). 356 units, each with hair dryer, coffeemaker, clothes iron, and other extras. Atrium restaurant, health club, heated indoor pool, sauna, massage therapy, rooftop tennis courts. Shuttle to downtown, on-site airline ticket office. Lower weekend rates. $$$–$$$$

Public Boat Launch

West Beach Park Shippan Avenue (203–977–4641 or 977–4692). Public ramp for boats up to 30 feet; $25 daily nonresident fee or $200 nonresident seasonal pass. Residents pay $5 daily or $35 seasonally. Restrooms, showers, phone, concession at nearby beach park.

For Further Information

Stamford Chamber of Commerce One Landmark Square, Stamford CT 06901 (203–359–4761). Call for its excellent seasonal calendars of events and its exceptional *Stamford Cultural Guide.*

Fairfield County Weekly For listings of evening entertainment in Stamford nightclubs and dance clubs, look for a free copy of the *Fairfield County Weekly*, a tabloid newspaper distributed at libraries, restaurants, drugstores, and so on.

Stamford Department of Parks and Natural Resources 888 Washington Boulevard (203–977–4641). Call for information on beaches and on nonresident use of boat launches, tennis courts, and public parks.

⛵ Darien

Hugging the shore less than an hour from New York City, the lovely residential town of Darien is safe harbor to throngs of commuters who emerge from the Metro-North trains or exit the highways at the end of the workday. These citizens are not typical worker bees, though: Darien ranks second among the state's 169 towns in per capita income and fourth in cost of homes. Throughout the town, tree-lined avenues flank manicured lawns and beautiful homes, and on the busiest corridors independent shops both classically traditional and trendily contemporary cater to the needs of affluent families. Excellent schools, a noteworthy library, and reliable services give Darien's townsfolk plenty of incentive to stay—but few good reasons for tourists to visit.

The larger cities of Stamford to the west and Norwalk to the east certainly offer more attractions, lodgings and restaurants, and a busier calendar of cultural arts and entertainments. In smaller, quieter Darien, the most exciting event to happen in a *long* time was the British raid on the parish church in 1781 when the Reverend Moses Mather and the men and boys of his congregation were carried right out of the services and carted off to prison for their Patriot sympathies. Since that date the most notable incidents in town have been its separation in 1820 from the town of Stamford and its rapid growth as a suburb after the completion of the New Haven Railroad in 1848.

For many visitors, the most attractive of Darien's features are its miles of Long Island Sound waterfront, fringed with beaches and yacht clubs. Unfortunately, Darien's snug relationship with the sea is closely guarded, and out-of-towners must either pay the hefty daily beach parking fee exacted from Memorial Day through Labor Day or wait until early fall to enjoy Indian summer on the Darien shore. Most day-trippers probably decide to head to less costly beaches in other towns. Stamford's Cove Island Park, Norwalk's Calf Pasture, or Westport's Sherwood Island, for instance, are a fraction of the price even at the height of summer.

Still, a day at the shore in Darien can be a rewarding experience for the traveler willing to patch together a crazy quilt of small adventures chosen from among the following options.

The Best of Darien

Bates-Scofield Homestead

Leave behind Darien's upscale hustle and bustle of the nearly twenty-first century and step into the eighteenth-century world of John Bates and his family. Situated on a small parcel of land not far from the Darien YWCA and the Goodwives Shopping Plaza, this beautifully restored saltbox structure is the only publicly held example of a pre-Revolutionary farmhouse in the area.

Built in 1736 and once recorded as a "mansion house," perhaps because of its somewhat atypical second story, the homestead in fact exemplifies the simplicity of a modest mid-eighteenth-century Connecticut residence. Around its huge central chimney the house features a formal parlor, a dining room, a kitchen, a buttery, and a number of bedchambers. An interesting variety of domestic tools, porcelain, toys, and wonderful Connecticut-made colonial furnishings are displayed throughout the house. Notable among these are a locally made tall-case clock, a late seventeenth-century painted blanket chest, and a charming baby tender. Although none of the authentic period furnishings are original to the house, they were all collected by the Society in duplication of the Bates family inventory.

Outdoors to the rear of the house, a garden is planted with heirloom specimens of culinary, medicinal, and fragrant herbs of colonial Connecticut and antique roses found in eighteenth-century Connecticut gardens. Guided tours of the house are given by docents, but visitors are welcome in the gardens at any time year-round. Visitors may also peruse the library and the small gallery of changing exhibitions in the modern wing of the Darien Historical Society, headquartered at this site.

45 Old Kings Highway North (203–655–9233). Open year-round. Research library and Darien Historical Society offices open Tuesday, Wednesday, and Friday from 9:00 A.M. to 1:00 P.M. and Thursday from 9:00 A.M. to 4:00 P.M. Tours of the house are usually Thursday and Sunday from 2:00 to 4:00 P.M. Admission is $2.50 per person for house tours; no charge to use library or view gardens.

Darien Ice Rink

At this privately owned indoor rink, the ice is ready all year long for skaters from beginner to expert. Lessons, a summer hockey camp, and frequent hockey games, skating competitions, and other exhibitions are also on the calendar. One of the most popular events is the five-day Open Figure Skating Competition in April, which brings in as many as 900 skaters from all over the United States. Visitors are welcome to watch these beautiful and exciting performances. Call for this year's dates and admission fees.

The ice rink is on Old Kings Highway North (203–655–8251). The rink is open for public skating every Sunday from 1:00 to 2:50 P.M., plus Monday through Thursday from noon to 1:45. Adults $5, seniors $3, children under 12 $4; skate rental $2.

Darien Town Beaches

The public beaches of Darien are not actually reserved only for the town's own citizens—it's the *parking* at the beaches that is restricted in the warm months. Residents of Darien purchase seasonal parking

Downtown Darien and Noroton Heights

Shoppers who would rather browse through one-of-a-kind boutiques than shuffle past the same old stuff at chain stores will probably enjoy a spree in Darien's charming owner-operated emporiums. Whether you're caught up in the holiday frenzy or merely window-shopping in any season, try the commercial areas of **Darien center**, which lies mostly along the Boston Post Road, its side streets, and part of Tokeneke Road, and **Noroton Heights,** a neighborhood sandwiched between the railroad, West Avenue, and I–95. Seek and ye shall find unique gift shops, galleries, antiques stores, and cafes.

Among the specialty shops are **The Complete Kitchen** (865 Post Road; 203–655–4055) for top-quality kitchenware plus a great lineup of cooking classes for children and adults; **Amanda & . . .** (977 Post Road; 203–655–7662) for pottery, pillows, teddy bears, jewelry, and women's and children's apparel; **The Compleat Angler** (987 Post Road; 203–655–9400) for fine tackle and other fishing gear and gifts, plus excellent advice, instruction, and leads for guided fishing trips; **Appalachian House** (1010 Post Road; 203–655–7885) for American handcrafts; **Rose D'Or** (1076 Post Road; 203–655–4668) for antiques, estate jewelry, and decorative arts; **Entre Nous** (23 Tokeneke Road; 203–655–0641) for Simon Pearce glassware, Italian ceramics, small furnishings, and unique clothing; and **Outlandish** (2 Tokeneke Road; 203–656–3811) for affordable, festive tableware and linens. If you need a quick pick-me-up, go directly to the **Alpine Bakery and Pastry Shop** (7 Tokeneke Road; 203–656–2777), **The Good Food Store** (863 Post Road; 203–655–7355), or **Uncle's Deli** (1041 Post Road; 203–655–9701).

passes for the privilege of enjoying their beaches in the most convenient way—that is, to be able to park in the lot near the concessions and restrooms, and so on. Nonresident visitors day-tripping in Darien by means of automobile are welcome to walk onto or bicycle into public beach areas if they can find legal parking for their vehicles elsewhere in town, or they may also pay a daily per-vehicle fee of $30 to enjoy the convenience of parking in the lot at Peartree Point Beach from Memorial Day to Labor Day or at Weed Beach from April through September. Outside of those dates, the parking restriction lifts, as does the daily fee.

If you'd like to explore the beaches, leave I–95 at exit 10 and take Noroton Avenue south to the Boston Post Road (Route 1). To reach Weed Beach, take a right onto the Post Road and a left onto Nearwater Lane, and go south toward the Sound, where the road bears to the right and leads directly to the beach. Lying just south of pretty Holly Pond, which separates Darien and Stamford, Weed Beach faces southwestwardly, across the cove from Stamford's Cove Island Park. The beach is wide and clean and has beautiful views of the Sound and Long Island. To reach Peartree Point Beach, take a left from Noroton Avenue onto the Post Road and a right onto Ring's End Road, cross the small bridge over Gorham Pond and Noroton Bay to Goodwives River Road, and bear right nearly immediately on Peartree Point Road to the beach. This smaller beach faces more directly south and has views of the boat clubs and marinas. A sandy picnic grove has grills and tables, and a simple picnic shelter perched on a small bluff provides a nice place to watch the marine traffic.

Weed Beach (foot of Nearwater Lane) and Peartree Point Beach (Peartree Point Road): Both beaches have picnic areas, restrooms, and concessions and assess $30 per-vehicle daily fee for nonresidents in season. For more information, call the Darien Parks and Recreation Department (203–656–7325).

Darien Arts Center

Founded in 1975, the Darien Arts Council, recently renamed the Darien Arts Center, followed in the hallowed footsteps of a group established in 1927 and named the Guild of Seven Arts. Today the Arts Center continues to provide an outlet for the dynamic energy of performing and visual artists engaged in a great variety of creative pursuits. Dance, theater, voice, and fine arts in many media are the main areas of focus, but surprising energies of all kinds manifest themselves here with regularity. The Center's 2,000-square-foot black-box

Weatherstone Studio is the usual site of three dramatic performances each year by the Darien Players; each of these runs two to three weeks and is appropriate for and affordable for (at $10–$15 per ticket) the whole family. The Darien Choraliers offer at least two annual concerts, and guest performances or cabaret productions round out the performing schedule.

An annual juried fine arts exhibition is held each June and is hung in the Weatherstone Studio when the flurry of local dance recitals subsides. Stop in at the Center (at the back of the Darien Town Hall) to view the current show. Call for dates and hours.

2 Renshaw Road (203–655–8683).

Gran Prix at Ox Ridge

On a sunny day in early June there can be no more beautiful outing in Darien than an afternoon at the annual **Ox Ridge Hunt Club's Charity Horse Show**. Celebrating nearly seventy years as Connecticut's oldest equestrian tradition, this seven-day event is recognized as one of the top five horse shows in the nation. In a classically country club setting at 512 Middlesex Road off Route 124 (Mansfield Avenue) north of Route 1, this exciting competition showcases the equestrian skills of more than 1,200 horses and riders, including the nation's top amateur and professional hunter/jumper riders from ages eight through adult.

Benefitting Darien's **Center for Hope** (1003 Post Road; 203–655–4693), a counseling center for children and families dealing with serious illness and bereavement, the Charity Show usually begins on Monday or Tuesday of the first full week in June and continues to the Grand Prix event the following Sunday. The Grand Prix is the United States Equestrian Team Regional Show Jumping Championship. Each day, from about 8:00 A.M. until late in the afternoon, the public is welcome to attend all of the equitation events as well as the other festivities of this benefit. Among these is an arts and crafts show featuring regional artisans and other vendors. A catered concession offers delicious lunches and suppers pleasing to all ages. Guests may also bring their own picnic hampers to enjoy in the stands or on the pretty lawns of this lovely club. Admission is $5 per vehicle Tuesday through Friday; $5 per adult and $3 per senior or child on Saturday; and $7 and $5 respectively for Sunday's $35,000 Grand Prix main event.

Ox Ridge (203–655–2559) also welcomes visitors to other horse shows throughout the season (typically June through September) and offers introductory horsemanship and riding lessons to the public.

Boat Excursions and Charters

Skinny Minni may be the name of the boat or the name of the man—the tip wasn't crystal clear, but the story is that Dan Wechsler (914-777-2812) offers guided fishing trips out of his slip on the Five Mile River. **Captain Ian Devlin** offers guided wade fishing trips from the Darien and Rowayton shore. Contact him at (203) 838-2912.

Places to Eat in Darien

Li's Brothers Inn of Darien 24-48 Old King's Highway, North, in the Goodwives Shopping Plaza (203-656-3550). Not a place to rest on a rave reputation as perhaps the best Asian restaurant in the state, Li's outdoes itself seven days a week with wonderful Hong Kong–style dim sum and authentic Hunan and Szechuan specialties. Open for lunch and dinner daily year-round, Li's is as wonderful for adult dining as it is welcoming to families. Relaxing, comfortable atmosphere and gracious service. $$-$$$

The Black Goose Grille 972 Post Road (203-655-7107). On the south side of the Post Road basically across from the train station, this restaurant features handsome oak paneling, tin ceilings, and black upholstered booths overhung with etched glass lamps—a lovely, smoke-free setting for casual dining on entrees of seafood, steak, chicken, and pasta and inventive appetizers and sandwiches. A pub room with a fireplace and magnificent bar originally from the Anheuser-Busch Brewery in St. Louis offers dining from the same menu. Smoking is permitted in the bar. Outside dining is possible on the patio tucked along the pretty alleyway that leads to the front door. Open daily year-round for lunch 11:45 A.M. to 2:30 P.M. and dinner from 5:30 P.M. $$-$$$

Dolcetti's 921 Post Road (203-656-2225). Bare wood floors, crisp white napery, and simple wooden furnishings add to the immaculate ambiance of this gracious restaurant known for its fine Italian cuisine as well as for its outstanding pizza. Adults as well as families will feel comfortable here, dining on reasonably priced antipasti, pasta dishes, seafood, veal, and chicken specialties, thin-crust pizza, crusty calzones, Italian sandwiches, and tempting desserts. Open for lunch Monday through Friday 11:30 A.M. to 2:30 P.M. and for dinner daily from 5:00 P.M. $$

Backstreet Restaurant 22 Center Street (203-655-9944). This small eatery is a favorite place for a casual dinner or lunch, especially in warm weather when you can enjoy its back patio. Sit under crisp green market umbrellas and choose from a menu of soups, sandwiches, salads, and appetizers, plus full entrees like steak, chicken, and pasta dishes. Cheerful service; affordable prices; reliably good food with a creative flair. $–$$

Post Corner Pizza 847 Post Road (203–655–7721). Well-recommended for families and casual dining, this local favorite is a sure thing for pizza and traditional Italian pasta, seafood, chicken, and veal specialties, plus salads, grinders and calzones. Open daily year-round for lunch and dinner from 11:00 A.M. to 11:00 P.M. $–$$

Uncle's Deli 1041 Post Road (203–655–9701). If you are here at the crack of dawn, this charming eatery in the heart of the shopping district and not far from the train station is the place to come for breakfast and coffee, or later, for lunch. Open year-round 6:00 A.M. to 5:00 P.M. daily. $

Place to Stay in Darien

Howard Johnson Lodge 150 Ledge Road, off I–95, exit 11 (203–655–3933). 72 units, outdoor pool, senior citizen rates. $$

For Further Information

Darien Chamber of Commerce 17 Old Kings Highway South (203–655–3600). Monday through Friday 9:00 A.M. to 1:00 P.M. Web site is http://www.darien.lib.ct.us.

Darien Parks and Recreation Department 2 Renshaw Road in Darien Town Hall (203–656–7325). Information on in-season nonresident use of town beaches and parks. Some Sound-related activities sponsored by the Rec Department may be open to nonresidents if space permits; among the possibilities are swimming, sailing, and sailboarding instruction. Open Monday through Friday 8:30 A.M. to 4:30 P.M.

State Welcome Center On I–95 between exits 11 and 13 northbound in the McDonald's Restaurant rest area (203–655–8289) with food court and restrooms open 24 hours daily. Tourism office open 9:00 A.M. to 6:00 P.M. daily from Memorial Day to Labor Day; 9:00 A.M. to 5:00 P.M. daily Labor Day to Memorial Day. Maps, brochures, and lodging and restaurant information.

Norwalk

Norwalk's interesting maritime history and attractive position on the Sound makes it one of Connecticut's most popular destinations for shoreline travelers. Long famed as a port and as one of the nation's largest producers of oysters, the city is experiencing a marvelous reawakening of its waterfront, a much-needed revitalization of a small city that began its nearly 350-year history in 1649. A decade or more in the remaking, the South Norwalk neighborhood is now especially redolent of salt air and fresh seafood, as manufacturing in the area has given way to a state-of-the-art aquarium, a new visitors' dock, scores of new restaurants, galleries, and shops, and a brand-new museum celebrating the city's history. Now the sounds of gulls and boat whistles and the rising of the Washington Street drawbridge compete with the happy sounds of the interactions of tourists, shoppers, and successful entrepreneurs who inhabit the busy streets of SoNo from morning to twilight and beyond.

Down in the quieter enclave of Rowayton near the Darien boundary at the Five Mile River, the sense of the sea is more apparent than in any other section of Norwalk. The quaintly twisting streets are lined with cottages, boatyards, and funky establishments that cater to an eclectic neighborhood of sailors, fishermen, artists, and weekenders from New York City. Just offshore are the sixteen Norwalk Islands, including Sheffield, Goose, and Chimon Islands, which provide habitat for colonial nesting waterbirds as well as migrating neotropical birds. Protected as units of the Stewart B. McKinney National Wildlife Refuge, they are now safe from developers who eyed the largest islands for their potential value as resort communities. Today Chimon Island is the most productive heron rookery in the state, supporting large populations of a dozen or more kinds of wading birds.

Explore the core and the corners of Norwalk, looking for the contemporary links to its history as a port. You'll have no trouble finding cruises and fishing charters, sailing lessons and regattas, oyster bars and boat shows. You name it—if it involves water, it's in Norwalk.

The Best of Norwalk

The Maritime Aquarium at Norwalk

The flagship, if you will, of the bustling SoNo neighborhood, this aquarium-cum-theater-cum maritime museum is a celebration of life near, on, and under the sea, particularly Long Island Sound. Located in a restored nineteenth-century foundry overlooking Norwalk Harbor, this major attraction includes twenty-two aquariums filled with nearly 150 species of marine life.

Visitors move from one marine habitat re-creation to another, beginning at the edge of the salt marsh and culminating at a 110,000-gallon tank with 9-foot sharks, stingrays, and other creatures of the open ocean. Harbor seals swim in an indoor/outdoor pool, and river otters tumble and slide in simulated woodlands habitat with underwater viewing windows. You can handle sea stars, horseshoe crabs, and other tidal pool inhabitants in the tidal touch tank. Interactive and video displays reveal the secrets of the fragile ecosystems of Long Island Sound and its estuaries.

In the maritime museum area, you can watch crafters build wooden boats in the centuries-old tradition of early New England boat builders. Changing exhibitions in the Aquarium may feature other creatures of the sea or birds of prey, perhaps. Even the Aquarium itself is changing, as construction proceeds on an Environmental Education Center, a cafeteria, and an expanded gift shop/bookstore. Before you go home, watch an IMAX film in the six-stories-high theater. Special events, lectures, educational camps, and workshops are commonplace at the Maritime Center; call to ask for a calendar of programs.

10 North Water Street (203–852–0700). Web site: www.maritimeaquarium.org. Open daily year-round, except on Thanksgiving and Christmas Day. Regular hours are 10:00 A.M. to 5:00 P.M.; from July 1 to Labor Day, hours are extended until 6:00 P.M. The IMAX theater runs on the hour from 11:00 A.M. to 3:00 or 4:00 P.M. and is also open for Friday and Saturday evening shows. Admission is charged to the Center alone, to the IMAX alone, or to both together. Adults are $7.75, $6.50, or $12, respectively. Seniors are $7, $5.50, or $10.50, and children 2 to 12 are $6.50, $4.75, or $9.50; under 2 are free. Parking is available at municipal lots adjacent to the facility at an additional cost.

The Norwalk Museum

The remarkably innovative Norwalk Museum seeks both to educate and entertain visitors by presenting the last hundred or so years of Norwalk history from a commercial and retail point of view. Located in the grandly restored 1912 former City Hall building just a block from the Maritime Aquarium, the museum focuses on the late nineteenth century and the first half of the twentieth. The Museum's centerpiece gallery, Merchants' Court, is created to bring to mind authentic businesses, industries, and artisans of earlier times. Celebrating the great number of goods invented or manufactured in Norwalk, it showcases dozens of products in their natural context and setting as merchandise. Each carefully researched storefront includes artfully arranged examples of items that added to the economy of the city while satisfying the needs of the populace.

Be sure to tarry a while in the museum shop, which offers merchandise manufactured, designed, or handcrafted locally. A second shop is a sort of year-round flea-market that will be a delight to unrepentant browsers. Rare book lovers may want to stop downstairs in the **Antiquarian Book Arcade** (203–853–6660) that shares the building with the Museum.

SoNo Historic District and SoNo Arts Celebration

The restored waterfront area called South Norwalk is listed on the National Register of Historic Places, and its comeback from decay is a tribute to the City of Norwalk. Centered on Washington, Water, and South Main Streets, SoNo is a picturesque neighborhood of boutiques, restaurants, art galleries, and other attractions. In addition to the Maritime Aquarium, you'll find the dock for the excursion boat *Island Girl,* the wonderful Norwalk Museum, and the **New England Brewing Company** (13 Marshall Street; 203–853–9110), which offers free thirty-minute tours of Connecticut's largest microbrewery. Lining the streets of SoNo are shops selling beads, dollhouses, hand-painted pottery, funky light fixtures, and everything else under the sun. t

If you like the arts, come to SoNo during the first full weekend in August for the three-day **SoNo Arts Celebration** held annually for more than twenty years (203–866–7916). Hundreds of juried fine artists exhibit their work in a sidewalk show spanning several blocks. Continual live-music performances, an antique auto parade, dance exhibitions, a silent film fest, and an extraordinary giant puppet parade are all part of the midsummer festivities. A children's area offers entertainment and hands-on projects specially designed for young artists.

North Main Street at the corner of Marshall (203–866–0202). Open daily year-round, except Thanksgiving and Christmas Day, from 10:00 A.M. to 5:00 P.M. Free. Ages 5 and older.

Lockwood-Mathews Mansion Museum

A National Historic Landmark, this lavish Victorian stone mansion is true extravagance. Originally built in 1864 as a summer home for Norwalk native Legrand Lockwood, Wall Street investment banker and railroad magnate, this remarkable four-story chateau redefines splendor and elegance as it displays the craftsmanship of the finest American and European artisans of the time. Incredibly fine inlaid woodwork, marble columns, frescoed walls, gold-leafed ceilings, crystal chandeliers, sweeping staircases, and decorative arts of all kinds are found throughout the fifty rooms that surround the mansion's magnificent skylit octagonal rotunda.

Hour-long guided tours of the mostly restored first and second floors are preceded by a short film describing the painstaking ongoing restoration. A Victorian gift shop and lovely grounds are also available for browsing and strolling. Annual events include a Victorian Ice Cream Social in early summer and a crafts fair in mid-July.

295 West Avenue, just a hair north of SoNo and I-95 (203–838–1434). Open February 1 to mid-December, Tuesday through Friday from 1:00 to 3:00 P.M. and Sunday from 1:00 to 4:00 P.M. Closed on major holidays. Last tour an hour prior to closing. Adults $5, seniors and students $3, children under 12 free.

Stew Leonard's Dairy Store

The original of the world's largest, most extravagant supermarkets is in Norwalk on Route 1, known here as Westport Avenue. Fresh baked goods, dairy products, fine seafood and meats, produce of every sort, cut flowers, and a huge hot and cold buffet of lunch and dinner foods are *not* the main attraction here, though.

We're sending you here for the rock 'n' roll dairy band, the strolling 6-foot cows who shake hands with awed toddlers, the guitar-and-banjo-strumming horse and dog in Civil War uniforms who croon toe-tapping tunes from velvet-draped stages overhead, the talking cow at the milk conveyor belt, the choir of singing lettuces and eggplants, and the barnyard animals in the mini-farm out front. If the crowds of folks who shop here don't slow you down, this amazing cast of characters will.

Aw, Shucks! Oysters!

The famed **Norwalk Oyster Festival** is held annually on the weekend after Labor Day. The huge waterfront festival celebrates Long Island Sound and its seafaring past, as well as the delicious Blue Point Eastern oysters that have made Norwalk's oystermen among the most successful farmers of the sea in history. Festival events include entertainment, an arts and crafts show, tall ship tours, an oyster shucking contest, and the typical foods and hoopla of summer festivals. Don't deny yourself the pleasure (203–838–9444).

100 Westport Avenue (203–847–7213). Open daily year-round from 7:00 A.M. to 11:00 P.M.

Island Girl Cruises to Sheffield Island

The clean and comfortable sixty-passenger, U.S. Coast Guard–approved *Island Girl* offers a thirty-minute cruise to the outermost of the Norwalk Islands, where one can disembark for an hour, an afternoon, or a whole day of beachcombing, bird-watching, sunbathing, picnicking, hiking, or touring the beautiful 1868 stone lighthouse.

The friendly and knowledgeable *Island Girl* crew and captain offer a lively narration on the trip to the island. Once on dry land out at the island, passengers are free to spend their time as they choose. Most folks take the fifteen- to twenty-minute tour of the ten-room lighthouse, of course. If you have time to spare, bring a picnic and spread a blanket under the oaks in the picnic grove for a leisurely lunch or brunch. No concessions are on the island, so bring your own snacks. Wear bathing suits and sunscreen so you can swim or comb the beach.

The sixty-acre island also includes the secluded **Stewart B. McKinney National Wildlife Refuge.** No trails are provided within its boundaries for humans, but you can encircle the refuge by simply walking the perimeter of the island. The last cruise departs the island at 3:00 P.M. on weekdays and 4:30 P.M. on weekends and holidays. The seating area on the *Island Girl* is covered to protect you from sun, wind, or inclement weather. Two bathrooms and a snack-and-drinks bar add to your comfort. The island is also open to private boaters. A dinghy service transports sailors from moorings to the island dock at a charge of $4.00 per adult on the boat.

The Island Girl *is at Hope Dock at the corner of Washington and*

Rowayton

One of Connecticut's most charming shoreline communities is Norwalk's tiny village of Rowayton, which hugs the border of Darien and edges out into the Sound at Noroton Point. A bare square mile of quaint seaside streets, it is lined with residences from delightfully unique renovations to traditional New England cottages in a variety of conditions dating from before the turn of the twentieth century. Boatyards, marinas, and beaches rub shoulders with tiny pocket parks, art galleries, and a small selection of restaurants and delis.

If you happen to be in Darien, follow Tokeneke Road across the Five Mile River to Cudlipp Street, then south on Rowayton Avenue to reach the diminutive center of "downtown" Rowayton. Or from South Norwalk, take Washington Street to Dr. Martin Luther King Jr. Boulevard to Wilson Avenue (Route 136 south) and wander into the enclave through the backdoor. An especially picturesque route is down Wilson Avenue to Bluff Avenue to Westmere, then a block south on Yarmouth, a right turn on Crescent Beach Road, a right turn up Ensign Road, a left on Pine Point to a right on Roton Avenue, and then a left on Crockett Street to Rowayton Avenue. This route is as wonderful for bikers and walkers as it is for drivers, taking visitors through the Bell Island and Roton Point sections and allowing time for stops at such sights as **Bayley Beach** or the tiny waterfront park near the base of Rowayton Avenue.

Stop for a meal at the outstanding **Restaurant at Rowayton Seafood** (see Places to Eat), the bright and artsy **Bistro du Soleil** (162 Rowayton Avenue; 203–855–9469), the dependable **Rowayton Pizza** (203–853–7555), or the **101 Deli,** where the hard-to-beat sandwiches and ice cream are available year-round from 6:30 A.M. **Pinkney Park** is a special delight in summer; if you are lucky you may catch its annual **Summer Arts Festival** or see one of its annual **Shakespeare in the Park** productions, held for four or five days in late June at 7:30 P.M. (call 203–851–1657 for information). Be sure to stop by the three galleries of fine art at the **Rowayton Arts Center** (145 Rowayton Avenue; 203–866–2744). Space constraints prevent full disclosure of all the pleasures of Rowayton. Discover its secrets as you explore.

Water Streets. Schedule and information (203–838–9444); special charters (203–334–9166). Weekends and holidays only from Memorial Day until the third week of June, with cruises at 10:00 A.M., 12:30 P.M., and 3:00 P.M. From late June through Labor Day, cruises depart at 9:30 A.M. and 1:30 P.M. on weekdays; three cruises are scheduled on weekends and holidays at the same hours as earlier in the season.

Seating is first-come, first-served. Adults and children $10; $1 discount on Wednesdays for seniors and children under 12. Thursday evening New England Clambakes (late May through late September, 6:00 to 9:30 P.M.) on the island are extra.

Boat Excursions and Charters

***Oceanic* Eco-cruises** From the Maritime Aquarium dock at the Norwalk River (203–852–0700, extension 206). If the displays at the Maritime Aquarium have sparked your interest in the sea, you might consider a two-and-a-half-hour cruise on its research vessel, the 40-foot trawler *Oceanic*. On winter weekends from December through March, weather permitting, public cruises set out to see the harbor seals that inhabit the Sound during the coldest months. Naturalists explain the marine plant and animal life and the laws protecting them. Summer cruises have on-board educators who explain the ecology of the Sound as participants study the marine life by collecting water samples, hauling a trawl net, examining the catch in the shipboard touch tank, and using a video microscope to view the tiny plants and animals that sustain life throughout the Sound. These Marinelife Study Cruises are Wednesday through Sunday at 1:00 P.M. from July 1 through Labor Day. All adults and children pay $15 for both summer and winter cruises. Reservations recommended.

White Creek Expeditions 99 Mayanos Road, New Canaan (203–966–0040). Freshwater and saltwater canoeing and kayaking; guided trips and instruction.

Small Boat Shop 144 Water Street (203–854–5223). Guided sea kayak tours of Norwalk Harbor and the Norwalk Islands, weekends and holidays from mid-May through October, weather permitting. No experience necessary; reservations required.

Sound Sailing Center 160 Water Street (203–838–1110). Private and group sailing instruction for all ages at all levels, plus rentals of sailboats, catamarans, and cabin cruisers.

Overton's Boat Livery 80 Seaview Avenue (203–838–2031). Rentals of 16-foot dories for sightseeing and fishing from May through October, weather permitting.

Places to Eat in Norwalk

Brewhouse Restaurant 13 Marshall Street (203–853–9110). This casual pub-style restaurant is an extension of the New England Brewing Company housed in a historic 1920s factory building in SoNo. Throughout the bi-level eatery is one of the nation's largest collec-

Life-in-Connecticut WPA Murals

Norwalk is home to yet another treasure, this one located right in its City Hall at 125 East Avenue. The hallways here are hung with a series of murals that are one of the nation's most important collections of Depression-era art. Bright and beautiful, these **Life-in-Connecticut murals** were a federal art project sponsored by the 1930s Works Progress Administration. Several of the nearly twenty restored paintings feature scenes of Connecticut history from the Indians selling land to Roger Ludlow to such events as the Great Connecticut State Fair at Danbury.

Contact Ralph Bloom, the city's historical curator (203–866–0202), if you'd like to arrange a $3 per person guided tour. The murals can be visited without a tour year-round, Monday through Friday from 9:00 A.M. to 5:00 P.M., unless City Hall is closed for a major holiday.

tions of brewing memorabilia and paraphernalia. Bratwurst, steamed mussels, battered fish, chicken and veal dishes, and sandwiches, salads, and appetizers are among the dishes that complement the award-winning brews produced here. Open daily for lunch from 11:30 A.M. to 5:00 P.M. and for dinner from 5:00 P.M. $$

Barcelona Restaurant and Wine Bar 63 North Main Street (203–899–0088). Wonderful hot and cold tapas, great crusty breads with olive oil, entrees like soft-shell crabs in season and delicious sweet pea ravioli. Save room for the outstanding Key lime cheesecake and the absolutely decadent chocolate indulgence. Casual and lively with bar, separate dining room, and warm-weather sidewalk cafe under a tent. Open for dinner daily from 5:00 P.M. $–$$$

Silvermine Tavern 194 Perry Avenue (203–847–4558). For romantic dining on fine New England-style cuisine in an eighteenth-century setting, the Silvermine Tavern is the tops in Fairfield County. Antiques and folk art, crackling fireplaces in winter, and al fresco summertime dining on a tree-shaded deck overlooking the pond are some of the features that lure regulars and travelers, the latter of which sometimes opt to stay overnight in the inn's guest rooms (see Places to Stay). Open year-round Wednesday through Saturday for lunch from noon to 3:00 P.M. and dinner from 6:00 P.M., plus Sunday champagne buffet brunch 11:00 A.M. to 2:30 P.M. and Sunday dinner 3:00 to 9:00 P.M. $$$

Amberjacks Coastal Grill 99 Washington Street (203–853–4332).

Fresh, innovative American cuisine with a creative flair for seafood. Sophisticated decor in a high-ceilinged dining room in a former bank building on the most colorfully revitalized street in SoNo. Outside dining terrace with great people-watching potential. Open daily for lunch from noon to 3:00 P.M. and for dinner from 5:30 P.M. $–$$

The Restaurant at Rowayton Seafood 89 Rowayton Avenue (203–866–4488). For outstanding seafood, great views, and an unbeatable ambiance overlooking the Five Mile River, try the restaurant adjacent to the fish market in the lovely hamlet of Rowayton. For lunch, try the barbecued shrimp sandwich on a Portuguese roll with Monterey Jack cheese and onions; for dinner indulge in oysters, scallops, salmon, and other seafood dishes, plus salads, appetizers, and more. Open daily year-round for lunch and dinner, plus Sunday brunch. $$$–$$$$

Famous Pizza 23 North Main Street (203–838–6100). Great for day-tripping families, Famous offers terrific pizza, calzones, grinders, pasta, fried chicken, club sandwiches, burgers, dogs, fries, and rings at very affordable prices. Steps from the Norwalk Museum and a block from the Maritime Aquarium. Open Monday through Saturday from 11:00 A.M. and Sunday from 2:00 P.M. for lunch and dinner. $

Shore Points
An Island Getaway

During the 1800s and early 1900s many families lived on the Norwalk Islands. One farmer raised his sheep on Sheffield Island and separated the ewes from the rams by driving the males across the sandbar at very low tide to a neighboring island, which soon became known as Ram Island. Once used by Mormon missionaries as a place to baptize converts without being bothered by onlookers, Ram Island was also the site of one of several noxious fish-oil rendering plants. Early environmentalists protested the smoke and odor that wafted from the islands to the mainland, and the plants were shut down in the late 1880s. The island has been renamed Shea Island in honor of Norwalk's Vietnam War hero Daniel Shea. Home to sparrow hawks, herons and egrets, the city-owned island has a swimming and picnic area that can be enjoyed by visiting boaters. Camping is allowed on the eastern shore near Ram Historical Park. Call the Norwalk Parks and Recreation Department (203–854–7806) for information.

Places to Stay in Norwalk

Courtyard by Marriott–Norwalk 475 Main Avenue (203–849–9111 or 800–647–7578). 145 units with one king-size or two double beds, plus 12 suites. Restaurant, lounge, health club, whirlpool, indoor pool, laundry facility, dry cleaning service. Moderate weekend rates; discounts for seniors. Complimentary breakfast buffet. $$$–$$$$

Norwalk Inn & Conference Center 99 East Avenue (203–838–5531 or 800–537–8483). 71 units, including 3 suites, restaurant, lounge, coffee shop, outdoor pool. Senior citizen rates. $$$$

Sheraton Four Points Hotel 426 Main Avenue (203–849–9828 or 888–806–4786). 127 units with 2 suites, restaurant, lounge, exercise room. Lower weekend rates and senior discounts. $$$

Club Hotel by Double Tree 789 Connecticut Avenue (203–853–3477 or 888–444–2582). 268 units, restaurant, lounge, indoor pool, fitness room. Senior discounts; lower rates on weekends. $$$$

Silvermine Tavern 194 Perry Avenue at Silvermine Avenue (203–847–4558). The most romantic place to stay in all of Fairfield County, this rambling 1785 country inn is set on the banks of the Silvermine River by a waterfall that lulls happy dreamers to sleep at night. Ten guest rooms, all with private bath, some with antique canopied double beds, some with two single beds. Award-winning restaurant (see *Places to Eat*) serves traditional New England cuisine; guests receive a complimentary continental breakfast featuring the tavern's famed honeybuns. $$$–$$$

Public Boat Launch

Norwalk Visitors' Dock Veterans Memorial Park (203–849–8823). Public boat launch ramp, water, pump-out service, snack bar, bait, dockage for 20 transient boats.

For Further Information

Norwalk Seaport Association 132 Water Street, South Norwalk 06854 (203–838–9444 or 888–701–7785). Information on boat charters, excursion cruises, special events in South Norwalk, events on Sheffield Island, public clambakes, and annual festivals such as the Oyster Festival (the weekend after Labor Day), the SoNo Arts Celebration (the first full weekend in August), and Norwalk Harborsplash (the third weekend in May), an annual festival celebrating the waterfront with harbor tours, walking tours, clam chowder cook-offs, boating activities, performing and visual arts.

Norwalk Parks and Recreation (203–854–7806). Information on nonresident use of the parks and beaches. **Cranbury Park** on Grumman Avenue has 8 miles of hiking and mountain biking trails, plus picnic areas and lawns for games and ball-playing. Nonresidents are welcome at any time at no charge. Nonresidents can park at **Calf Pasture Beach** at any time at no charge in the off-season and for $15 daily from Memorial Day to Labor Day. No cooking is allowed at Calf Pasture. Adjacent **Shady Beach** allows cooking but does not offer nonresident parking. If you want to cook, park at Calf Pasture and walk to Shady Beach.

Westport

Westport usually needs no introduction. Long famous as a haven for writers, actors, artists, and other glitterati, it is well-known as the suburb of suburbs with a dash of panache rivaled only by its imitators. Though more crowded with high-priced automobiles than ever before, it still has the same old zing. Travelers are often drawn to Westport by the hype about its astonishing shopping opportunities and its famed residents. The truth lies somewhere in the midst of the many lines of hyperbole—you *might* be able to be seated next to Paul Newman at his favorite Italian restaurant, and you *might* run into Redford or some other seasonal resident at the Baskin Robbins ice cream emporium, but chances are you won't. Better to enjoy the shops, the restaurants, and the entertainments for what they can more obviously offer to you.

Travelers intent on discovering the natural wonders of Westport will be attracted to its beaches and woodlands. While few of the town's typical tourists would start a tour of Westport in its quieter corners of nature, most would agree that once the thrill of browsing and buying in the shops wears off, the spirit is restored by the more prosaic qualities of the woodlands and wetlands. In whatever order you choose to enjoy Westport's attractions, be sure to save time for an evening performance at one of its equally famed stages. More than in any other place on the Connecticut shore, the stars come out in Westport.

The Best of Westport

Nature Center for Environmental Activities

Open 365 days a year from dawn to dusk, the Center's 62-acre wildlife sanctuary includes 3 miles of trails for all ages. A Swamp Loop Trail, an open field habitat, and a trail for the blind are among the several options outside.

Inside the Center's 20,000-square-foot museum, a large live-animal hall with many species of indigenous animals is often the site of live animal demonstrations. A Discovery Room with changing displays on ecology and, animal biology, a working water-quality lab, a wildlife rehab center, a variety of dioramas and aquariums, a marine touch tank, and a great gift shop are all here.

Perhaps best of all, though, are the special events, workshops, guided walks, outdoor classes, and summer camp programs. Beach walks, maple sugaring, birdbanding, Earth Day activities, junior nauralist groups, a holiday fair, and more are open to all visitors. Some are free; others require reservations and tuition. If none of those options appeal, still come to this little slice of wilderness—wild turkeys, pheasants, red foxes, deer, hawks, songbirds, and more await you.

10 Woodside Lane (203–227–7253). Open year-round Monday through Saturday from 9:00 A.M. to 5:00 P.M. and Sunday from 1:00 to 4:00 P.M. Closed on major holidays. Adults are invited to donate $1; children, 50 cents.

Sherwood Island State Park

One of the state's most popular sites on the Sound, this park's mile-and-a-half-long beach is preceded by 200-plus acres of open space, two picnic groves, and several sorts of drives, footpaths, and walkways. Swimming, fishing, and scuba diving or snorkeling are permitted (scuba divers must register at the ranger station) at all times, but lifeguards are on duty only from Memorial Day to Labor Day; during this time they won't let you bring inflatable water toys, boats, canoes, or kayaks into the water.

On the Scene Downtown

Go ahead and get the urge out of your system—trendy and upscale downtown Westport is the ideal place for an all-day shopping spree in any season. Both national chain stores and one-of-a-kind boutiques are densely but pleasantly packed into a relatively small area, also crammed with dozens of eateries purveying everything from egg creams and bagels to lobster thermidor. From army-navy surplus to haute couture, the clothing shops are filled with an array of goods matched only in Greenwich. If you can't put your finger on what you want in the environs of Main Street, Riverside Avenue, and the immediate stretch of the Post Road East near these two north-south arteries, you probably won't find it anywhere. If compelled, however, amble or drive a while farther along the east-west Post Road any distance from Norwalk to Fairfield—this route is basically wall-to-wall stores and nary a mall in sight.

Bargain-hunters should be sure to come to Westport in summer (for the exact dates, call the Westport Chamber of Commerce at 203–227–9234) for the **annual sidewalk sale**. The best of its kind probably anywhere, it is an unbelievably popular event with amazing goods sold at deeply discounted prices. Real detectives may want to peruse the famed racks of the **Westport Goodwill** (203–259–3943) on the Post Road, where a black cashmere Ann Taylor sweater can be salvaged for $5 as easily as a $30 Armani suit. For renewal at the end of an exhaustive spree, Sal Gilbertie's famous herbs, flowers, essential oils, and other wholesome garden goods are all on display and for sale in the beautiful greenhouses and shop (203–227–4175) at **Gilbertie's Herb Garden** on Sylvan Avenue off Riverside Avenue.

Come here for saltwater shore fishing and clamming, kite-flying, volleyball, badminton, horseshoes, softball, bocce, and bicycling. Bring your own equipment for all of the above. No animals are allowed in the park in the summertime. From September 30 to April 15 you can bring them, but dogs must be leashed.

The park's appeal to lovers of Long Island Sound is enhanced by a self-guided interpretive nature trail that points out flora, fauna, and special areas of interest to the Sound, its freshwater estuaries, and its shoreline. Just a half-mile long, the trail is perfect for seniors and families with young children. A small and very good nature center includes a touch tank, live-animal exhibits of native reptiles and amphibians, and shorebird specimens. The nature center is open

10:00 A.M. to 4:30 P.M. between Memorial Day and Labor Day, except on Mondays. A bird observation deck provides an overview of the shore habitat; bird-watchers are welcome year-round.

The park provides public restrooms, changing rooms, and showers at no additional charge. Only the restrooms function in the winter. The concession stand at the beach's large pavilion offers food, drink, candy, and some souvenirs and folks are welcome to picnic or barbecue.

Off I-95 exit 18. Turn south at the end of the ramp and drive directly into the park (203–226–6983). Open daily year-round, dawn to one half-hour before sunset. Admission per vehicle, $5 with Connecticut plates, $8 with out-of-state plates from Memorial Day to Labor Day on weekdays. On weekends and holidays from Memorial Day to Labor Day these rates are $7 and $12 respectively. Off-season parking is free, except on weekends in May and September when the charge is $5 Connecticut and $8 out-of-state.

Westport Country Playhouse

Over more than half a century, this wonderful summer-stock playhouse has offered hundreds of professional productions starring such legends as Henry Fonda, Helen Hayes, Jessica Tandy, Gene Kelly, Liza Minnelli, Cicely Tyson, and many, many others. Located in a cow barn-turned-tanning factory and now a rustic country theater with post-and-beam construction and red-cushioned bench-style seating, the Playhouse is a Fairfield County fixture and one of the few remaining professional stock theaters in the Northeast. Approximately six shows per season, from late June until early September, bring musicals, comedies, dramas, and classics such as Shakespeare's *Taming of the Shrew* to the stage. Refreshments are served outside in the Playhouse courtyard. Pre-show performances by local musicians greet theatergoers as they arrive.

If you have young children in your party, call for a schedule of the theater's second-most famous productions—its Children's Summer Theatre. For nine weeks every summer, a new show is produced each week on Fridays at 10:30 A.M. and 1:00 P.M. Fairy tale productions, a mini-circus, puppet theaters, magic shows, and concerts are among the possibilities. Tickets are $6 or $7.50 (depending on which part of the theater you'd like) per ticket for children and adults.

25 Powers Court, just off Route 1 (203–226–0153 or 203–227–4177). Ticket prices vary; subscriptions as well as single tickets are sold for the season's series.

Saugatuck Valley Trails

A cooperative effort of Westport's Aspetuck Land Trust, the Bridgeport Hydraulic Company, the Connecticut Audubon Society, and the Nature Conservancy, with support from the towns of Weston and Redding, has resulted in the limited development of protected lands for hiking and some horseback riding in areas surrounding the Saugatuck River and its beautiful reservoir. Open to the public at no charge, the trails are open year-round. Open meadows, shaded mountain laurel groves, cascades and pools, marshes, and forested uplands are among the habitats and features in twenty-four separate preserves. Free maps of these areas are mailed to interested hikers who write to Aspetuck Land Trust, P. O. Box 444, Westport CT 06880. The trail map is considered a hiking permit, and all users must have one. Day-trippers can find the maps at the Westport Town Hall or the local libraries of Westport, Redding, or Weston. The maps show the location of parking areas and toilets. Adequate footwear is a must for these easy to strenuous trails.

White Barn Theatre

The brand-new work of well-known as well as up-and-coming playwrights and performers are staged at this fifty-year-old venue run like an English theater club with two-night performances of each of five works in the monthlong August series. All performances are at 8:00 P.M. on Saturday and Sunday only; a Saturday night reception allows the audience to mingle with writers and actors in the converted rustic country barn setting.

452 Newtown Avenue (203–227–3768). Tickets are $30; subscriptions for the five-show August-only season are $125.

Levitt Pavilion for the Performing Arts

Don't miss the festival atmosphere at the Levitt. Right on the banks of the Saugatuck River, this open-air series has offered approximately sixty evenings of entertainment every summer, from late June through late August, for the past quarter-century. Bring a blanket, and a picnic to the lawn in front of the band shell and enjoy the absolutely free performances.

Monday is Potpourri night—maybe swing, maybe the community band, maybe stories for children. Tuesday is Concert and Show Bands. Wednesday is Family and Children (theater, mime, puppetry, magic, storytelling, sing-alongs). Thursday is

Classical/Cabaret/Theater; Friday is Party Time (maybe folk, reggae, bluegrass, or classic rock 'n' roll); Saturday is Pop/Rock; and Sunday is Big Band/Blues/Jazz. On some Mondays, there is no show, and occasional special events do have an admission charge. Call for a calendar.

Showtimes vary from 7:00 P.M. to as late as 8:30 P.M. Fridays and Saturdays are designated as alcohol-free evenings. Park in one of the municipal lots in back of the Westport Public Library on Jesup Road off the Post Road East (Route 1) and walk up the gravel path toward the brownish band shell at the side of the river.

Jesup Road, behind the Westport Public Library (203–226–7600).

Boat Excursions and Charters

Longshore Sailing School 260 South Compo Road (203–226–4646). In addition to lessons with sailboats, catamarans, and sailboards for all skill levels from ages nine and up, this well-reputed sailing school offers rentals of sailboats, canoes, sea kayaks, sailboards, or rowboats. Available June through August.

Places to Eat in Westport

Miramar 2 Post Road West (203–221–1351 or 800–628–4255). This restaurant recently put the finishing touches on a thorough transformation of everything except its award-winning continental cuisine and impeccably elegant style. Lunch and dinner daily at this four-star establishment continue as before; inquire about any new dining opportunities like brunch or outdoor seating. After your meal, take a stroll along the riverfront boardwalk in this restored historic wharf area on the Saugatuck River. $$$$

Da Pietro 36 Riverside Avenue (203–454–1213). This self-described romantic storefront cafe transports patrons to the south of France or the north of Italy with the award-winning menu of owner/chef Pietro Scotti. A relaxing and enticing dining experience rated excellent by the *New York Times* and voted Best Italian in the state by readers of *Connecticut* magazine. Open for dinner only, Monday through Saturday. $$$–$$$$

Splash 260 Compo Road South (203–454–7798). Rave reviews for this refreshing contemporary restaurant in Longshore Club Park. Pacific Rim cuisine means lots of fresh seafood and other dishes with a creative, tropical flair. Outdoor dining on a wraparound porch in warm months. Views of the Sound indoors and out. Open daily for lunch 11:30 A.M. to 2:30 P.M. and dinner from 5:30 P.M. $$$–$$$$

A Taste of Westport History

The 1795 Wheeler House is the home of the Westport Historical Society, the docents of which would be happy to let visitors in on some of the local lore and legend. Westport enjoyed quiet beginnings in the mid-seventeenth century, with settlements in what were then parts of both Fairfield and Norwalk. Not too much happened in the area except some nasty dealings with the natives and some fairly efficient forest clearing and farmstead building. During the Revolution, a little action came to Westport in the form of a notable raid by the Brits on Compo Beach and some handy efforts at retaliation on the parts of the colonial minutemen, some of whom followed the Redcoats to the Battle of Ridgefield and skirmished with them again in Westport after their retreat from Danbury.

After that first Fourth of July, Westport went back, for the most part, to farming, small manufacturing, shipping, and warehousing goods bound for other parts of the world. For a hundred years or so, not a lot changed until the railroad brought the cityfolk to town and Westport became a New York suburb with a flair for the dramatic.

The Wheeler House re-creates the nineteenth century pretty tidily in its restored Victorian parlor, bedroom, and kitchen, its costume collection, its unusual octagonal-roofed cobblestone barn, and its changing exhibitions on Westport history from prehistoric to contemporary times. The museum is open year-round Tuesday through Saturday from 10:00 A.M. to 3:00 P.M. (203–222–1424). A donation is suggested.

Allen's Clam and Lobster House 191 Hillspoint Road (203–226–4411). A landmark for more than a generation, overlooking the Sherwood Mill Pond north of Compo Cove. Waterside seats from which to savor fine seafood all year round. Closed Mondays; open Tuesday through Sunday for lunch and dinner. $$$

The Beach House 23 Hillspint Road (203–226–7005). Right on Old Mill Beach with superb views of the Sound, this casual establishment specializes in "domestic coastal cuisine" with generous influences from the Mediterranean and Caribbean coasts as well. Delightful seasonings, surprising combinations, all delicious. Open Wednesday through Monday for lunch and dinner and Sunday brunch. Closed Tuesday. $$$

Bridge Cafe 5 Riverside Avenue (203–226–4800). Casually elegant Continental restaurant on the Saugatuck River serving exceptional seafood, delicious veal, poultry, and beef, creative pastas, and outstanding desserts. Tile floors and stuccoed walls in soft colors inside;

Shore Points
The Great Race

One of the most entertaining Westport festivities is the annual **Great Race** on the Saugatuck River. A series of small-craft competitions for canoes, kayaks, and racing shells underscores the serious side of the race, but an amusing collection of homemade vessels of every description adds a whole lot of levity to the spectacle. Judged for the creativity and originality of their appearance and for their propulsion method, the watercraft ride the tides sometime in mid-July, often coinciding with the excellent two-day **Westport Outdoor Art Show** in downtown Westport and along the banks of the Saugatuck. The put-in point for the race is usually somewhere close to the Post Road bridge across the river; the best viewing spots are in the riverside park on the eastern bank (behind the Westport Public Library at the Levitt Pavilion) or from various vantage points along Riverside Avenue on the western shore. Call for further information on the race (203–454–6564) or the art show (203–226–4261).

outdoor patio in warm seasons. Open for lunch Monday through Friday 11:30 A.M. to 2:30 P.M. and Saturday and Sunday until 3:00 P.M. Open for dinner Monday through Saturday from 5:30 P.M. and Sunday from 5:00 P.M. $$$–$$$$

Acqua 44 Main Street (203–222–8899). Marvelous Mediterranean menu with an emphasis on seafood. Excellent appetizers, wonderful pastas, inventive thin-crust pizzas made in wood-burning oven. In the heart of the downtown shopping district, this casual but sophisticated restaurant has an upstairs bar with views of the river. Open for dinner Monday through Saturday from 5:30 P.M. Closed Sunday. $$–$$$$

Places to Stay in Westport

The Westport Inn 1595 Post Road East (203–259–5236 or 800–446–8997). Moderately priced full-service hotel with 116 units, indoor pool, fitness center, whirlpool, sauna, restaurant, lounge, entertainment. Senior discounts and weekend packages. $$$–$$$$

The Inn at Longshore 260 Compo Road South (203–226–3316). Formerly a summer estate, built in the 1890s, this seaside inn at town-owned Longshore Club Park offers lodging right on the Sound. The eleven comfortably decorated rooms (including 3 suites) have a New England flair. Some rooms have wide-angle views of the Sound;

others offer limited seascapes. Among the extras are an outdoor pool and beach swimming, boating, tennis courts, a golf course with guest privileges and options for cross-country skiing in the winter, and a children's playground. Complimentary continental breakfast. $$$$

The Inn at National Hall 2 Post Road West (203–221–1351 or 800–628–4255). Fabulously luxurious inn in historic 1873 National Register Italianate brick building overlooking the Saugatuck River in the heart of downtown. Fifteen rooms, including 7 suites, each equally stunning but all unique. Top-of-the-line everything is everywhere; this inn is a cut above the cream of the crop. Massage services can be arranged; guest privileges at the Westport YMCA are complimentary, as is continental or full breakfast. Award-winning Miramar restaurant on the first floor (see Places to Eat). $$$$

Public Boat Launch

Saugatuck River Ramp Access on eastern bank under I–95. Take Route 136 south onto Compo Road; first right to launch area. Parking for twenty-five cars. Seasonal weekend and holiday parking fee.

For Further Information

Westport Chamber of Commerce (203–227–9234). Maps, brochures, information on lodging, restaurants, annual events.

Westport Parks and Recreation (203–341–5090). Information on nonresident use of beaches and parks. Policy has been $10 per car for nonresidents on weekdays and $25 per vehicle on weekends and holidays. Inquire about use and launching of car-top boats. The beach parks at Compo Beach and the Longshore Club have playgrounds, snack bars, showers, changing rooms, restrooms, grills, and picnic tables. For information on use of golf course at Longshore Club Park, call (203) 341–1833.

Westport Community Theatre 110 Myrtle Avenue (203–226–1983). Nearly half a century of comedies, musicals, and classical and contemporary drama by such playwrights as Hellman, O'Casey, Wilde, Shakespeare, and Williams. Intimate theater located in back of the Westport Town Hall. Call for calendar of September through June productions and ticket information.

Westport Arts Center 431 Post Road East, Suite 8 (203–226–1806). This center for the performing and visual arts offers exhibitions, performances, and workshops throughout the year. Call for information on programs and special events.

 # Fairfield

Fairfield's position on the coast of Long Island Sound was no mere coincidence when it was settled by the English in 1639. A string of such settlements along the shore had sprung from the importance of the estuary as a maritime highway in a time when sailing vessels provided the quickest means of transporting people and goods. In the seventeenth century, bedraggled colonists traveling by land struggled through Connecticut's swamps and marshes, hacked their way through forests, and depended on rudimentary ferries to carry them across rivers. When Captain John Mason and Roger Ludlow, deputy governor of the Connecticut colony, arrived in the native village of Unquowa after harrying the Pequots from Mystic all the way to the swamp at Sasqua, they were no doubt exhausted. Apparently a fair amount of adrenaline, combined with a belief that the Divine Lord *wanted* the English to destroy the fearful Pequots, helped Ludlow complete the colony's mission of decimating the tribe's remaining eighty warriors. Ludlow and his compatriots spared the 200 old men, women, and children who hid in the thickets of the swamp, then promptly claimed the land for the colony and renamed its native villages Fairfield and Southport.

Beleaguered area tribes (who had themselves suffered at the hands of the dominant and often vicious Pequots) were all too happy at the time to give land to the triumphant English who had subdued their enemy. At the completion of the negotiations, Ludlow had secured nearly 140 square miles of shoreland and woodland that comprised Fairfield. Soon the fair fields of Unquowa and Sasqua had been sown with English seed, and farming and shipping interests replaced the less intrusive lifeways of the natives. Fairfield's entrepreneurial citizens capitalized on its location on the Sound, and by the eighteenth century the development of water-powered mills and shipping wharves led to the growth of the grain, lumber, cider, textile, and shipbuilding industries.

Populated mostly by farmers, tradesmen, sailors, and shipbuilders through much of the eighteenth century, the town was burned in

1779 by Hessian troops under the command of British Major General William Tryon. Rebuilding was slow but determined, and soon the community had rallied as the busy Southport and Black Rock harbors helped to reestablish Fairfield's place as an important port of entry. Two centuries later, Fairfield's shoreline location still influences life in this thriving, comfortable community. Today the interstate highway system, railroads, and air transportation relieve the town's dependence on the Sound, leaving its coastline open for mostly recreational activities. The onion fields that once flourished in Southport are long gone; the mills and factories supported by an immigrant workforce are mostly closed. Now largely residential, Fairfield attracts newcomers looking for a suburban setting within commuting distance of larger cities. As one of Connecticut's oldest towns, Fairfield holds beautiful historical homes and still-quaint village centers within its now 30 square miles. These classically New England sights plus 8 miles of shoreline and sophisticated options for entertainment, dining, and shopping keep Fairfield on the map for shoreline day-trippers.

The Best of Fairfield

Ogden House and Gardens

An excellent historical site for those interested in pre-Revolutionary life, Ogden House is a 1750 saltbox farmhouse furnished to portray the lives of its first inhabitants, Jane and David Ogden. Owned by the Ogden family for 125 years, the house has been meticulously restored and accurately outfitted with artifacts mentioned in the original household inventory. An eighteenth-century kitchen garden and a native wildflower woodland garden are also on the picturesque property overlooking Brown's Brook near Mill River.

In addition to annual events celebrating the gardens and the seasons, Ogden House offers workshops, lectures, and activities for visitors of all ages. A Hands-On History Camp for children eight to eleven is held annually during the second week in July, and high school students can make reservations to participate in the archaeological dig taking place on the property.

1520 Bronson Road (203-259-6356 or 203-259-1598). Public tours of the house and gardens are offered from mid-May through mid-October on Saturdays and Sundays from 1:00 to 4:00 P.M. Adults $2, children $1.

The Dogwood Festival

While you visit the northern reaches of town, explore the neighborhood a bit. Graced by vintage homes as well as more modern mansions, the winding country roads take you through lightly populated residential enclaves and into a perfect antique village center punctuated by one of the nation's most stately Congregational churches. Known as Greenfield Hill, the area is heavily planted with dogwoods and is famed for its annual **Dogwood Festival** in mid-May—a great outing for Mother's Day or any other reason.

To celebrate the gorgeous pink and white blossoms that open on more than 30,000 dogwoods, the Greenfield Hill Congregational Church (1045 Old Academy Road) plans a weeklong schedule of festivities that include an arts and crafts show, a plant sale, walking tours and sit-down luncheons, musical programs, a children's games and crafts area, and a white elephant sale. Buy food here or bring a picnic. For information, call the Fairfield Town Hall and ask for the current Festival Committee telephone number.

Fairfield Historical Society

In its Georgian-style brick home near the Town Green, this wonderfully curated small museum offers seasonal changing exhibitions as well as a permanent collection of paintings, prints, maps, costumes, furnishings, and fine decorative arts. Three spacious galleries showcase objects from pre-Revolutionary vintage to contemporary significance. In addition to household implements, tools, locally made furniture, and toys are artifacts that relate to the town's role as a seaport during the eighteenth and nineteenth centuries. Notable among the museum's collections are its textiles, costumes, and an intriguing assortment of walking sticks.

636 Old Post Road (203–259–1598). Open 9:30 A.M. to 4:30 P.M. weekdays and 1:00 to 5:00 P.M. weekends. Closed on major holidays. Adults $1, children 50 cents.

Birdcraft Museum and Sanctuary

This six-acre enclave was founded in 1914 as the first songbird sanctuary in the United States. Documented records of more than 120 species of birds have been kept for this vest-pocket site. Huge maples and century-old rhododendrons are along the trail that runs through the woodlands and across a beautiful wooden boardwalk above a shallow pond.

Sit awhile at the gazebo and listen to the birds and frogs. Look for the nesting night herons.

Inside the turn-of-the-century museum, designated as a National Historic Landmark, browse through galleries featuring the birds and mammals of New England, grouped in diorama displays by habitat and by seasons, and of Africa. The murals here are exceptional.

You can stroll through the Birdcraft on your own or take a one-hour guided tour, arranged by appointment. Be sure to come the second Saturday of May for the annual International Migrating Bird Day, a festival of bird-watching, crafts, a book sale, and lessons on how to landscape your own yard to attract birds.

314 Unquowa Road (203–259–0416). Museum and sanctuary open year-round Tuesday to Friday from 10:00 A.M. to 5:00 P.M. and Saturday and Sunday from noon to 5:00 P.M. Adults $2; children under 14, $1.

Roy and Margot Larsen Bird Sanctuary and Connecticut Audubon Center at Fairfield

Created on reclaimed farm property, this 160-acre tract of New England woodland in the north end of town was built as a model wildlife sanctuary juxtaposing habitats and trails to allow people maximum opportunity to experience the diversity without disturbing the refuge. Marsh, wetlands, streams, vernal pools, meadows, coniferous forest, and second-growth areas of mature hardwoods are among the sanctuary's habitats. Laced throughout the property are 6 miles of trails, including a Walk for the Disabled. A butterfly meadow designed to attract native butterfly species and other indigenous insects features native vegetation that had been supplanted by invasive imported plants.

On site is the Connecticut Audubon Center at Fairfield (with natural science exhibits, discovery room, non-circulating library, live animal displays, and an excellent gift shop/bookstore) and the Educational Animal Compound of non-releasable animals the Audubon Society has rehabilitated. Summer camps, workshops, naturalist-guided walks, junior naturalist programs, field trips, and other special events are open to visitors.

2325 Burr Street (203–259–6305). The Audubon nature center is open year-round, Tuesday through Saturday, from 9:00 A.M. to 4:30 P.M. and Sunday (except in July and August) from noon to 4:30 P.M. Closed on Mondays and major holidays. Admission is free. The bird sanctuary is open daily, year-round, from dawn to dusk; adults $2, children under 12 are 50 cents.

Quick Center for the Arts

This facility on the campus of Fairfield University brings nationally and internationally acclaimed performers to the stage throughout the season from September to June. From student productions featuring the University choral groups and instrumental ensembles to such star talents as Judy Collins, the Alvin Ailey Dance Company, or Le Cirque Bohemien, the Quick Center offers single tickets and series subscriptions to its music, dance, and theater productions. A Young Audience series provides entertainment ranging from puppetry and magic shows to interpretations of classic literature and folk storytelling.

The Quick Center also has an outstanding gallery for fine arts exhibitions. Called the Thomas J. Walsh Art Gallery, it focuses on the works of contemporary painters, printmakers, sculptors, and photographers as well as exhibitions showcasing masterpieces of past centuries.

At Fairfield University; enter on North Benson Road (203–254–4010). Call this number for ticket information or for full calendar of events and exhibitions. Walsh Gallery open Tuesday through Saturday 11:00 A.M. to 5:00 P.M. and Sunday from noon to 4:00 P.M.

J. Russell Jinishian Gallery

Visitors with an appreciation for the beauty of the sea and ships may enjoy a visit to this outstanding gallery of marine and sporting art. Boasting a collection like none other in the United States, the gallery displays the work of the world's most prominent marine and sporting artists of contemporary times as well as American and European works from the nineteenth century. Although the works are all museum-quality, this gallery is not, of course, a museum. The artworks are for sale and typically range in price from $500 to $50,000. Appreciative browsers are welcome to enjoy a look at these magnificent pieces before they find good homes.

At the Greenwich Workshop Gallery, 1657 Post Road (203–259–8753). Open to the public Tuesday through Saturday from 10:00 A.M. to 5:00 P.M. and by appointment. No charge to visit the collection.

Places to Eat in Fairfield

Voila! 70 Reef Road (203–254–2070). This "bistro française" is Fairfield's most charming eatery, tiny and lace-trimmed, French-owned and utterly delicious. Soft pink walls and black-and-white napery give a pleasing and promising message that lovely surprises will follow—

Beachin' It

Public access to Long Island Sound has long been a priority for the town of Fairfield. Five public beaches allow residents and visitors to enjoy fishing, swimming, boating, and beachcombing throughout the year. From Memorial Day to Labor Day, nonresidents must pay a day-use fee to park at either Jennings or Penfield beaches, payable in cash at the gate of either beach: $15 per vehicle on weekends, $10 during the week. To get a seasonal pass for unlimited use of the beaches throughout the summer season, purchase a windshield sticker ($50) at Independence Hall next to the Fairfield Town Hall at the corner of Beach Road and the Old Post Road. For further information, call the Fairfield Parks and Recreation department (203–256–3144).

Penfield Beach (Fairfield Beach Road) and **Jennings Beach** (South Benson Road) are the only two beaches open to nonresident vehicles. Both facilities have pavilions, concessions, restrooms and showers, and playgrounds. In addition to its other amenities, Jennings Beach features the Sandcastle, a play structure for children; it is also a great place to watch the annual fireworks extravaganza on or near the Fourth of July.

Southport Beach (Pequot Avenue) is less crowded and has great sandbars for young children, restrooms, and a small concession. Its small parking area is restricted to resident vehicles, but walkers and bikers are welcome. This beach is also just past the pretty historic village center of Southport—a pleasant place to stroll and shop. For picnic goodies, pick up traditional American delicatessen staples at its classic **Southport Market** (203–259–8377; open 8:00 A.M. to 6:00 P.M. daily), also on Pequot Avenue, or at the **Spic and Span Market** (203–259–1688; open 7:30 A.M. to 6:00 P.M. Monday through Saturday) across the way for goods with a gourmet flair. You can take your picnic to picturesque **Perry's Green** on Harbor Avenue adjacent to the Pequot Yacht Club, a five-minute walk from the village center, or park along the street right at the park at no charge.

and they do. Try the coquilles St. Jacques Provençale, the marvelous cheese soufflé, or the pan-fried monkfish. Perfect crusty breads, excellent desserts made in the patisserie at the rear of the same building, and a well-chosen wine list make lunch or dinner here a complete delight. Open Monday through Saturday for lunch from noon to 2:30 P.M. and dinner from 6:30 to 10:00 P.M. $$$

Spazzi 1229 Post Road (203–256–1629). This popular establishment presents Northern Italian cuisine with an emphasis on creative

Pequot Library Book Sale

If you are in Southport in late July, stop at the **Pequot Library's annual five-day book sale**. Nearly 100,000 books are collected each year, and the selection is fantastic. On the first day, book dealers and casual collectors alike arrive in droves to vie for the most desirable volumes. On this day (Friday), buyers pay twice the marked price; big spenders laying out $250 or more receive 20 percent off the doubled price. On Saturday and Sunday, the books are priced as marked; on Monday they are half of the marked price; and on Tuesday, all remaining books are free!

No admission is charged; the tents and doors open at 9:00 A.M. daily. On Friday the dash for the best titles ends at 8:00 P.M. On Saturday, Sunday, and Monday, the feeding frenzy is stopped at 5:30 P.M., and on Tuesday, you and your wheelbarrow have to be out by 3:00 P.M.

Built in 1887, the recently restored Romanesque Revival library (203–259–0346) is a Southport landmark, located at 720 Pequot Avenue just before you round the bend to Southport Beach.

pasta specialties and wood-oven pizza. Other delicious entrees include a hickory-grilled portobello mushroom tower, pan-seared tuna, Black Angus sirloin, lobster ravioli—but the menu changes according to the seasons and the creativity of the chef. Indoor seating or outdoor patio. Open daily for lunch, brunch, dinner, late supper. $$–$$$

Southport Brewing Company 2600 Post Road (203–256–2337). This rising star offers a smoke-free, 200-seat dining room with views of its gleaming chrome and stainless-steel microbrewery from every table in the house. The talented chef adds an Italian influence to the generous pasta dishes, fresh seafood, thin-crust pizza, crisp salads, and beef and chicken dishes. Soups, sandwiches, and pasta dishes are the focus at lunch. Muraled walls inside depict the process of making the brewery's ten original brews; a patio outside provides extra seats in warm weather. Live entertainment on Thursday nights. Open Monday through Saturday for lunch from 11:30 A.M. to 3:00 P.M. and dinner from 5:30 P.M., and for dinner only on Sunday from 4:30 P.M. $$

Firehouse Deli 22 Reef Road (203–255–5527). Major sandwiches, grinders, tacos, salads, quiche, soup, bagels, cheesecake, giant cookies, much more. Take-out or sit-down self-service. Outside seating in nice weather. Open Monday through Saturday 7:00 A.M to 6:00 P.M. and Sunday 8:00 A.M. to 5:00 P.M. $

Driftwood Coffee Shop Pequot Avenue (203–255–1975). This Southport landmark is a wonderful throwback to the good old days—come for great breakfast specials, freshly made chicken salad sandwiches, top-quality roast beef cooked right here, house-made soups just like your mother (or grandma) used to make, and other traditional favorites in a down-home luncheonette-style setting. Breakfast and lunch year-round daily from 8:00 A.M. to 4:30ish. $

Places to Stay in Fairfield

Fairfield Inn 417 Post Road (203–255–0491). Convenient, clean, cream-of-the-crop motor inn. 80 units, outdoor pool. $$$

Merritt Parkway Motor Inn 4180 Black Rock Turnpike (203–259–5264). Perched atop a hill at north end of town. 40 units, restaurant, continental breakfast. $$

Seagrape Inn at Fairfield Beach 1160 Reef Road (203–255–6808). 14 suites in an impeccably renovated Fairfield landmark that hadn't always enjoyed a crystal-clean reputation. Today the entire place sparkles in its new incarnation. A kitchenette, balcony, and sitting room is in every immaculately redecorated suite. A renovated restaurant is also on the premises. Daily, weekly, and monthly rates. Open year-round. $$$$

Public Boat Launches

South Benson Marina in the Jennings Boat Basin on the inside of Ash Creek Harbor to the west of Black Rock Harbor. Town-owned ramp for resident use primarily; nonresidents cannot purchase day-use permits, but seasonal permits ($70) are available by prior arrangement at the Parks Department (203–256–3010) at Independence Hall at the corner of Beach and Old Post Roads. Bring driver's license, vehicle registration, and boat registration.

Ye Yacht Yard at Southport Harbor (203–259–1384). Public boat launch ramp that operates exactly like the one at South Benson (see entry immediately above).

For Further Information

Fairfield Conservation Trust (203–256–3071). For map of 650 acres open for low-impact hiking, fishing, swimming, and mountain biking on Conservation Trust land. Areas of special interest may be **Lake Mohegan and the Cascades,** for swimming, hiking, fishing, and, with a permit, primitive camping; **Ash Creek,** for salt marsh, meadow, and creek habitats as well as a children's playground, walk-

Shore Points
Sound Reflections

Although thousands of residences crowd nearly rafter to rafter in private beach areas, most of the 5 million people who live along the shores of Long Island Sound only occasionally consider that America's Mediterranean, as it has been called, is a precious treasure that needs vigilant protection.

Fairfield is a good place from which to reflect on the importance and value of the ecosystem to which we also belong. Notable for its commitment to preserving public ownership and stewardship of coastal areas, Fairfield also is home to a large population that actively uses the Sound for recreation and transportation. Sit a while on Jennings Beach and notice the many indications of the complex issues that affect the future of the Sound: the busy commercial and recreational boat traffic, the signs of air and water pollution especially common in the western end of the estuary, the erosion of wildlife habitats as humans jostle for space along the sand and attempt to control the sea with jetties and seawalls. Juxtapose these concerns with the pleasures of listening to the rustling grasses on the restored dunes, breathing the fresh salt air, watching the sun rise on the eastern horizon, sifting through the sand for simple treasures like sea glass and shells.

Remember that this waterway teems with life and that human behavior constantly impacts the health of its plants, animals, and the water itself. In Fairfield and everywhere in the Long Island Sound watershed, human responsibility is essential to the preservation of this sea and all of its gifts to us.

ing trails, and opportunities for boating and fishing; **Brett Woods,** for a stocked trout pond and horseback riding trails; **Springer Glen,** for walking, fishing, picnicking; and **Pine Creek Marsh,** for boating and fishing at a 113-acre tidal salt marsh with wildlife.

Fairfield Parks and Recreation Department Independence Hall at the corner of Beach and Old Post Roads (203–256–3010). Information on beaches, parks, tennis, golf, boating, and permits for public boat launch ramps.

Fairfield Chamber of Commerce 1597 Post Road (203–255–1011). Maps, brochures, and information on lodging, businesses, restaurants.

⚓-Bridgeport

Heavily industrialized Bridgeport is unlikely to be the first municipality that comes to mind when travelers consider a visit to a coastal Connecticut town. At first glance, its virtues seem limited to manufacturing ventures, and its connection to the Sound appears a wholly unromantic one.

And yet, the state's largest city is also one of its busiest ports, its harbor offering dockage to massive tankers and cargo vessels loaded with goods destined for shipment to all of New England. Its beaches and salt marshes comprise the longest public waterfront in the state, and its many marinas and yacht clubs offer slips and moorings equal to the best of the better-known sailors' ports along the coast. One of the nation's oldest lighthouses is in Bridgeport, and, although its beacon is extinguished now, it once guided to safe anchorage the commercial fleet that still plies the offshore fishing grounds for lobsters and Connecticut's famed Blue Point oysters.

If you decide to forgo a visit to Bridgeport, you will miss a wealth of activities linked to the city's golden history as a center of industry, culture, and trade. Bridgeport has more designated historic districts than any other Connecticut municipality (including 3,000 structures on the National Register of Historic Places) and among its many greenswards are two expansive parks designed by famed landscape artist Frederick Law Olmsted.

Settled in 1639 on the site of a Native American village known as *Pequonnock,* or *cleared field,* after their cultivated acreage north of the natural harbor, Bridgeport was, for more than a hundred years, a scant collection of perhaps a dozen houses between the larger towns of Stratford and Fairfield. The deepest port between New York and New London was at Bridgeport's Black Rock. Consequently, Bridgeport's early economy focused on maritime trade, whaling, and shipbuilding.

During the Industrial Revolution, inventors, entrepreneurs, and major manufacturers flooded the "cleared field," establishing the city as a center of industry and a mecca for the immigrant population in search of jobs. Elias Howe had his sewing machine mass-produced here, Alexander Graham Bell's gramophones burst into song here, and Frisbie's pies made history first for their culinary excellence and later for the clever recycling of their tins as the world's first frisbees.

Ethnic enclaves enriched the city's cultural life, public parks and monuments punctuated wide boulevards lined with mansions and magnificent public buildings, and trains and trolleys brought visitors from the suburbs to the city's theaters and restaurants. Unfortunately, all that glittered was not gold. Greed, graft, and a notorious political patronage system, along with street crime, overcrowding in substandard schools, and poorly constructed housing hastily built to shelter tens of thousands of immigrant laborers led to the deterioration of the gilded city.

Now, in the last quarter of the twentieth century, much has been done in Bridgeport to polish up the urban landscape. New royal-blue street signs help usher visitors to the best-kept secrets of life in this reawakening shoreline city. It's not too early to celebrate the renaissance of Bridgeport. Come to enjoy the city's seaside parks, its excellent museums and theaters, the state's only zoo, and the diverse ethnic communities that infuse the culture of the city with energy and vitality.

The Best of Bridgeport

Discovery Museum

Hands-on in nearly every way, this family-friendly museum contains more than 100 interactive exhibits in the areas of art, science, and a smattering of industry. Although all are of general interest to visitors of all ages, the displays have been specially designed for the entertainment and education of children ages four to twelve.

Built to represent an artist's studio, the first floor's Interactive Art Gallery offers lessons about color, line, and perspective. You can "paint" with a computer, spin color wheels to "mix" new colors, shift stained "glass" puzzle pieces to create mood changes, or duck into a cavelike structure that plays red, blue, and yellow music.

Upstairs, past the fine art gallery, visitors learn about nuclear energy, electronics, electricity, magnetism, and light. Take a simulated bumper car ride to test your reaction time, hear Alexander Graham Bell's first telephone transmission, measure your height electronically under the giant Stanley Powerlock measuring tape, and use your body to create a swirling wall of color in the Pepsico Light Gallery.

The lowest floor includes a gallery of simple machines and "Discovery House," a learning space for children under five, with simplified hands-on science and art for the youngest visitors. The lower level is also home to the **Henry B. Dupont III Planetarium.**

The museum is also the site of one of the nation's sixteen **Challenger Learning Centers,** a computer-simulated mission control and space station where participants perform experiments and collect data as astronauts would. Afternoon mini-missions are offered to the public on weekends; these thirty-minute sessions cost $3 and are limited to visitors older than age ten. Five-hour missions, also for visitors aged ten and up, cost $25 per person and are planned for selected Saturdays throughout the year. For either option, call ahead for reservations.

4450 Park Avenue (exit 47, Merritt Parkway) (203–372–3521). Open year-round Tuesday to Saturday 10:00 A.M. to 5:00 P.M. and Sunday noon to 5:00 P.M., and on Mondays 10:00 A.M. to 5:00 P.M. in July and August. Closed on major holidays. Adults $6, seniors and children ages 3 to 18, $4; children under 3 are free. Extra fee for Challenger missions.

The Beardsley Zoological Gardens

This 36-acre zoological park inside 130-acre Beardsley Park specializes in rare or endangered species of North and South America, including red wolves, scarlet ibises, sandhill cranes, golden lion tamarins, spectacled bears, and ocelots. A beautiful trio of Siberian tigers also live here, an unusual departure from the Americas theme—and a lucky one for zoo visitors who admire this magnificent species. Among the 120 other species are river otters, toucans, timber wolves, and macaws. A New England farmyard enclosure is a petting zoo that features bunnies, goats, geese, sheep, a red-headed pig, and a Scottish Highland cow. Inside the New World Tropics building is an outstanding South American rainforest re-creation. Wooly monkeys, tortoises, and marmosets live with tropical birds in this excellent open-aviary exhibit.

The zoo's small size and accessible facilities plus frequent special events such as the ZooFolk concert series and teddy-bear picnics make Beardsley Zoo a popular site for families. Pony rides, a children's stage, a gift shop, a snack bar, and a large picnic grove are on the grounds. Also here is a marvelous pavilion housing exhibits from the beautiful antique **Pleasure Beach carousel** as well as its operating modern replica.

As you leave the zoo, ask the parking attendant for directions back to Route 8/25 South (which takes you to Route I–95 north or south) or North (which takes you to the Merritt Parkway north or south). It's a different route out of the zoo than in because of a one-way street or two.

1875 Noble Avenue (203–394–6565). Open daily from 9:00 A.M. to 4:00 P.M., except for Thanksgiving, Christmas, and New Year's Day. Adults $4, children ages 3 to 11, $3; under three are free. Zoo-only visitors do not have to pay the parking fee ($3 for Connecticut vehicles, $5 for out-of-state vehicles) charged to users of Beardsley Park.

Barnum Museum

Located in the heart of downtown on Main Street a block south of State Street is one of the best museums between New York and Boston. If you only have one day to spend in Bridgeport, make sure this "Greatest Show on Earth" is one of your stops.

Dedicated to the life and times of Phineas Taylor (P. T.) Barnum, the museum also celebrates the industrial heritage of Bridgeport and the culture of the circus in general. The first floor concentrates on Barnum the showman, entrepreneur, politician, and journalist. The successful juggler of half a dozen careers during his eighty-one years, Barnum bragged that his circus was "the most expensive and marvellous combination of the world's wonders ever brought together." You'll be easily drawn in to his magic from the minute you step inside the museum.

Be sure to watch the excellent clip from the movie *Barnum* so you get a fix on who Barnum was. Born in 1810 in Bethel, Connecticut, Barnum was a study in contradictions—hoaxster of outrageous proportions when it came to entertaining (and bilking) the masses, the clever Barnum was also mayor of this city, responsible for one of its greatest periods of growth and the conservation of its valuable parklands.

On the third floor, step right up and enter the circus. See Barnum's Fejee Mermaid, the two-headed calf, a real Egyptian mummy, Tom Thumb and Lavinia Warren's clothing and furniture, clown props, memorabilia of singer Jenny Lind, and the incredible five-ring Brinley's circus, hand-carved completely to scale and massive even in miniature.

820 Main Street (203–331–9881). Open year-round Tuesday through

The Barnum Festival

The annual **Barnum Festival** is a multifaceted celebration that culminates with the Great Street Parade and the Seaside Park fireworks on or near each Fourth of July. Among parades held across the nation, Bridgeport's has historically been second in size only to Macy's Thanksgiving Day extravaganza. A fabulous marching band competition called Champions on Parade, a Jenny Lind voice competition, and a children's Wing-Ding parade and carnival at Beardsley Park are among other festival events that out-of-town visitors can enjoy. For a schedule, call the **Barnum Festival Society** (203–367–8495).

Those visitors charmed by the beguiling Mr. Barnum and his tiny companion, Tom Thumb, may wish to visit **Mountain Grove Cemetery** on Dewey Street at North Avenue, the final resting place of Barnum and Charles Stratton, the tiny man who toured the world as General Tom Thumb. Call for hours and directions (203–336–3579).

Saturday 10:00 A.M. to 4:30 P.M. and Sunday noon to 4:30 P.M. Also open Monday in July and August, 11:00 A.M. to 4:30 P.M. Adults $5, seniors $4, children 4 to 18, $3; under age 4 is free.

The Housatonic Museum of Art

In the midst of the magnificently restored neighborhood surrounding lovely McLevy Green is Bridgeport's Housatonic Community–Technical College, which houses a small art museum with a noteworthy collection of 4,000 pieces. American and European artists of the nineteenth and twentieth centuries are represented here, along with African and Asian ethnographic collections, contemporary Latin American art, and works by Connecticut artists.

Among the paintings, graphics, prints, photos, masks, wood carvings, and sculpture are works from Cassatt, Miró, Rodin, Cézanne, Matisse, Picasso, Marsh, Lichtenstein, Rauschenberg, De Kooning, and Warhol. When you visit, you will see only a portion of the whole collection in the galleries as you walk into the main building at 900 Lafayette Boulevard. New shows are hung in this space every several weeks. Look for the wall racks that hold self-guided tour brochures to the rest of the collection in various campus sites.

900 Lafayette Boulevard (at State Street) on the downtown campus of Housatonic Community–Technical College (203–332–5000). Open September through May, Monday through Friday, from 8:30 A.M. to

The Bridgeport Bluefish

The continuing revival of Bridgeport is apparent in the new stadium constructed in 1998 as the first component of the sports arena and transportation complex to be completed over the next five years or so near the city's waterfront. The Bridgeport Bluefish are the Park City's new Class A baseball team playing in the also-new Atlantic League, a professional minor league club with no major league affiliations.

Constructed by the same firm that built the Norwich Navigators' Dodd Stadium, the 5,300-seat ballpark squats on the former site of the Jenkins Brothers Valve Company just blocks from the water and a mere stroll away from downtown. A superlative success in its 1998 opening season, the ballpark has fine views of the Sound, and the ferry docks and its box seats, club seats, and even skyboxes ensure a great view of the game. A supervised play area, a barbecue picnic area, food and souvenir concessions, restrooms, and on-site parking add to the park's appeal. Not since the 1940s when the lights went out on the Bridgeport Bees who played in the old Colonial League in the North End's Candlelight Stadium has Bridgeport been this excited about baseball.

The Bluefish play at 500 Main Street (off exit 27 on I-95) at the Connecticut Ballpark at Harbor Yard (203–333–1608 or 203–334–8499). Single-game prices range from general admission reserved tickets at $2 for children under 12 and seniors over 65 and $4 for adults to premium box seats at $10. The on-site parking fee is $2. Call for schedule and reservations.

5:30 P.M. *Closed during college recess in summertime and midwinter. Free, but donations are appreciated.*

Downtown Cabaret Theater

Revamped with a new sound system, comfortable seating, handicapped access, and better lighting, this theater produces professional, award-winning shows from Broadway hits to original musical revues every weekend of the year. Matinee and evening performances are given cabaret-style; patrons sit at round tables and bring their own picnics and refreshments or purchase snacks and set-ups from a concession. Many of the evening performances are suitable for children older than eight.

An enormously successful slate of musical productions for children ages 4 to 12 is offered every weekend from October through May. A great bargain for exposing youngsters to theater are the subscriptions to all six shows each season for $45. Security parking ($2) for all performances is available in the City Hall lot on Golden Hill Street, directly across from the Cabaret.

263 Golden Hill Street (203–576–1636). Open year-round; performances Friday at 8:00 P.M., Saturday at 5:30 and 8:30 P.M., and Sunday at 5:30 P.M. Single tickets generally range from $16 to $25; subscriptions available for whole season. Children's matinee series October through May; performances Saturday at noon and 2:30 P.M. and Sunday at noon. Single tickets $9.50; subscriptions available to part of or whole series.

The Polka Dot Playhouse

Called by the *New York Times* "the quintessential community theatre," Bridgeport's oldest continuously running live performance company is proudly celebrating its own renaissance as a professional theater. For more than forty years, the Playhouse staged four productions each summer season from its island home at Pleasure Beach Park. Tragedy struck in 1996 when the charming, white wooden bridge to the island went up in flames.

Now relocated to a new home in an amazingly revitalized area in the heart of downtown and beneficiary of a $2 million portion of a State of Connecticut fund set aside to revitalize Bridgeport's sinking economy, the Polka Dot has cut the ribbon on a fabulous 223-seat theater newly created inside a magnificent 1911 bank building in one of Bridgeport's historic districts. Just a block from the Barnum Museum and the Housatonic Museum of Art, the Polka Dot is now a year-round venue, offering musical revues, Broadway hits, and dramas led by Executive Director Rose Lodice. Here in this incredibly transformed district is an affordably priced opportunity to enjoy great theater.

167 State Street (203–333–3666). Performances usually on Friday and Saturday at 8:00 P.M. and Sunday at 3:00 P.M. All ages.

The Bridgeport to Port Jefferson Steamboat Company

The huge white boat at the rebuilt pier just a block from the downtown transportation terminal is a ferry that sails Long Island Sound 365 days a year. Still more excursion boat than commuter transportation, it can be used as a pleasure cruiser or as a means of getting by car to the prettier parts of Long Island more quickly than you'd go via New York City or the Throgs Neck Bridge.

You can go on foot, with bicycles, or with your car to Port Jefferson, New York, a village of shops and restaurants that cater to day-tripping crowds from the ferry. Theatre Three (516–928–9100) on Main Street in Port Jefferson presents live summer theater including reasonably priced, well-known hits suitable for the whole family. Special children's matinee productions are offered in July and August.

The sailing time on the ferry is about an hour and twenty minutes each way. Charters, moonlight cruises, dance cruises, and other specials are available.

Water Street Dock, Bridgeport (888–443–3779) or 102 West Broadway, Port Jefferson (516–473–0286). Operates year-round. Rates and schedules vary. Call for reservations, brochure, or information on Port Jefferson attractions.

Captain's Cove Seaport

One of the finest examples of Bridgeport's gradual recovery from blighted pockmark to merry dimple in the cheek of the Sound is this busy place at the edge of historic Black Rock Harbor. Part marina, part museum, and part shopping arcade, Captain's Cove is the baby of Kaye Williams, the friendly and imaginative Black Rock native and lobsterman who began the clean-up of this derelict area in the early 1980s. Along with the totally refurbished marina with new docks and slips and a boat repair shop are a 500-seat restaurant, a fish market, and a charming boardwalk filled with tiny boutiques and galleries, most of which are open only in the warm months.

Most notable of the many vessels at Captain's Cove is HMS *Rose*, a fully-rigged, twenty-four-gun British frigate and the only example of a Revolutionary-era warship afloat today. The world's largest operational wooden vessel, the beautifully restored *Rose* is often used as a sailing school training ship or as a goodwill ambassador to other ports. When she's home, you can tour her (adults $3; children $2).

The Seaport also includes a small museum on the first floor of the restored Victorian Dundon House. Exhibits are on the maritime history of Black Rock harbor as well as the environment and economy of Long Island Sound and its fisheries and oyster beds. Photographs depict the history of three local lighthouses that guided sailors and fisherfolk, and a collection of interesting items salvaged from nearby waters provides an eye-opening look at nautical litter. Admission is $2 for adults, $1 for children.

The surprises that await you at Captain's Cove are as variable as the New England weather. Sea chantey sing-alongs, band concerts,

Seaside Park

At the city's southernmost tip at the shore of Long Island Sound lies Seaside Park, a 325-acre expanse donated to the city by P. T. Barnum and designed by famed partners Frederick Law Olmsted and Calvert Vaux. The park is reached through the magnificent Perry Memorial Arch over Park Avenue. Designed by Henry Bacon in the same year (1916) he designed the Lincoln Memorial in Washington, the arch is the gateway to the small peninsula that features a shoreline drive, a wide, white-sand beach, playing fields, a band shell, concessions, walking paths, and rest areas.

Nonresidents wishing to drive through or spend a day at the park and beach must stop at a checkpoint to purchase a day-use pass. Connecticut vehicles are charged $5, out-of-state vehicles are charged $10, from Memorial Day weekend through Labor Day weekend. Swimming is occasionally limited in the summer season due to pollution, but the water is usually perfect for wading and cooling off, and the sand at Seaside is exceptionally fine and clean.

If you're in the mood for beach walking, follow the walkway along the long spit westward to Fayerweather Island and its nineteenth-century lighthouse. The perfect place for watching the boat traffic to the small marinas in the area and for photographing HMS *Rose* as she sails in or out of port, this site also offers a view of the sewage treatment plant and the now-grassy city landfill. Notwithstanding these inconsistencies, Fayerweather Island is a pretty place, offering great views of the Sound, the Seaport, and St. Mary's-by-the-Sea. A public boat launch ramp is out this way, as is a public fishing pier. The park is widely used year-round and is open from dawn until sunset. Call the Bridgeport Parks Department (203-576-7233) for more information.

food festivals, and other events are planned daily. Harbor cruises and chartered fishing trips are easily arranged here. Harbor cruises on *Mr. Lucky* or similar passenger launches are offered on Saturday and Sunday from noon to 5:00 P.M. (about $5 per adult, $4 for seniors, and $3 for children under twelve). Private charters can also be arranged on some of these tour boats.

One Bostwick Avenue (203–335–1433). Seaport stores open roughly April 1 to October 1 from 11:00 A.M. Closing time varies with the day, the crowds, and the weather. Restaurant, bar, and fish market open year-round; call for off-season schedule. Free admission to Seaport. Small fees for entrance to boats and Dundon House.

Boat Excursions and Charters

***Mr. Lucky* and other harbor tours** at Captain's Cove 1 Bostwick Avenue. Narrated public cruises around historic Black Rock, Burr Creek. For further information, call the office at Captain's Cove Seaport (203–335–1433) to ask for telephone numbers of the captains currently offering cruises or private charters. For the 1998 season the following boats offered fishing charters:

Carol Marie Captain Terry Thomas (203–264–2891). A 29-foot sportfishing boat offering fishing, diving, and cruising charters; departs Captain's Cove mid-April through October.

Daystar Captain Bob Bociek (203–333–1912, extension 212, or 203–876–2190). Departs Captain's Cove Seaport mid-April through November

Somertime Captain Bill Somers (203–438–5838). Departs Captain's Cove mid-April through November

Coastal Charter Company Captain Richard Scofield (203–334–9256). The 53-foot Hatteras motor yacht *China Clipper* offers lunch/dinner cruises, sightseeing; overnight cruises for up to six passengers. April 15 to November 15.

Places to Eat in Bridgeport

Fishing Buddies 211 State Street (203–335–7255). This downtown coffeehouse/bagel bakery was inspired by the happy memories of two cousins who wanted to motivate youngsters toward positive childhood experiences that enrich life. Designed as a fishing lodge, its hickory furniture and muraled walls are a great backdrop for its outstanding array of breakfast, lunch, and picnic foods such as bagels and spreads, sandwiches, muffins, and scones. Official suppliers of coffee for the Bridgeport Bluefish, Fishing Buddies also offers cappuccinos and lattes—it's no surprise that the shop's slogan is "one drop and you're hooked." Open weekdays from 6:30 A.M. to 5:00 P.M. $

Arizona Flats 3001 Fairfield Avenue (203–334–8300). Close enough to Captain's Cove Seaport if you've rejected their seafood and fries, this comfortable Southwestern-style restaurant serves tasty Tex-Mex cuisine. Great margaritas and warm blue-corn tortilla chips take the edge off your appetite while you wait for lunch or dinner. Popular bar, with an equally popular but quieter restaurant. Open for lunch Monday through Saturday 11:30 A.M. to 3:00 P.M. Dinner Monday through Saturday 5:00 to 11:00 P.M. and Sunday 4:00 to 11:00 P.M. $$–$$$

Ralph's and Rich's 121 Wall Street (203–366–3597). Right across

Shore Points

St. Mary's-by-the-Sea

In Black Rock, close to the city's border with Fairfield at Ash Creek, **St. Mary's-by-the-Sea** is one of the prettiest spots along the Connecticut coast. Below a natural bluff, a seawall edged with riprap keeps the waves from washing over the grassy shoreline park and promenade that borders the Sound. Across the curving boulevard that separates the park from the adjacent residential neighborhood are some of Bridgeport's most beautiful mansions.

Once the site of a small wooden church called St. Mary's-by-the-Sea, the park is now popular with walkers and joggers of all ages, families pushing strollers, and lovers ambling hand in hand. The cement promenade with a low wooden rail overlooks a wide-open vista across the Sound. Linger here, if you can, to watch the sun set and the moon rise and the lights come on across the water on Long Island. Benches along parts of the park and promenade provide a place to rest, but no other facilities are here. Small beaches lie at either end of the walkway, so you can add beachcombing to the simple pleasures you can enjoy at this lovely spot. Parking in the summer season is limited to Bridgeport residents and is strictly enforced. If you have been to Seaside Park earlier in the day, however, you can use your day-use pass at both parks. Otherwise, come from Labor Day to Memorial Day to savor the sights and smells that are free to all visitors.

To reach the mile-long park, take Fairfield Avenue (Route 1) west from downtown Bridgeport or east from Fairfield to Courtland Avenue. Go south on Courtland one long block to Gilman Street. Take a right on Gilman and follow it along the curve of Ash Creek and the salt marshes. As the road curves to the left near the mouth of the creek, it becomes Grovers Avenue, which is the wide boulevard that stretches along the promenade. Stop if you can, then continue along Grovers Avenue to Brewster Street. Take a left there to return to Fairfield Avenue.

from the Bridgeport Holiday Inn, this downtown gem is often SRO on weekend evenings. Offering continental cuisine a bit weighted toward Italian dishes, it also brags about its Black Angus beef and other hearty chops and steaks. Happy patrons say this is no boast; superb daily specials, excellent pasta, great bread, interesting sandwiches, and good service are a reality. Live piano music in the lounge on Friday and Saturday nights. Lunch Monday through Saturday 11:30 A.M. to 3:00 P.M.; dinner Monday through Saturday from 5:00 P.M. $$–$$$

Bloodroot 85 Ferris Street (203–576–9168). Tucked at the edge of Cedar Creek, this unassuming little place near Black Rock harbor is a marvelous place for wholesome-food lovers. Nourishing soups, crispy salads, whole-grain breads, and tasty vegetarian and vegan casseroles made with organic produce, aromatic grains, and root vegetables are some of the reasons a loyal following will come from out of state just to enjoy the food and the enlightened spirit that infuses the casual dining room. Enjoy a look at the terrific bookstore focusing on women's literature, poetry, health, and spirituality; it's to the left of the dining room as you walk in. Open for lunch Tuesday and Thursday through Sunday from 11:30 A.M to 2:30 P.M. and for dinner Tuesday and Thursday from 6:00 to 9:00 P.M. and Friday and Saturday from 6:00 to 10:00 P.M. $–$$

La Scogliera 697 Madison Avenue (203–333–0673). Bridgeport's Little Italy is centered on Madison Avenue at Capitol Avenue and is also known as the MAMA district, truthfully an acronym for Madison Avenue Merchants Association but symbolically a reminder of the great home cooking available at the many Italian restaurants, markets, and bakeries near this intersection. Just a few blocks south of the intersection, this restaurant on Madison between Capitol and North has offered authentic Italian cuisine for twenty years, and rumor is that no one has been disappointed yet. Housemade pasta, flavorful sauces, and tasty seafood and poultry dishes are what you might try before indulging in the delicious desserts. Open for lunch and dinner year-round, Tuesday through Thursday 11:30 A.M. to 10:00 P.M., Friday and Saturday 4:30 P.M. to midnight; Sunday noon to 9:00 P.M. $$

Micalizzi Italian Ice 712 Madison Avenue (203–366–2353). It's not fancy—it's just plain delicious. If you are visiting Bridgeport in the warm months, don't leave without stopping for the soft and creamy Italian ice that has made this home-based North End business a Park City classic. The wholesale end of the operation supplies restaurants throughout the state with some of the best ices and ice creams ever made, but the retail stand draws a stream of patrons who line up at the service window for their favorites of the twenty-two flavors produced inside this quintessential Little Italy residence. Open daily in summer, Monday through Saturday from noon to 10:00 P.M. and Sunday from 1:00 to 10:00 P.M. $

Places to Stay in Bridgeport

Bridgeport Holiday Inn 1070 Main Street (203–334–1234). Full-service hotel in convenient downtown location. 230 rooms, including 2 suites. Health club, indoor pool, restaurant, P.T.'s lounge, coffee shop. Sunday brunch from 9:00 A.M. to 1:00 P.M. Kids stay free. Inquire about senior citizen rates and weekend packages. $$$

Trumbull Marriott 180 Hawley Lane, Trumbull (203–378–1400). Convenient to Merritt Parkway and Route 8 and all Bridgeport attractions. Health club with sauna, indoor and outdoor pools, piano lounge. 320 rooms with data ports, hair dryers, coffeemakers, and more; children stay free. Two restaurants, including award-winning Ashley's Grille and Gratzi; Sunday brunch from 10:30 A.M. to 2:00 P.M. Half-price meals for kids 5 to 12 and complimentary meals for under-fives. $$$

Public Boat Launches

Seaside Park Ramp I–95 exit 27, south on Park Avenue, right on Waldemere Avenue to Barnum Dyke (203–384–9777). City launch ramp. Park is open roughly at dawn; gates lock at sunset. $5 fee for non-city residents. Parking for 60 cars.

Brewster Street Ramp Call Bridgeport harbormaster (203–576–8107) or Bridgeport Port Authority (203–384–9777). Improved ramp near Black Rock Harbor; no fee.

For Further Information

Bridgeport Convention and Visitors Commission 303 State Street (203–576–8491). Calendar of events, maps, brochures for attractions, information on lodging, dining, and transportation.

ARTFORCE (800–290–ARTS). Civic organization dedicated to the arts in the city. Call for calendar of annual events. Sponsors the Showcase Shuttle, a seasonal tour bus that leaves the ferry terminal and stops at major attractions throughout the city, on Saturdays only from 9:00 A.M. to noon; 25 cents per rider.

Bridgeport Parks Department (203–576–7233). Information on park hours, fees, special events.

Bridgeport Chamber of Commerce (203–332–1995). Maps; brochures on local attractions and businesses.

Wonderland of Ice 123 Glenwood Avenue (203–576–8110). Tournament-class indoor rink near Beardsley Park. Public skating sessions year-round. Call for schedule and fees.

Stratford

This small municipality often gets lost in the shuffle as travelers and commuters rush past it on I-95 but an afternoon here offers a few rewards for the educated tourist. It's true that few folks traveling through on the interstate highway would pick Stratford out as one of the most picturesque towns along the Sound, even though it has had ample time to establish itself as such. One of Connecticut's earliest English settlements, founded along with Fairfield in 1639, Stratford actually predates the hulking city of Bridgeport across the Pequonnock River. In those early days Bridgeport was a mere dozen houses in a place called Newfield, and Stratford was far more important as the place where the ferryman brought Post Road travelers across the wide Housatonic on its eastern border.

Although today much of Stratford maintains a close link to the quiet charms of the sea and busies itself with the simple commerce of a largely residential suburb, during the nineteenth century Stratford grew along with Bridgeport as a center of industry. Well known for its production of machine products, brake linings, hardware, and chemicals, the city also celebrates its unquestionable role in aviation history as the workshop of Igor Sikorsky, inventor of the first practical single-rotor helicopter. Today dwarfed by Bridgeport, Stratford still stays on the map as producer of the magnificent

Antiques Bonanza

Perhaps the artifacts of the Judson House have whetted your appetite for furnishings and accessories of days past. If so, head to the **Stratford Antique Center** (400 Honeyspot Road; 203–378–7744), an enormous blue warehouse filled to the brim with the wares of more than 200 dealers. Located not far from exit 31 off I-95, this group shop covers more than 16,000 square feet with furniture, statuary, jewelry, glassware, pottery, and thousands of other collectibles and one-of-a-kind artifacts both functional and decorative. Open at no charge daily from 10:00 A.M. to 5:00 P.M. year-round, and until 9:00 P.M. on Thursday evenings in November and December. Closed Thanksgiving, Christmas Day, and Easter Sunday.

whirlybirds of Igor's imagination at the Sikorsky Aircraft Division of United Technologies. From its earliest days to the present, Stratford has enjoyed only a modest reputation in Connecticut history in spite of its notable bird. A closer look reveals a few little-known attractions at the edge of the Sound.

The Best of Stratford

Catharine B. Mitchell Museum and Captain David Judson House

Visitors curious to discover exactly what Stratford has been all about these past 350 years should come here to its town museum. The home of the Stratford Historical Society, this small complex between Stratford's Main and Elm Streets includes two buildings open to visitors. A walk through the past is the main treat at the handsome red home of Captain David Judson. Built about 1750 on the site of his great-grandfather's 1639 stone homestead, this carefully restored post-and-beam, central-chimney colonial has a beautiful broken-scroll pediment doorway, a huge kitchen fireplace, paneled walls, and many examples of original Stratford-made furniture.

The Catharine Bunnell Mitchell Museum adjacent to Judson House contains permanent exhibits on Stratford history and changing exhibitions taken from the collections of the Historical Society. Among its artifacts are a fine collection of baskets, objects from the Native Americans who inhabited the area prior to European settlement, and items from early African-American history.

967 Academy Hill (203–378–0630) Open mid-May through October 31, Wednesday, Saturday, and Sunday from 11:00 A.M. to 4:00 P.M. and other times by appointment. Genealogy library open Tuesday and Thursday from 9:00 A.M. to 2:00 P.M. year-round. Guided tours of the Judson House; self-guided tours of Catharine Bunnell Mitchell Museum. Adults $2; seniors and students $1.

Short Beach Park

On the east-facing cove that cups the mouth of the Housatonic River, Stratford's city-owned Short Beach lies just north of the beach community of Lordship at the southernmost part of town. Popular with town residents as well as visitors, Short Beach offers tourists the best day-tripping bargain of all the public beaches along the Connecticut shore.

Ballfields, a playground, a nine-hole golf course, a miniature golf course, and tennis, basketball, and paddle tennis courts are all here. Picnic tables and grills help to make a visit a daylong affair. If barbecuing seems like too much of a chore, buy snacks at the concession (summer months only).

Short Beach Road (Stratford Parks and Recreation Department: 203–385–4052). Open year-round dawn to dusk. Lifeguards mid-May through Labor Day. Concession, restrooms, outside showers. Nonresident day use fee $3 per vehicle; season pass $100 per vehicle for unlimited use from Memorial Day to Labor Day.

Children's Garbage Museum

If young children are in your party, a visit to this innovative museum may be a worthwhile lesson. Twenty-two interactive exhibits teach children about the importance of recycling and the responsible treatment of garbage. One of the exhibits is a soft-sculpture compost pile in which children can crawl around in a simulated worm tunnel to see how organic

Shore Points

Long Beach

The sand spit at Long Beach offers some of the best beach walking in Fairfield County—and also demonstrates some of the powerful ways natural erosion, storm weather, and artificial beach "armor" like boulders, groins, and jetties can affect the condition of a beach. Park at the base of Washington Parkway among the restaurants near Marnick's Motel and walk from Point No Point, at the eastern end of the seawall, toward the west, where Stratford's Long Beach stretches toward Bridgeport's Pleasure Beach.

The armor of boulders at **Point No Point** that protects the Lordship residents from storm tides also robs its beach of sand. A walk along here from east to west reveals how the beach widens from only yards across to more than a quarter-mile across as the sand stretches westward. At the western edge of the spit a 700-foot-wide inlet was cut between Long Beach and Pleasure Beach by the hurricane of 1938. Closed over a period of years by the construction of a series of groins and by renourishment of the beach through the dumping of hundreds of thousands of cubic yards of sand, this Lewis Gut no longer threatens the Great Meadows marsh or its nearby human residents. Conservationists predict that another catastrophic storm is likely to destroy the spit, but for now, beachcombers enjoy the wind and the wildlife in this secluded spot.

matter decomposes into soil. The museum's mascot of sorts is Trash-o-saurus, a 24-foot-long dinosaur constructed from trash.

Visitors to the museum generally spend about an hour at the hands-on exhibit area, then take a tour of the next-door Southeastern Connecticut Regional Recycling Plant, where recyclables are sorted and prepared for sale to remanufacturers. Often a visit here ends with a return to the museum area for creation of a craft made from recycled or reusable material.

1410 Honeyspot Road Extension (I-95 exit 30; 800-455-9571). Open to school groups daily throughout the academic year; open to families the first Saturday of every other month, beginning with October, from 10:00 A.M. to 2:00 P.M., and in the summertime on Thursday only from 1:00 to 3:00 P.M. Suggested donation, $2 per person or $5 per family of four.

Long Beach Skateland

A whirl around this old-fashioned roller skating rink is sure to lift the spirit and raise the heart rate of every visitor, young or old. Owned and operated by the same family for the past forty-plus years, the rink now welcomes the kids of the kids who skated here in the fifties and sixties. To protect their specially coated wooden floor, they allow only traditional quad skates—no new-fangled in-line skates. Bring your own skates if you still have them or borrow a pair here, then let the rhythm of the music set your pace around the rink. You might want to consider your taste in tunes when choosing a time to visit: Most sessions feature contemporary Top Forty hits that kids and teens seem to love, but Sunday evenings feature the charming lilts of organ music harking back to the heyday of rollerskating dance competitions. A competition team practices here still, and you may get to see their graceful artistry if you come on Sunday evening.

Washington Parkway (203-378-9033). Open year-round, Friday 7:00 to 9:00 P.M., Saturday 2:00 to 4:00 P.M. and 7:30 to 10:00 P.M., and Sunday 2:00 to 4:00 P.M. and 7:00 to 9:00 P.M. Admission $4.50 per person regardless of age. Skates available at no extra charge. Snack and soda machines.

Stratford Shakespeare Festival Theater

Set in the midst of fourteen beautiful acres on the banks of the Housatonic, the Stratford Festival Theater was commonly known as the Shakespeare Theater from its opening in 1955 to its closing in 1982. Renowned during that time for its full-stage productions of the works of Shakespeare, the theater itself was modeled after the design believed by scholars to most closely resemble the bard's own Globe Theater in London. The theater's stage darkened in the early eighties when funding was lost, and deterioration of the theater as well as its surrounding parkland began.

A private, nonprofit organization spearheaded by the theater's artistic director Louis Burke has now taken on restoration of the park and renovation of the theater. In 1999, look for news of the grand reopening.

Two entirely new theaters are being added to the original structure. One is likely to concentrate on children's productions; the other is tentatively slated for theater workshops and dramatic arts classes. The main stage will feature the works of Shakespeare, classic plays by other famed dramatists, and perhaps Broadway musical hits and other twentieth-century works.

1812 Elm Street. Call SNET Information (411) for new listing of theater box office.

Boothe Memorial Park and Museum

This thirty-two-acre park overlooking the Housatonic River was once the site of an estate most recently shared by two wealthy but apparently eccentric brothers whose family had successfully farmed the site for more than 300 years. Today the park includes two of the original Boothe homesteads, plus a trolley station, a tollbooth plaza, a model lighthouse, a miniature windmill, an icehouse, an outdoor basilica with an organ house, an 1844 chapel, a barn with a weaving loom and other objects related to nineteenth-century farm life, a working blacksmith shop that boasts forty-four corners and forty-four vertical outside walls, a clocktower museum, and an amazing redwood monument called the Technocratic Cathedral. Did I mention that the brothers were eccentric?

Surrounding this intriguing conglomeration are acres of park grounds offering a beautiful rose garden, walking paths, picnic groves with tables, barbecue grills, and shelters, a children's playground, ball-playing areas, and restrooms. The buildings and restrooms close in November, but ice skating and sledding are permitted in the off-season when the weather cooperates.

134 Main Street, Putney (203–381–2046 or 203–381–2068). Park grounds open year-round daily from approximately 8:00 A.M. to dusk. Buildings open for guided or self-guided tours June 1 through November 1; call for schedule. Free.

Boat Excursions and Charters

Reel Thing **Boat Charters** (203-375-8623). Operates from Brown Boat Works, 638 Stratford Avenue. Chartered fishing trips May 1 through November 1. Capacity up to 16 passengers; day trips 7:00 A.M. to 3:00 P.M.
Reel Joy III (203-877-7164). Leaves from Spencer's Marina, Milford.
Mako (203-261-8821). The *Mako* docks at Birdseye Street municipal ramp at Beacon Point. Chartered fishing trips April to mid-November.

Places to Eat in Stratford

The Shell Station Main Street at the railroad station (203-377-1648). A friendly little place that has enjoyed a long-standing reputation for great seafood, handmade pasta, and freshly made-on-the-premises desserts. The Victorian decor in this historic depot adds to the quaint ambiance of this casual establishment. Soups, salads, sandwiches, and interesting appetizers round out the menu. Open year-round for lunch Monday through Friday 11:30 A.M to 2:30 P.M. and for dinner Monday through Saturday 5:00 to 10:00 P.M. and Sunday from noon to 9:00 P.M. $$-$$$
Amigos 7365 Main Street (203-378-8808). This classic Mexican eatery offers a festive ambiance for dining on traditional fare like tacos, fajitas, nachos, tostadas, and rellenos, plus chicken, seafood, and pork specialties. Views of Acapulco on the muraled walls and an authentic Mexican fountain complete the ethnic theme. Open for lunch Tuesday through Friday and dinner Tuesday through Sunday. $$
Knapp's Landing 520 Sniffens Lane (203-378-5999). Knapp's Landing sits at the mouth of the Housatonic at Sniffens Point, just north of Short Beach. Delicious continental cuisine, a charming sunken fish pond left from its former incarnation as a Japanese restaurant, and an open deck with patio seating in warm weather make this a great place to enjoy lunch or dinner on the Sound. The chef offers an eclectic menu of chicken, seafood, and pasta dishes, plus steaks, sandwiches, and salads. Open for lunch and dinner year-round, Tuesday through Sunday. $$
Allen's East 60 Beach Drive (203-378-0556). A classic seafood restaurant basking in the sun at Long Beach in Lordship, Allen's East is a spin-off from the famed Allen's Clam and Lobster House in

Westport. Overlooking the Sound, with gorgeous views from inside as well as from its beautiful outdoor patio, Allen's is well known for its outstanding seafood, its delicious Boston-style clam chowder, and its fast, friendly service. Full bar; lunch and dinner daily year-round. $$$

Seascape Restaurant 14 Beach Drive (203–375–2149). Seascape adds an Italian or even a Cajun flair to its creative seafood and pasta dishes. Tasty appetizers, veal, chicken, and New York strip, plus other treats for meat-lovers and vegetarians alike. An all-you-can-eat Sunday brunch is offered from 11:00 A.M. to 3:00 P.M. Early-bird dinner specials include soup or salad and a basket of bread for the table. Open weekdays for lunch and every day for dinner, plus Sunday brunch. $$

Marnick's Restaurant 10 Washington Parkway (203–377–6288). Attached to Marnick's Motel on the water, this casual family-owned eatery offers waterside dining with window tables overlooking the Sound. From sirloin steak and fresh seafood to sandwiches, salads, burgers, and fries, this Stratford classic is perfect for casual dining or family fare, reasonably priced. Open daily year-round. $–$$

Places to Stay in Stratford

Nathan Booth House B&B 6080 Main Street (203–378–6489). In the Putney section of town, south of the Merritt Parkway, this beautifully restored 1843 Greek Revival farmhouse on the National Register of Historic Places offers four lovely guest rooms decorated with period antique furnishings. A full country breakfast for all guests each morning may include fresh eggs from the innkeepers' own chickens, fresh honey collected from their honeybees, and treats like banana-blueberry pancakes, decadent French toast, or herb-baked eggs, plus juice, coffee, and teas. Smoke-free; no pets or children under age 13. $$$$

Marnick's Motel 10 Washington Parkway (203–377–6288). Updated and redecorated with a fresh face for the new century, this waterfront motel has been family owned for thirty-plus years. Of its twenty-nine simply but comfortably furnished rooms, all those facing the Sound have balconies, microwaves, and refrigerators. All rooms have private baths, cable color TV, and either two double beds or a king-size bed. Some rooms are reserved for nonsmoking guests. Rollaways and cribs are available. Guests are welcome to use the motel's private beach for swimming and shore fishing. Restaurant serves three meals daily. $$

Ramada Inn Stratford 225 Lordship Boulevard (203–375–8866).

145 rooms, restaurant, lounge, Friday and Saturday night live entertainment, Saturday night prime rib buffet. Indoor pool. Senior citizen
rates. $$$–$$$$

Days Inn 360 Honeyspot Road (203–375–5666). 92 units, indoor
pool, complimentary continental breakfast, senior citizen rates. $$

Public Boat Launches

Stratford Municipal Ramp Birdseye Street to Beacon Point
(203–377–9114). Permit required; inquire about day and season use.

Knapp's Landing Sniffens Lane at Sniffen's Point (203–375–6184).
Seasonal ramp with gas/diesel dock; restaurant.

For Further Information

Stratford Parks and Recreation Department (203–385–4052).

Milford

Settled in 1639 by families from New Haven and Wethersfield, this
community is Connecticut's sixth-oldest municipality. Now home to
enough citizens to qualify as a small city, Milford nonetheless retains
the charm of a New England shore town. In fact, Milford revels in its
intimate connection with the sea and the rivers that lap its 17 miles of
freshwater and saltwater shoreline.

On the town's eastern border, the wide Housatonic River empties
its fresh water into the Sound near beautiful Milford Point after making the 148-mile passage from its headwaters in the Berkshires. On
Milford's western border with West Haven, the boundary is formed by
the Oyster River, once the site of native encampments and later oystering concerns. In the center of town, the Wepawaug and Indian
Rivers flow gently into Milford Harbor and Gulf Pond before adding
their waters to the Sound, providing quiet shelter and safe anchorage
for the thousands of anglers and boaters who play here nearly three-
quarters of the year. Even the pretty duck ponds and small waterfalls

that characterize downtown remind the visitor of Milford's undeniable link to the water.

Back in 1639 one Thomas Tibbals literally stumbled upon Milford when he and a few others were busy chasing the Pequots from Mystic to Fairfield. He hurried back to his congregation and told them of the fair harbor and rich and goodly meadowlands he had found at the banks of the Wepawaug. The congregation set out by land and by sea to their new home, which they purchased from the Paugusset for the typical assortment of kettles, cloth, axes, and such. A year later, the English built a grist mill near the narrows between the river and the harbor and named their plantation Milford.

By the late seventeenth century Milford was well established as a mill town, with two grist mills, a sawmill, and two fulling mills for the production of cloth. By 1690 it had begun construction of its first shipbuilding wharf and sent its brigs to establish a brisk West Indies trade. Later the town gained a reputation as a producer of fine quality seed, straw hats, carriages, boots, shoes—and oysters.

Milford has made remarkable efforts to protect or restore its most valuable assets near the shore. Its coastal wildlife sanctuary is one of the most important tidal salt marsh refuges on the Sound, and its shellfish beds are among the healthiest and most productive in the state.

The Best of Milford

Connecticut Audubon Coastal Center at Milford Point

This pristine 840-acre habitat comprised mostly of salt marshes that border the Sound and the mouth of the Housatonic River provides visitors the opportunity to see one of the last surviving unaltered coastal properties in Connecticut. Opened in 1995, the Coastal Center is located at the very end of Milford Point Road.

A pathway provides access to the area's beach, a serene and secluded place for exploring and enjoying the native flora and fauna. Observation platforms at the beach edge help you gain a better view of the shorebirds and other wildlife. This is not a park, so no picnic areas or trash receptacles are provided. Swimming is prohibited, as are collecting and dune walking.

At the coastal environment education center, you can climb to the top level of a marvelous observation tower for a crow's-nest view of this land- and seascape. The displays inside the center include a 300-gallon saltwater tank with a diamondback terrapin and other speci-

Milford Beaches

Milford offers out-of-towners a chance to enjoy its public beaches for active fun.

Gulf Beach Gulf Street. Visitor parking $5 per vehicle from Memorial Day through Labor Day. Concession, restrooms, lifeguards, birdwatching/fishing pier. From here you can walk to legendary Charles Island, about half a mile offshore, at low tide. This adventure is not recommended by officials for nonswimmers but is perfectly doable even for adult-supervised children if you're aware of the tides. Be aware that a swift current crosses the fully submerged bar when the tide rises. On the partly wooded isle you can observe nesting seabirds and look for signs of the legendary treasure of Captain Kidd, supposedly buried somewhere on the south side of the island. Perhaps you'll return to the mainland draped in jewels.

Walnut Beach Corner of East Broadway and Viscount Drive. Parking $5 or free street parking. Large beach, small pavilion, restrooms, picnic tables, lifeguards. Nice, wide-open views, great sandbar access to the famed Charles Island, and convenient location adjacent to Silver Sands State Park. Officially open on weekends only from 11:00 A.M. to 3:00 P.M. from Memorial Day to July and from mid-August through Labor Day; open daily from 10:00 A.M. to 4:00 P.M. between July 1 and mid-August. These are the hours when the concession operates and lifeguards are on duty.

Silver Sands State Park (Call Milford Parks and Recreation at 203-783-3280 or the Hartford Office of State Parks at 860-424-3200.) Off Mayflower Avenue between Robert Treat Drive and Nettleton Avenue. Contiguous with Walnut Beach, this property of approximately 250 acres of shoreline includes Silver Sands Beach. Ongoing development at this state-owned, but city-run property will eventually make this a popular destination for the crowds; a boardwalk, first aid station, and restrooms are among the slated projects. Lifeguards and portolets are the only current amenities; bring your own drinking water, picnic foods and beverages, and trash bags.

Anchor Beach Beach Avenue off Chapel off Merwin Avenue in the Woodmont section of town. Free (but limited) street parking, no concession, portolet. Small, pretty crescent beach in mostly residential beach neighborhood.

mens native to the area, along with exhibits on shells, eggs, birds, and Long Island Sound ecology. Inquire about the lecture series, summer camp programs, and family activities.

Among the most popular events here are the naturalist-guided canoe trips through the Charles E. Wheeler State Wildlife Management Area, which is the official name for all this beautiful wetland and waterway system that surrounds the Coastal Center. Reservations are strongly recommended for the day and evening trips from mid-May through late September. Fees are $8 for Connecticut Audubon Society member, $12 per nonmember, if you bring your own canoe; for those who borrow center-owned canoes, the fees are respectively $10 or $14 per person.

One Milford Point Road, off Seaview Avenue (203–878–7440). Open

The Milford Green

The Milford town green, the second largest in Connecticut, was used in colonial times to graze cattle and sheep. Today the green, which lies between North and South Broad Street in the center of town, is used mostly for cultural events like craft fairs, art shows, and annual festivals. Free concerts are held on selected Friday nights from mid-June through August. Visitors are welcome to join town residents at these relaxing hourlong events. Call the **Milford Chamber of Commerce** (203-878-0681) or the **Milford Fine Arts Council** (203-878-6647) to obtain a schedule of the fairs and entertainment.

One of the green's best-known events is the **New England Arts and Crafts Festival,** held in early July, usually on the weekend following Independence Day. This colorful fair celebrates the creativity of scores of the region's finest crafters and fine artists. Visitors can enjoy musical performances and other entertainment throughout the two-day festival. A food court set up on the green by area restaurants helps keep the crowds happy. The festival hours are 9:00 A.M. to 5:00 P.M. both days.

The green is surrounded by boutiques and restaurants, so even without a planned activity, visitors will have no trouble finding ways to enjoy this pretty spot. On the north side of Broad Street in a charming structure that was once the site of the first telephone company in Milford is Lori Massi's **Somewhere in Time** boutique (203-877-6763) with Victorian-style gifts, preserved flowers and wreaths, and scented toiletries. Right next-door is the incomparable **Rainbow Gardens Inn** (203-878-2500) at 117 North Broad Street. (See Places to Eat and Places to Stay for details.)

year-round. Outdoor areas open dawn to dusk at no charge. Center open Tuesday through Saturday from 10:00 A.M. to 4:00 P.M. and Sunday noon to 4:00 P.M. Adults $2; seniors and children 3–12 $1; under 3 free; family rate $5. Free bird walks from 9:00 to 10:00 A.M. every second and fourth Saturday, year-round.

Milford Landing

At the head of Milford Harbor at the mouth of the Wepawaug River is an establishment that bends over backward to be the best of its kind anywhere. An all-transient docking facility for visiting boaters, this city-owned marina features fifty slips for vessels up to 65 feet, a launch ramp, 30- and 50-amp service, free pump-out service for overnight dockage, concierge service, and trained dock staff to assist at tie-up and so on. Handicapped access, restrooms, shower facilities, ice and water, and a laundromat help make visitors comfortable. Six public tennis courts, basketball courts, and a picnic pavilion are in the adjacent Wilcox Park.

37 Helwig Street. For slip reservations and further information, call Operations Director Dick Hosking (203–874–1610) or reach him by fax (203–874–1619).

Historic Wharf Lane Complex

Revisit the past through a visit to the three historic eighteenth-century homes maintained by the Milford Historical Society. Named for the old street that once ran from the old town wharf near Milford Harbor to the Milford Green, the Wharf Lane site was once a busy place lined with warehouses, tanneries, and general stores. Today a peaceful spot on a small bluff overlooking the harbor at the lower end of High Street, Wharf Lane is now but a road back in time. Featuring the 1700 Eells-Stow House, the 1780 Clark Stockade House, and the circa 1785 Bryan-Downs House, the complex portrays three centuries of life in New England through the furnishings, artifacts, and tours given in the trio of homes.

The Eells-Stow House is claimed to be the oldest surviving house in Milford. Built by Samuel Eells, this home has some significant architectural details and Milford-made eighteenth-century furnishings. See some Eells family artifacts and portraits, and hear the story of second owner Stephen Stow, who gave his own life in an effort to minister to the needs of two hundred American soldiers returned from a British prison ship with smallpox.

The Bryan-Downs House contains the Claude C. Coffin collection of Native American artifacts, touted as one of the finest archaeological records ever gathered in the state of Connecticut. Baskets, pottery, and stone tools are among the outstanding specimens providing clues to 10,000 years of prehistory in a coastal community. Also in the Bryan-Downs House is a re-creation of a general store, with barrels of candy and wooden toys, local histories and lore and walking tour guides. Outside the house is a period garden.

The **Clark Stockade House** was the first house in Milford to be built outside the original stockade. Moved to this site from its original location near the western end of the green, the house served as Milford's first hospital and also as a teahouse. Enjoy the thrill of walking down the same stone steps that General Washington trod when he visited Clark's Tavern during the Revolution.

34 High Street (203-874-2664). Open Memorial Day through Labor Day on Saturdays and Sundays from 2:00 to 4:00 P.M. Free; donation appreciated. Call to inquire about Christmas in July festivities and candlelight tours in early December.

Center for the Arts

In a landmark railroad station just north of Broad Street and the green is the Milford Fine Arts Council's own Center for the Arts, site of an ongoing schedule of events in the arts. Full dramatic productions by

Christmas in the Mansion

A unique Milford tradition is the annual holiday fair at Lauralton Hall, a private Catholic girls' high school of the Sisters of Mercy. The school's picturesque campus a short distance north of the town green was originally a country estate owned by Charles Hobby Pond, who built his early Victorian mansion there in 1864.

The school's principal fund-raiser takes festive advantage of the romantic ambiance of the mansion. Christmas in the Mansion, held on the weekend following Thanksgiving weekend, is a three-day arts and crafts fair. Decorated with luminaria, garlands, living wreaths, and thousands of lights, the mansion's rooms and hallways are filled with the wares of dozens of talented regional artisans. A Chinese auction allows visitors to take a chance on beautiful themed Christmas trees created by local decorators and florists, and the festival includes complimentary wassail and an affordable self-serve luncheon of quiche, soup, and sandwiches.

Lauralton Hall is located at 200 High Street. For further information, call (203) 877-2786.

Milford Oyster Festival

Slap on the sunscreen and load your wallet with cash for the irresistible fun at this annual celebration of the gustatory delights of the homely but delicious oyster. Why all the fuss for a simple shellfish? Well, Milford is famed for its oyster beds. The Paugusset tribe gathered oysters for centuries not far from the Wepawaug riverbank where their village was located, and the colonists became oyster gatherers too. By the mid-1800s, oystering had become big business.

The second full weekend in August is the usual date of the Oyster Festival, which draws tens of thousands of visitors to the harbor, the green, and Fowler Field on New Haven Avenue a block or so east of the green. An arts and crafts, a classic car show, entertainment, children's activities, a canoe race, a moonlight music and dance party, and a food court featuring oysters, of course, as well as many other treats from the sea are all part of the fun.

Admission to the Oyster Festival is free, but the food and the crafts will cost you at least a little something. Call (203) 878-5363 for more information.

the Eastbound Theater Company have included such popular shows as *A Lion in Winter* and *The Butler Did It;* among children's performances staged in the summertime have been *A Secret Garden* and other productions taken from classic literature. Poetry readings, coffeehouses on the last Friday of each month, a jazz concert series in the fall, a fine arts exhibition in October, and a photography exhibition in April are among the events visitors might enjoy here.

If you visit in summer, ask about the Council's annual sandcastle competition planned in July or August according to the best tide. Inquire also about the Council-sponsored summer concerts and fairs and festivals on the green.

40 Railroad Avenue South (203-878-6647). Open Monday through Friday from 9:00 A.M. to 1:00 P.M. plus other times for exhibitions, coffeehouses, performances. Free exhibition center; special performances $10 for adults; $8 seniors and students; $5 for children's performances.

Places to Eat in Milford

Stonebridge Restaurant 50 Daniel Street, off Broad Street at the memorial stone bridge (203-874-7947). Just a short walk from either the green or the harbor, this pretty restaurant overlooking the Wepawaug River and its waterfall offers casual patio dining in the summertime, plus more intimate seating in the cozy inside dining room, open year-round. Salads, sandwiches, fresh seafood, chicken, steaks, and vegetarian dishes are the mainstay here, as is evening entertainment in the pub room. Open Sunday to Thursday from 11:30 A.M. to 10:00 P.M and Friday and Saturday until 2:00 A.M. $–$$$

Scribner's 31 Village Road (203–878–7019). Tucked into a mostly residential beach community called Woodmont, Scribner's serves the freshest fish available anywhere. Wood-paneled dining rooms and a booth-lined lounge offer a comfortable ambiance for enjoying fine seafood and other culinary treats. Wonderful early-bird dinners served Sunday through Thursday from 5:00 to 6:00 P.M. are specially priced at under $12; they include a cup of Scribner's famed clam chowder. Open daily for dinner year-round from 5:00 P.M.; lunch Monday through Friday from 11:30 A.M. to 2:30 P.M. $$$

Jeffrey's 501 New Haven Avenue (203–878–1910). From inventive appetizers to delicious entrees, Jeffrey's offers one taste sensation after the other. Located just east of the center of town near Old Gate Lane, the restaurant overlooks the salt marshes bordering Gulf Pond. Open year-round for lunch Monday through Friday from 11:30 A.M. to 3:00 P.M., dinner Monday through Saturday from 5:30 P.M., and Sunday for a dinner menu only from 2:00 to 8:00 P.M. $$$

Rainbow Gardens Inn 117 North Broad Street (203–878–2500). Just across from the gazebo on the town green, this colorful Victorian home serves equally colorful and delicious meals year-round at lunch and dinner. Marvelously creative multicultural meals measure up to their intriguing names: discover the culinary delights of Rising Sun Stir Fry, Bayou Bliss, Medallions of Gold, or Heaven and Earth. Open for lunch Monday through Saturday 11:00 A.M. to 3:00 P.M.; dinner is served Tuesday through Thursday 5:00 to 9:00 P.M., Friday and Saturday until 10:00 P.M., and Sunday 4:00 to 8:00 P.M. $$$

Paul's Famous Hamburgers 829 Boston Post Road (203–874–7586). Skip the national fast-food chains and come instead to this classic drive-in burger shack, offering the finest in burgers, dogs, grilled chicken, and other typical American fast-fare, all prepared to order in a decidedly casual setting. Eat at the tables inside and out, or take it on the road. The author's husband swears Paul's are the best burgers on the planet. Open Monday through Saturday for lunch and dinner. $

Places to Stay in Milford

Comfort Inn 278 Old Gate Lane (203–877–9411 or 800–221–2222). 120 units, including 4 suites; sauna, indoor and outdoor hot tubs, continental breakfast. $$

Hampton Inn–Milford 129 Plains Road (203–874–4400 or 800–HAMPTON). 148 units; continental breakfast, senior citizen rates. $$

Red Roof Inn 10 Rowe Avenue (203–877–6060 or 800–THE–ROOF). 110 units, with 1 suite; children stay free; pets okay; senior citizen rates. $$

Susse Chalet Inn 111 Schoolhouse Road (203–877–8588 or 800–5–CHALET). 102 units; outdoor pool, continental breakfast; senior citizen rates. $$

Howard Johnson Lodge 1052 Boston Post Road (203–878–4611 or 800–I–GO–HOJO). 165 units with 3 suites; restaurant, coffee shop, lounge, in-room refrigerators, health and exercise facilities, sauna, whirlpool, playground, indoor and outdoor pools, miniature golf. Airport limo; senior citizen rates. $$

Rainbow Gardens Inn 117 North Broad Street (203–878–2500). This beautifully restored 1855 Victorian home on the green offers three cheerfully decorated rooms with antique furnishings, special luxuries like down pillows, a full country breakfast, and room service. For a truly indulgent treat, guests can arrange for a massage, facial, or aromatherapy. The inn is smoke-free and air-conditioned. Dinner & Stay packages are available. Open year-round. $$$$

Public Boat Launches

Housatonic River State Boat Launch Ramp and parking area in Devon section of town on Naugatuck Avenue north of Route 1, under the I-95 bridge between Stratford and Milford. Access upriver as far as the dam in Derby; downriver through Charles E. Wheeler Wildlife Refuge and out to Long Island Sound. Parking fee in summer only.

Milford Town Dock near Milford Landing at the head of the harbor (203–877–9990). Boat launch ramp; daily or seasonal fee.

For Further Information

Milford Chamber of Commerce (203–878–0681). 5 North Broad Street, 06460. Hours 8:30 A.M. to 4:30 P.M. Monday through Friday. Web site is http://www.milfordct.com. Maps, brochures, information on lodging or dining.

West Haven

Nearly 60,000 residents share West Haven's 10 square miles, leaving little room to entertain tourists in this suburb of New Haven. Settled by the English in 1648, this area was at first called West Farms and was considered part of the New Haven Colony. By 1711, West Farms had formed a separate parish with the area now called Orange, and eventually the two sections became known as the town of Orange. Late in the nineteenth century, a borough called West Haven was created, and in 1921 it became a town.

Today, rows of modest homes with neatly groomed yards characterize many neighborhoods; in others commercial establishments are flanked by apartment complexes and condominium developments right down to the shoreline. Nevertheless, the foresight of the city planners reserved a wide swath of beach for the use of all residents—and, thankfully, out-of-town guests. On your way to towns with sexier attractions, pause for an hour or so to savor the seascape.

The Best of West Haven

Bradley Point Park and West Haven Promenade

Grab a picnic cooler and a colorful kite and ride down to the West Haven shore to enjoy one of the most wide-open views of Long Island Sound accessible to the public. Along West Haven's Ocean Avenue and Captain Thomas Boulevard, walkers, bicyclists, and motorists can soak up the sounds and smells of the waves and the sea breezes as they explore 3 miles of roadway, pathway, and beach.

In the first half of the twentieth century, this beach was home to one of the Northeast's most famous amusement centers. At the height of its popularity from 1927 to 1957, the Savin Rock amusement park included dozens of carnival rides, not least of which were one of the world's highest Ferris wheels and a colossal—and scary—wooden roller coaster called the Thunderbolt that took its screaming fans right out over the water. After ninety years of happy, dizzying activity, the park became dilapidated and a center for activities of a more unsavory nature, and it finally was bulldozed in the early 1960s.

Today, by comparison with past decades, the completely restored and redeveloped beach is a quiet place, and the promenade that stretches across the former site of Savin Rock park is frequented mostly by gulls wheeling overhead, seniors playing bocce, and anglers waiting patiently at the fishing pier for a tug on their lines. On breezy days the sky here is often filled with the merry dance of literally dozens of kites. Come with your own kite, or just watch the beautiful aerial acrobatics of other flyers. Bring a picnic (leaving out anything that requires cooking—open flames are prohibited), beach gear, and bicycles to enjoy a full day here.

Food vendors often set up in or near park, and several restaurants along the boulevard provide sit-down meals of all descriptions. Another public park lies farther east of the Promenade, after Captain Thomas Boulevard shifts south one block and becomes Beach Street; called Morse Park, it has a playground and pavilion and is not far from the town boat launch ramp and the marinas that dot the western edge of New Haven Harbor. At this turning point, Beach Street becomes First Avenue, which heads northward to hug the harbor shore. To leave West Haven, follow First Avenue right up to I-95.

Bradley Point Park is on Captain Thomas Boulevard at Bradley Point (203–937–3651). Take exit 42 off I-95 and follow the signs for Route 162 south, to Platt Avenue, and then south to the shoreline. Open dawn to dusk year-round. Parking in lot or on side streets; constable on duty from Memorial Day to Labor Day; non-residents pay per-vehicle fee of $10 per day or $5 after 4:00 P.M.

Shore Points
Fun after Dark

Fireworks over the Sound are a special event in West Haven on or near the Fourth of July. Launched from a barge offshore, the display is among the best in the state. The popularity of this event means that parking becomes a serious issue, so plan to arrive early in the afternoon and stake out your place on the beach or promenade for the best views. A certain amount of holiday hoopla accompanies the show. Along with your beach chairs and blankets, be sure to bring a bit of extra cash for balloons, ice cream, and neon necklaces. Plan, too, to deal with a delay in the traffic flow after the show; unless you skedaddle mid-display, the wait in the parking lots and main avenues of egress will almost certainly exceed the twenty- to thirty-minute pyrotechnic extravaganza. Call the West Haven Park and Recreation Department (203-937-3651) for information on this year's display.

Places to Eat in West Haven

Chick's Drive-In 183 Beach Street (203–934–4510). A shoreline classic established in 1950, this quintessential drive-in seafood shack is the perfect place to stop if you want to be as close to the beach as possible when you celebrate summer with an orgy of fresh fried clams, a brimming lobster roll, or a plate of soft-shell crabs. If seafood doesn't float your boat, pair one of Chick's famed West Haven split dogs with an order of excellent homestyle onion rings. Indoor and outdoor seating. Open daily year-round. In-season hours Sunday through Thursday from 10:00 A.M. to 11:00 P.M.; Friday and Saturday until midnight. Winter hours shorter. $

Beach Street Waterfront Grille 343 Beach Street (203–934–3554). This "new" kid on the block is the reincarnation of the Original New England Food and Beverage Company, with a facelift that makes "creative flair" sound like a weak description. Star-studded fiber optic ceilings, colorful murals, and a wide-open view of the Sound accompany dozens of updates to the menu itself. Pastas, grilled seafood, shrimp pesto, a raw bar, and much more. Entertainment in the bar on Friday and Saturday nights; open daily for dinner year-round; lunch also on Friday and Saturday, plus the dinner menu from noon onward on Sunday. $–$$$

Captain's Galley 19 Beach Street (203–932–1811). Some folks say this is the best of all the seafood restaurants nearby; it certainly is delicious. Fresh seafood almost any way you like it; housemade chowders, fresh salads, plus chicken, prime rib, and pastas. Inside dining and outside patio in warm weather. Open year-round for lunch and dinner daily. $$

Jimmie's of Savin Rock 5 Rock Street (203–934–3212). Probably the most widely known of all the seafood restaurants along this part of the shore. Long lines attest to its popularity. All the shore seafood favorites, plus lots of other American standbys. Overlooks the Sound, but no outdoor seating. Open year-round for lunch and dinner daily. $$

Biagetti's Restaurant 77 Campbell Avenue (203–934–7700). Not far from the beach but with no view, this restaurant has offered fine Italian-American cuisine for twenty-six years. If you love good food, trade the view for wonderful specialties just like Mama made. Everything is homemade from sauce to soup, and the family-style ambiance keeps the place comfortable and affordable for adult as well as young diners. Open year-round for dinner Tuesday through

Saturday from 5:00 P.M. and Sunday from 1:00 P.M. $$

Places to Stay in West Haven

Econolodge 370 Highland Street (203–934–6611). 79 basic units; no meals. $$

Courtyard by Marriott New Haven/Orange 136 Marsh Hill Road, off I–95 exit 41, in Orange (203–799–2200). 121 rooms, including 6 suites, some with Jacuzzi, balcony; outdoor pool, health club, breakfast restaurant. $$$$

Days Inn Hotel–West Haven 490 Saw Mill Road, off I–95 exit 42 (203–933–0344 or 800–DAYS–INN). 102 units; restaurant, lounge, indoor pool, whirlpool, fitness center. Senior citizen rates; shuttles to airports. $$

Public Boat Launch

West Haven Public Ramp At foot of Monahan Place off First Avenue floating dock and launch ramp (203–946–8546).

For Further Information

West Haven Chamber of Commerce 259 Elm Street, second floor (203–933–1500). Open year-round Tuesday to Thursday 11:00 A.M. to 2:00 P.M. Maps, brochures, and listings of businesses, lodgings, restaurants.

Outdoor Summer Concerts (203–937–3510). John C. Ireland Bandstand on the West Haven Center Green, Friday evenings at 7:00 P.M. from June through August. Free. Call for schedule.

New Haven

Since its earliest days an important center of industry, education, and culture along the Connecticut shore, New Haven also remains one of the most vital cities in the state. Although Connecticut's capital city of Hartford is also steeped in history and strongly rooted in the arts and education, New Haven sports a more sophisticated, cosmopolitan style. Perhaps its location on I–95 between New York and Boston contributes to this ambiance. Undeniably, its inseparable association with Yale University enriches its artistic and intellectual aspects, and its diverse community of citizens adds to its cultural panache.

Long a center of life for the Native Americans who once fished its waterways and hunted along its traprock ridges, New Haven has also been home to European newcomers for the better part of four centuries. Once the site of a village called *Quinnipiac,* which means *long river place,* New Haven was renamed by the five hundred English settlers who arrived from Boston in 1638 and established a colony here in 1640. Led by a charismatic Puritan minister named John Davenport and a wealthy Puritan merchant named Theophilus Eaton, the New Haven colonists were better off financially than any other group of settlers in New England. Their wealth showed in the stately homes they built around the New Haven Green, and their confidence defined their settlement as one of great importance. From 1701 to 1875, in fact, New Haven served, with Hartford, as joint capital of the Connecticut Colony and then of the state.

New Haven became known best for the superior quality of its products. By 1810 and for more than fifty years, for instance, New Haven was famed as the producer of the country's finest carriages, and America's first assembly line, in fact, was right here in James Brewster's Carriage Factory. Perhaps the most notable manufacturer of New Haven was Eli Whitney, Yale-educated lawyer and inventor. Whitney's cotton gin changed the economy of the South—as well as contributed to the rise (and tragedy) of slavery—and was produced in his New Haven factory.

Simultaneously with all this activity, New Haven's Yale College developed its reputation as one of the nation's finest educational and research institutions. By 1810, it had established a medical school and the nation's first school of science. Shortly thereafter, it added other professional schools, including one of the country's first law schools and what is to this date the oldest continuous forestry school in the United States. In 1832, it established the nation's first university art museum and the nation's first art school. Be sure to spend at least a few days exploring this fascinating urban campus.

The Best of New Haven

West Rock Ridge State Park

If the layout of the city mystifies you, you might want to start a tour of New Haven high above the urban clamor. Overlooking the entire city, West Rock is one of two ridges of basalt forced skyward through volcanic action some 200 million years ago. The state park here runs along the top of the western ridge and has hiking trails, a fishing pond, and a picnic area.

A scenic drive traverses parts of the park. Its southern portion is open to motor vehicles only on a seasonal basis, usually April through November; call for opening dates. The northern section is closed to vehicles but open to hikers, cyclers, and skiers year-round. Folks in cars wishing to hike when the scenic drive is closed can park at the Nature Center on Wintergreen Avenue. The park entrance is about 200 feet south of the Nature Center entrance, also on Wintergreen Avenue.

The park's blue-blazed main trail, called **Regicides Trail**, is accessible at the top of the ridge via the scenic drive or you can walk in off-season from the Nature Center. Situated just off the roadway that also leads to the park's South Overlook, this 6.3-mile footpath begins near a parking area close to the summit at Judges Cave. It follows the crest of the West Rock Ridge range northward, ending at its junction with the Quinnipiac Trail, which leads to Sleeping Giant State Park in Hamden. The trail offers beautiful views of the harbor and, of course, leads through pretty woodlands. Wear proper footgear because the path, although not consistently strenuous, can be difficult in some spots.

The most infamous site on the trail is the **Judges Cave,** where in 1661 Edward Whalley, John Dixwell, and William Goffe hid from bounty hunters (agents of Charles II) who were hoping to claim the reward for their capture as traitors against the Crown. Charles II intended to execute the men, who had been among nearly sixty

Englishmen who had signed the death warrant against Charles I many years earlier. The trio eluded the pursuers, and each of the men lived in New Haven for at least some time after the agents gave up the search. Today, three of the city's avenues are named for the regicides.

Wintergreen Avenue (203–789–7498). Open year-round daily from 8:00 A.M. to sunset. Entrance fee for cars, in season, $1.

West Rock Nature Center

Owned and operated by the city and visited most frequently by school-children, this separate area just north of the entrance to West Rock Ridge State Park on Wintergreen Avenue covers forty acres. Short nature trails take visitors along the Wintergreen Brook ravine, over Wintergreen Falls, past a small pond, and so on. The center's Old Nature House and other indoor and outdoor exhibits have wildlife displays such as native birds, reptiles, and small native mammals, and a small demonstration organic garden. Winter is also pretty here. If you come on a snow day with sleds and toboggans, a guaranteed good time awaits.

1020 Wintergreen Avenue, at Baldwin Drive, not far from exit 59 off Route 15 (203–946–8016). Center open Monday through Friday 10:00 A.M. to 4:00 P.M. Closed holidays. Grounds open dawn to dusk daily, year-round. Free.

East Rock Park

The twin of West Rock, East Rock is on the other side of the city, recognizable by its matching sandstone and traprock cliffs. Its 425-acre park is city-owned and is best known for its spectacular views of the city and harbor from its monument-topped summit. Long-range binoculars, benches at the scenic overlook, and a large, grassy picnic area with barbecue grills add to your enjoyment.

A new environmental education center is slated to open in the park by 1999. Called the Trowbridge Environmental Center, the building will have a pre-school focus and will contain displays about local wildlife and plant life.

Elsewhere in the park, walk on the 10 miles of hiking trails, including the cliff-side ascent called the Giant's Steps Trail. A bird sanctuary, a self-guided nature trail, picnic pavilions, playgrounds, an ice skating rink, a basketball court, and opportunities for sledding, fishing, and kite flying are also located within the park boundaries. Stop at the ranger station in College Woods for a map.

Enter from East Rock Road in New Haven or Davis Road in Hamden. Playground and ranger station in College Woods at corner of Cold Spring and Orange Street (203–946–6086). Station open year-round Monday

Yale University Visitor Information and Walking Tours

As you might guess from its worldwide reputation, Yale is a wonderful university to tour. See the gloriously Gothic splendor of the Sterling Memorial Library. Walk through Phelps Gate into the Old Campus quad and listen to the bells in Harkness Tower. Stop at the statue of Yale grad Nathan Hale outside the 1750 Connecticut Hall, where Noah Webster, Nathan Hale, and William Howard Taft perfected their studies. Learn about the development of the university into a world-class research and education center.

You can join a free, student-guided **Yale University Walking Tour** on Saturday and Sunday at 1:30 P.M. and on Monday through Friday at 10:30 A.M. and 2:00 P.M. (but not on Thanksgiving, Christmas Eve, Christmas Day, New Year's Eve, or New Year's Day). The one-hour tour leaves from the **Yale Visitor Information Center** (203-432-2300) at 149 Elm Street, across from the north side of the New Haven Green. No reservations or tickets are necessary; simply arrive about ten minutes prior to departure. You can also pick up a self-guided tour pamphlet from the Visitor Center (open year-round, Monday through Friday from 9:00 A.M. to 4:45 P.M. and Saturday and Sunday from 10:00 A.M. to 4:00 P.M.) and tour the campus on your own.

A second tour option is the perfect complement to the university tour; offering a special focus on the city's history and architecture, the **New Haven Walking Tour** covers important downtown sites near the New Haven Green. Those tours are given from April through October on Thursdays at noon. Plan to arrive at the Yale Visitor Center five minutes or so before noon. No reservations or tickets are necessary for this tour either, but you may call for information (203–432–2302).

through Friday from 8:30 A.M. to 4:30 P.M. Call for info on the Trowbridge Environmental Center. Park open daily year-round from sunrise to sunset. Summit Road open daily from April 1 to October 31, 8:00 a.m.to sunset, and at the same time on Fridays and weekends only from November 1 through March. Two other roads are closed to vehicles but open to cyclists, in-line skaters, and walkers. Hiking trails are closed to mountain bikes. Free.

Yale University Art Gallery

Founded in 1832, the oldest university art museum in the United States, the gallery's 100,000-piece collection provides an excellent overview of the history of art from ancient to modern times. Come here to see objects from ancient Egypt, elsewhere in the Middle East and Africa, the Pacific islands, and the Far East. The American paintings and decorative arts are exquisite, as are the collections of American furniture and silver. O'Keeffe, Kandinsky, and Pollock are among the twentieth-century artists, but earlier treasures abound, including masterpieces of the Hudson River School and American Impressionists. The European collection includes Van Gogh, Manet, Monet, Picasso, and many more famed artists.

In addition to special exhibitions of works from the permanent collection, the museum hosts changing exhibitions of work that may never again be collected in one place in this area. The museum also offers tours, lectures, and concerts.

1111 Chapel Street at York Street (203–432–0600). Open from September through July, Tuesday through Saturday from 10:00 A.M. to 5:00 P.M. and Sunday from 1:00 to 6:00 P.M. Closed in August and on December 24, 25, and 31 and January 1. One-hour guided gallery tours throughout the season, usually on Wednesday and Saturday at 1:30 P.M. plus other dates with special speakers. Free; donation suggested.

Yale Center for British Art

Home to the largest collection of British art outside Great Britain, the center exhibits magnificent oil and watercolor paintings, drawings, prints, rare books, decorative arts, and sculpture from the Elizabethan period to the present. Works by Stubbs, Gainsborough, Hogarth, Turner, Constable, Blake, and Reynolds are among its treasures. Aligned with a research institute, a reference library and photographic archive, and a paper conservation laboratory, the museum has a serene and serious aura, but visitors of all ages are most welcome. Although the museum's calendar of lectures, symposia, gallery tours, Sunday afternoon concerts, and films are specifically directed to art students and adult aficionados, programs suitable for children occasionally appear on this schedule.

1080 Chapel Street at High Street (203–432–2800). Usually open year-round Tuesday through Saturday 10:00 A.M. to 5:00 P.M. and Sunday noon to 5:00 P.M. Closed major holidays. Free.

Beinecke Rare Book and Manuscript Library

In the midst of the Yale campus and bordered by a sunken courtyard garden featuring the sculpture of Isamo Noguchi, the Beinecke Rare

The Audubon Arts District

Tucked primarily into the two short blocks of Audubon Street between Whitney Avenue and State Street, the Audubon Arts District is a small neighborhood with a focus on the visual and performing arts. In this enclave, galleries, studios, and art and music schools attract visitors as well as serious artists and aspiring students. Serving their other needs are a fair number of restaurants, cafes, and boutiques with a personal flair. In addition to the **Creative Arts Workshop** (203–562–4927) at 80 Audubon Street, visitors may want to visit or inquire about special exhibitions and/or performances at such establishments as the **Educational Center for the Arts** (203–787–5191) at 55 Audubon Street, the **Neighborhood Music School** (203–397–2709) at 100 Audubon Street, the **Small Space Gallery** (203–772–2788) at 70 Audubon Street, and the **Wave gallery** and shop at 15 Whitney Avenue.

Of particular note in the neighborhood is **Artspace** (203–772–2377), at 70 Audubon Street. Its studios usually hum with the vibrations of creative energy, and its gallery and some studios are open to visitors Tuesday through Saturday from 11:00 A.M. to 5:00 P.M. (summer hours may differ).

The **John Slade Ely House** (203–624–8055) at 51 Trumbull Street is just a block north of Audubon Street between Whitney Avenue and Orange Street. Housed in a 1905 mansion, this center for contemporary visual arts and humanitarian activities offers eight galleries displaying works from New Haven's oldest art guilds. The center is open at no charge from September through June from Tuesday through Friday 1:00 to 4:00 P.M. and Saturday and Sunday 2:00 to 5:00 P.M.

Out of the district but not far away is **Erector Square** (203–865–5055) at 315 Peck Street, Building 20, former site of the historic A. C. Gilbert Toy Factory that once manufactured erector sets and American Flyer toy trains. Now the building houses eighty artists who display and sell their work in the gallery/shop and occasionally open their studios to guests. Open from September through May, the gallery has nine exhibitions each season. Hours for the gallery and the gallery shop are Wednesday through Saturday from 1:00 to 4:00 P.M.

Book and Manuscript Library contains remarkable treasures within its dimly lit galleries. The only natural light that enters this nearly sacred space is filtered through translucent slabs of Vermont marble, which protect the manuscripts, illuminations, and rare prints from the damage of solar radiation. One of the largest rare book collections in the world, the Beinecke contains well over 500,000 printed volumes and several million manuscripts. Among the library's most famed holdings are a Gutenberg Bible, the prints of artist and ornithologist John James Audubon, and the original collection of the Yale College Library. Along with these are amazing medieval illuminated manuscripts, priceless volumes printed before 1500, and journals, first editions, and rare editions of books by the world's greatest authors. Awe-inspiring and yet welcoming to visitors of all ages, the library presents four special changing exhibitions annually.

121 Wall Street (203–432–2977). Open year-round Monday through Friday from 8:30 A.M. to 5:00 P.M. and Saturday from 10:00 A.M. to 5:00 P.M. Closed on Sundays, major holidays, and on Saturdays in August. Free.

Carillon Concerts at Harkness Tower

If you are in New Haven in the summertime on Friday night at 7:00 P.M., grab a blanket and a picnic dinner and head to Harkness Tower near the Old Campus between Chapel and Elm Streets. Enter the quad from High Street, and, there in the courtyard, relax a while and listen to the incredible music of the 221-foot-tall tower's fifty-four chromatically tuned carillon bells. Students of the art as well as international artists play here several times each summer for about an hour. Don't pack anything crunchy and noisy in your picnic and make sure you close your eyes for the full and unforgettable effect of the glorious classical and popular pieces on each concert's program.

For schedule of these free performances, call Yale Guild of Carillonneurs (203–432–2309) or Yale Events Hotline (203–432–9100). In case of rain, a listening room is opened in Phelps Hall at 344 College Street.

Peabody Museum of Natural History at Yale

The Peabody, built in 1866, houses one of the nation's oldest and largest natural history collections. Just imagine dinosaurs, dinosaurs, dinosaurs, plus fossils, birds, insects, seashells, rocks, shrunken heads, minerals, meteorites, mummies, mastodons, and mammals. An enormous mural in the Great Hall depicts scientists' best guesses as to how the dinosaurs might have looked. (Called *The Age of Reptiles,* this Pulitzer Prize–winning mural painted by Rudolph Zallinger from 1942 to 1947 has also been partially reproduced on one of the oil storage tanks near New Haven Harbor.)

In other galleries, excellent wildlife and cultural dioramas from many habitats and periods include studies of Neolithic, Pacific,

Mesoamerican, ancient Egyptian, and Connecticut Native American peoples. Of interest to those traveling with children may be the Discovery Room, which has been designed especially for young visitors who need to touch, feel, and smell the displays.

Changing exhibitions and tons of special events, classes, workshops, and hands-on activities are offered throughout the year. The museum has a gift shop and restrooms but no food concession.

170 Whitney Avenue (203–432–5050). Open year-round daily, Monday through Saturday 10:00 A.M. to 5:00 P.M. and Sunday noon to 5:00 P.M. Adults $5, children 3–15 $3.

New Haven Colony Historical Society

This beautiful building designed by famed architect and architecture historian J. Frederick Kelly expressly as the museum of the Colony of New Haven is alone worth a visit. A colonial revival masterpiece built in 1930 in the late Georgian style, it has a lovely skylit rotunda, marble staircases, an alluring salmon-colored ballroom, and magnificent moldings at every doorway. The exhibits focus on the history of the colony, the development of the city, and the inventions and industries begun in New Haven County. See Eli Whitney's cotton gin, Charles Goodyear's rubber inkwell, an organ made by the New Haven Organ Company, an original Mysto Magic Erector Set, and a three-story dollhouse with a thousand details of decoration. Along with these displays are historical photographs, maps, ships' models, a wonderful ongoing *Amistad* exhibit that includes Nathaniel Jocelyn's portrait of Joseph Cinque, and changing exhibitions.

114 Whitney Avenue (203–562–4183). Open year-round Tuesday through Friday 10:00 A.M. to 5:00 P.M. and Saturday and Sunday 2:00 to 5:00 P.M. Closed major holidays. Adults $2; children 6–16 $1.

Amistad Memorial

Lessons of courage, honor, and justice are to be learned at the base of the marvelous bronze sculpture outside New Haven's City Hall. Created by Kentucky artist Ed Hamilton, the *Amistad* Memorial reminds visitors of the bravery of Joseph Cinque and the commitment of his American supporters to take a moral stand against the outrage of slavery and the illegal capture of free Africans from their homelands.

The story of the *Amistad* Africans started in the seas off Havana, Cuba, in 1839 when fifty-three Mendi captives seized control of the merchant ship *La Amistad,* which was taking them closer and closer

Elm City Firsts

Historians, archivists, and ordinary diehard fans of New Haven have had some fun compiling lists of the city's famous "firsts." Of course, counterclaims have occasionally refuted these assertions, but New Haven buffs aver that the world as we know it would be entirely different if not for these local inventions:

Football The story goes that Yale freshmen and sophomores—en masse—regularly accosted one another in a kind of chaotic romp involving a round ball, a large field, and two goalposts. The older and wiser sophomores eventually decided that perhaps only twenty of each class should meet on the field, and Walter Camp organized the gridiron pattern and created the rules that made the wild rumpus into a new game called American football.

Frisbee Mrs. Frisbie's pies—and their metal tins—were made in Bridgeport, but Yalies who had finished their pies took the tins to the New Haven Green and sent them whirling in a new twist, so to speak, on the game of catch. Soon plastic versions replaced the tins, and now students play Ultimate Frisbee all across the nation.

Hamburgers In 1900 Louis Lassen couldn't bear to throw away the tender meat scraps from his thin-sliced steak sandwiches, so he ground them up, packed them together in a patty, and made history. (Stop in at Louis' Lunch, 263 Crown Street, for the full story.)

Hot Dogs Who's to say who really wrapped the first bun around a plump sausage? Some say it happened here, and the proof rests at least partly in the Yale student newspaper that printed, in about 1900, the first written reference to the immediately popular sandwich.

Pizza Frank Pepe is the father of American pizza and that's all there is to it. (Try a taste test at Pepe's Pizzeria Napoletana, 157 Wooster Street.)

Lollipops The word (and the sweetmeat or candy treat for which it stood) has existed since the late eighteenth century, but New Haven says lollipops as we know them were invented here in 1892 by George Smith of the Smith Candy Company, who was the first fellow to put a stick in it.

to the unspeakable ordeal of a lifetime of slavery. Eventually apprehended by the U.S. Navy as the ship met the waters of Long Island Sound, the slavers accused their captives of piracy, and the Africans were taken into custody and held in the New Haven jailhouse, formerly on a site just opposite the present City Hall. Here the captives awaited trial, as abolitionists and attorneys and even former

President John Quincy Adams joined the battle to restore the freedom of the Africans.

The heroic acts of the group's leader, Sengbe Pieh, also known as Joseph Cinque, are celebrated on the 14-foot, three-sided bronze sculpture that stands near the site of the jailhouse where the illegally kidnapped Mendi Africans were imprisoned. Although the morally laudable and eventually triumphant teamwork of the principal players in this incident did not lead directly or immediately to the release of other captive Africans, it did contribute greatly to the abolitionist movement and inspired the courage of countless other Africans who sought, fought for, and won their own freedom.

165 Church Street at the New Haven City Hall. Accessible year-round and round the clock at no charge.

Creative Arts Workshop

Just a few blocks from the New Haven Green and the university, this three-story workshop houses studios for masters and students of painting, drawing, pottery, jewelry, printmaking, sculpture, photography, and weaving. Children as well as adults can participate in studio tours and classes. Call ahead to find out what artists might be crafting on a particular day. All visitors may also admire the exhibitions in the Hilles Gallery and purchase the works for sale in the shop.

During the workshop's annual holiday exhibition and sale, more than 400 juried artisans from around the country display more than 10,000 pieces of artwork in the gallery. Called the *Celebration of American Crafts,* this exhibition showcases fine art as well as decorative and functional artworks in all media. Shop from mid-November through December 24.

80 Audubon Street (203–562-4927). Open year-round. Gallery and shop open Monday through Friday 9:00 A.M. to 5:00 P.M. and Saturday 9:00 A.M. to noon. Different hours during annual holiday exhibition and annual Sunday Open House.

New Haven Symphony Orchestra

The fourth oldest orchestra in the United States, this symphony offers an October to June concert season in beautiful Woolsey Hall at the corner of College and Grove. Under the direction of Michael Palmer, the symphony performs with internationally known artists in the NHSO Series and the Merrill Lynch Great Performers Series. Subscriptions and single tickets are available for both series.

The orchestra also plans at least two Sunday matinee concerts of special appeal to children and at budget-conscious prices, held at the Lyman Auditorium of Southern Connecticut State University. Before each performance, youngsters may meet the musicians and touch and try the orchestral instruments. Tickets for the two-concert series are $20 for adults; $12 for children; single tickets are $12.50 and $7.50, respectively. In addition to these series, the NHSO presents pops concerts. Also inquire at the box office about the free concerts given in New Haven and on nearby town greens in the summertime.

Offices at 33 Whitney Avenue; concert hall at Grove and College. For tickets and information, call the box office (203–776–1444 or 800–292–NHSO).

Shubert Performing Arts Center

This recently refurbished theater offers all-new seats and a state-of-the-art sound system for your comfort and pleasure in seeing Broadway musicals, ballet, opera, modern dance, comedy, mime, and much more in a full season from September through May. Located just off the green in the heart of downtown not far from the university, the Shubert has entertained theater-lovers from its opening in 1914. Many legendary successes have premiered here and gone on to Broadway; among these are such musical classics as *My Fair Lady* and *Damn Yankees,* and plays by Neil Simon and Tennessee Williams. In true Shubert tradition, Neil Simon's Broadway-bound *Proposals* opened the 1997–1998 season.

Tickets are available singly or through the pre-season Early Bird Buyer program, series subscriptions, or group sales. Some shows are aimed especially at families and are offered at special prices as low as $10 per ticket. A Starter Student Series offers special hourlong daytime performances for children at $5 per student. School groups and homeschoolers should call Ruth Feldman (203–624–1825) for further information.

247 College Street. For a calendar of performances or to order tickets, call the box office (203–562–5666 or 800–228–6622). E-mail: shubert@shubert.com. Web site is http://www.shubert.com.

Long Wharf Theatre

This thirtysomething theater won a Tony Award in 1978 for Outstanding Regional Theater, two Pulitzer Prizes for Drama, and two Drama Critics Circle Awards for Best Play—but it's not resting on its laurels. Although it remains in its original home in New Haven's Long Wharf district near the Sound, big changes have taken place within. Artistic Director Doug Hughes and Managing Director Michael Ross

More New Haven Parks

Edgerton Park On Whitney Avenue and Cliff Street near the Hamden line; enter observatory area at 75 Cliff Street (203-777-1886). Comprised of twenty-two acres on the National Register of Historic Places, this property was originally owned by Eli Whitney and later became the site of the now-demolished Edgerton mansion built at the turn-of-the-twentieth-century as a wedding present for the wife of Frederick Brewster. The park's design was planned according to an eighteenth-century English landscape garden to emphasize the importance of open space. Its Crosby Conservatory of tropical plants has a simulated rain forest path and horticultural exhibits such as carnivorous plants, cacti, and succulents; Greenbrier Greenhouse offers culinary herbs and seasonal plants for sale year-round. A community garden blooms throughout summer, and a horticultural library is located nearby in the Carriage House. Seasonal fairs and concerts draw visitors to the park's flower gardens and its walking, biking, and cross-country skiing paths, and its picnicking areas. The grounds are open daily year-round from dawn to dusk; the conservatory and garden center are open year-round Monday through Friday from 10:00 A.M. to 5:00 P.M. and on weekends until 4:00 P.M.

Edgewood Park 720 Edgewood Avenue between Whalley Avenue and Chapel Street (203-946-8028). One-hundred twenty acres with nature walkways, playground, ranger station with wildlife displays and programs, duck pond, tennis and basketball courts, playing fields, Holocaust Memorial, and Spanish-American War monument.

Wooster Square Green On Chapel Street between Academy and Wooster Place. Near New Haven's Little Italy, a restored historic district of some of New Haven's prettiest architecture designed in the early 1800s around a central square as if it were in fact in the heart of London. Linger a while in this grassy oasis named for New Haven's Revolutionary War hero David Wooster. Have a look at the monument to Christopher Columbus, then get in line behind all the other hungry patrons drawn to the pizzerias, ristorantes, and trattorias on the outer edges of this tiny enclave.

have recently overseen a revitalization of the theater's lobby and other interior spaces to underscore the energy of the gifted performers who regularly light up the two stages here.

With the guidance of acclaimed directors and the support of nationally known set designers, such actors as Julie Harris, Joanne Woodward, Al Pacino, and John Lithgow have dazzled the audiences who fill the 491 seats of the intimate auditorium of the Newton

Shore Points

A Whirl by the Sea

Lighthouse Point Park was once the popular last stop on the New Haven Trolley line. In those days the park had bathhouses, boat rides, amusement rides, and baseball games, with such legends as Babe Ruth and Ty Cobb playing here on Sunday afternoons in the Roaring Twenties. Today only one of its famed rides remains. Housed in a landmark building on the National Register of Historic Places is the Lighthouse Point Carousel, a well-restored treasure. Jumping horses that slide on gleaming brass poles stand four abreast, alternating with the steadfast steeds, which stand shoulder to shoulder in rows of three. Climb aboard for only 50 cents.

The 82-acre park also has the pre-Civil War **Five Mile Point Lighthouse** and a great little nature center at the East Shore Ranger Station. A marine touch tank displays common shore plants and creatures, and a ship's deck provides a great play space for youngsters to pretend on.

The park's beach is clean and safe, with a first aid station, a snack bar, spotless changing rooms and showers, a small wooden playground, swing sets, and a picnic grove. A public boat launch, a fishing pier, volleyball nets, a nature trail, and excellent bird-watching areas in the bird sanctuary are also here. Hawk, falcon, and eagle watching during the annual migration from late August through November brings birders from all over the state.

The park is at 2 Lighthouse Road. Take exit 50, Woodward Avenue, off I-95 northbound, or exit 51, Frontage Road, southbound; follow the signs down Townsend Avenue to Lighthouse Road and the park (park manager 203–946–8005; ranger station 203–946–8790). The park is open daily year-round, 6:00 A.M. to sunset, without charge from Memorial Day to Labor Day when each out-of-town carload pays $6 per day. The carousel operates from Memorial Day to Labor Day on Tuesday through Friday from 3:00 to 7:00 P.M. and on Saturday and Sunday from 11:00 A.M. to 7:00 P.M. and on the holidays.

Schenck Stage. From Tuesday through Sunday in season, the stage sizzles with the works of playwrights such as Arthur Miller, Donald Margulies, William Inge, and Eugene O'Neill. On other days, Stage II lights up; this 199-seat proscenium theater also stages full productions. Single tickets and subscriptions for adults and children ages 10 to 17 are available for the October through May season.

22 Sargent Drive (box office 203–787–4282). Tickets generally $15 to $39 for single performances. For subscription information and sea-

son calendar, call the box office or write to Long Wharf Theatre, P.O. Box 9507, New Haven, CT 06534, or on the Web at http://www.long-wharf.org.

Yale Repertory Theatre/Yale School of Drama

From Shakespeare to Shaw and Chekhov to Soyinka, from drama to musical, from hilarious comedy to profound philosophy, the Yale Rep never fails to engage its audiences in its full-scale productions from September or October through May. The Rep itself is the professional arm of this award-winning organization. Some productions are special projects of the graduate program of the School of Drama, with student apprentices working with a professional director in various roles from actor to set designer to producer.

The season at the Rep/YSD may include intriguing interpretations of classic plays as well as contemporary and world-premiering works. Staged in the marvelous space created in 1970 within the landmark 1868 Calvary Baptist Church, performances are usually Tuesday through Saturday at 8:00 P.M. and Monday at 7:00 P.M. Matinees are scheduled for some productions on Wednesday and Saturday at 2:00 P.M. Call for a detailed calendar of the season and subscription possibilities.

222 York Street at the corner of Chapel and York in the former Calvary Baptist Church (203–432–1234). Single tickets $25 to $30; subscriptions to 6- or 10-play series or make-your-own-series of 3 to 5 plays also available.

Pardee-Morris House

This beautifully simple 1780 homestead on Morris Cove overlooking New Haven Harbor is owned and operated by the New Haven Colony Historical Society. Originally built in 1750 on land acquired by Thomas Morris in 1671, the first structure on this property was burned to the ground by the British in 1779 when they invaded New Haven during the Revolution. Subsequently rebuilt on the remaining foundation, the current structure is noted for its stone ends and its third-floor ballroom. With many period and original furnishings, the wonderfully preserved Pardee-Morris House offers a peek into the eighteenth century through the story of the well-to-do family who lived here.

325 Lighthouse Road; exit 50 from I-95 (203–562–4183). Open for guided tours June through August on Saturday and Sunday from 11:00 A.M. to 4:00 P.M.; call to inquire about exact dates and special *events. Adults $3; seniors and children 6 to 16 $1.50; under age 6 is free. Two weeklong children's history day camps with daily sessions from 3:00 to 5:00 P.M. in mid-July and from 10:00 A.M. to noon in mid-August. Tuition for each session is $50 per child. Call educational director Jeff Nichols to register.*

Fort Nathan Hale and Black Rock Fort

After a visit to the Pardee-Morris House, you might want to make another historical pit-stop as you travel north again on Townsend Avenue. Take a left on Fort Hale Park Road to visit two of New Haven's oldest historic sites. **Black Rock Fort** was built in 1776 by order of the Connecticut Colony to protect the Port of New Haven from the British. Unfortunately, by the time Major General William Tryon arrived on July 5, 1779, with three thousand British troops, only nineteen defenders remained at the fort; they were swiftly captured by the enemy, which then marched on to New Haven. (Amazingly, the Brits were repelled the next day in the city by a mere several dozen colonial soldiers.)

Fort Nathan Hale was built near the same site in the early 1800s as the British and Americans prepared again to fight. This time, during the War of 1812, the defenders successfully quashed the British invaders right here. Rebuilt in 1863 with new ramparts, bunkers, a drawbridge, and eighteen guns, the fort was prepared for Civil War action, but it never came.

Now you can make a self-guided tour of both sites. The drawbridge, its moat, the ramparts, bunkers, and other fortifications either still exist or have been restored. In addition to the remains of the forts, there is a handsome statue of the young Nathan Hale, a colorful flag display, and some signage and self-guided tour brochures at the information booth at the entrance to the site.

Woodward Avenue (203–787–8790). Open daily Memorial Day to Labor Day from 10:00 A.M. to 4:00 P.M. Free.

Schooner, Inc. Cruises

If you want to see New Haven from the Sound and get a history/ecology lesson and a great boat ride to boot, call this tour operator during the warm months. Weather permitting, they'll take you out on chartered half-day, full-day, and sunset sails aboard the *Quinnipiack,* a beautiful 91-foot gaff-rigged wooden schooner.

Two kinds of public sails are offered from late May through September. The Sea Adventures are educational trips with an onboard naturalist who helps passengers identify and examine specimens caught in the schooner's trawl net. The sunset cruises are purely relaxing, with great storytelling thrown in for entertainment. On both types of cruises, passengers are welcome to bring picnic lunches or dinners and beverages. Wine or beer is permitted aboard for adults.

Schooner, Inc. also offers weeklong summer day camps for children in grades kindergarten through high school. Sea Sprites (grades K–4) explore marine habitats, study marine animals, and do arts, crafts, and games. Seafaring Scientists (grades 5–8) make day sails on the *Quinnipiack* for Long Island Sound exploration. Source to Sound (grades 9–12) allows older explorers to canoe from the headwaters of the Quinnipiac River all the way to New Haven Harbor.

60 South Water Street, departing from the Long Wharf Pier off I-95 exit 46 (203-865-1737). Private charters from April to November. Public sails from late May through September: Educational Sea Adventures on Wednesday and Friday from 6:00 to 9:00 P.M. or Sunday from 1:00 to 4:00 P.M. Sunset Cruises on Sundays from 5:00 to 8:00 P.M. Adults $15, children under 12 $10.

Boat Excursions and Charters

Sail the Sound Oyster Point Marina (860-355-9210 or 207-773-8230). Late April through October. Call for current schedule. The simple, sibilant pleasures of sun, sky, sails, stars, salty spray, and solitude are the gifts you'll enjoy if you charter *Quiet Passage,* a 45-foot ketch that cruises out of New Haven Harbor and into the Sound for half-day, full-day, and overnight adventures on the sea. For overnight cruises, two to four passengers can be accommodated; for all other charters, a maximum of six can come aboard.

Places to Eat in New Haven

Louis' Lunch 263 Crown Street (203-562-5507). Louie Lassen opened this landmark luncheon stand in 1895 and claimed responsibility for the first hamburger cooked in America in 1900. Now in its second century, this famed eatery has a place on the National Register. Now Louis' octogenarian grandson, Ken Lassen, and his great-grandson, Jeff Lassen, are behind the counter, making fresh-daily, hand-formed burgers and cheeseburgers, served on toast in adult and child-sized portions. You can also get steak sandwiches, or, on weekend nights, a hot dog or two. Tuna salad made by Jeff's mom, Lee, is served year-round on Fridays. For lunch or dinner, come here for a taste of culi-

Outdoor Summer Festivals and Performances

New Haven is well known for the enormous variety of outdoor entertainments it offers in the summertime. Most of these performances are free and appropriate for all ages. Here is a selective list of the best events.

Outdoor Summer Concerts on The Green/New Haven Jazz Festival Presented by the New Haven Office of Cultural Affairs (203–946–7821). These free summer concerts in July and August on selected Saturday evenings feature outstanding jazz artists from around the globe. At about 6:00 the warm-up music starts; the main act may not begin until 8:00. Bring a blanket and picnic or eat at the food booths set up at the edge of the green. Dance in the twilight with music all around you.

International Festival of Arts and Ideas (203–498–1212 or 888–ART–IDEA; Web site is http://www.artidea.org). Acclaimed performers come from nearly every continent to unify the global community and raise our awareness and our spirits in an outpouring of artistic energy that spans five days late in June each year. Of the hundreds of indoor and outdoor performances staged on or near the New Haven Green and on the Yale campus, most are free. See classical and modern dance. Hear opera, folk, salsa, reggae, jazz, and classical artists. Participate in Native American dances and pageants, listen to engaging discussions of matters of the heart, the mind, music, and other arts. Open your eyes to the amazing arts, crafts, traditional dances, food, and cultural themes of New Haven's own citizens and its global neighbors.

Summertime Street Festival (203–946–7821). A mid-August extravaganza on Chapel Street from College to Park Streets brings folks out for four days of music, dancing, arts and crafts, children's activities, and food galore. Five music stages, nationally known performance artists, and strolling entertainers keep the streets lively Thursday and Friday from 5:00 to 11:00 P.M. and Saturday and Sunday from 1:00 to 11:00 P.M. A finale concert makes the New Haven Green the place to be on Sunday evening. Free.

Greater New Haven Acoustic Music Society (203–468–1000). This contemporary folk music society sponsors acoustic concerts and workshops featuring national and regional touring artists and local performers. Fall and spring performances are generally held at the University of New Haven, but ten summer performances are given at the Eli Whitney 1816 Barn across from the Eli Whitney Museum in Hamden, on Whitney Avenue just north of the New Haven line. Call for a calendar of performances.

nary history. Open Tuesday and Wednesday 11:00 A.M. to 4:00 P.M., Thursday through Saturday from noon to 2:00 A.M. Closed Sunday and sometimes Monday and for the entire month of August. $

Pepe's Pizzeria Napoletana 157 Wooster Street (203–865–5762). Some would argue that no better pizza has ever been made, even in Italy. Most folks claim Frank Pepe's famous white clam pie is the most delicious item on the menu, but those who eschew clams swear on their own favorites. Be ready to wait for pizza this perfect—it won't matter how early you get here, other aficionados will have staked a place before you. $–$$

Sally's Pizzeria 237 Wooster Street (203–624–5271). Throw out the guidebooks that say that "her" menu includes New Haven's finest pizza—they haven't been here. Anyone who loves this place knows that Sally was the late, great Salvatore A. Consiglio and that *he* learned some of the tricks of his trade from his uncle Frank Pepe down the street. Following in his celebrated footsteps are his talented descendants who still throw the best pies in the neighborhood into the 12- by 12-foot coal-fired brick oven that pushes out twenty pies at once. Even so, a line of fans often stretches out the door as Flo, Sal's widow and the matriarch and hostess of this place, tries to seat everyone as quickly as possible. Order your favorite pie—no matter where else you've asked for a similar combo, you won't have had it so good until you eat it here. Closed Mondays. $–$$

Claire's Corner Copia Cafe 1000 Chapel Street at corner of College (203–562–3888). Close to the New Haven Green, Yale University, and the Art Gallery and British Art Center, Claire's offers the best soups made in the city, plus other amazing and fla-vorful vegetarian and vegan dishes from lasagnas to pasta salads, sandwiches, chili, quesadillas, great breads, pastries, and cakes, and much more. Take-out or tables with a semi-self-service, casual flair that works equally well for students, shoppers, and families. Open for breakfast, lunch, and dinner year-round daily from 8:00 A.M. to 10:00 P.M. $

Gennaro's Ristorante D'Amalfi 937 State Street (203–777–5490). This elegant restaurant is closed on Sunday—that's the only strike against it. Come here for the finest Italian cuisine in New Haven for lunch (Monday through Friday 11:30 A.M. to 2:00 P.M.) and dinner (Monday through Saturday 5:00 to 9:30 P.M.) Reservations required. Every dish is a symphony of flavors; the service is helpful and discreet; the ambiance and decor refined and relaxing. $$–$$$

Union League Cafe 1032 Chapel Street (203–562–4299). Just across from Yale's Old Campus in an 1860 landmark building once home to the Union League, the elegantly informal cafe presents country French cuisine with a delightful homespun flair that defies the American misperception of "bistro" fare. Time, talent, and creativity define the philosophy here. Ask for a table by the fireplace in winter or at the windows overlooking the passersby on Chapel Street in spring and summer. Open for lunch on weekdays and for dinner daily year-round. $$$

Pika Tapas Cafe 39 High Street (203–865–1933). Casual, contemporary setting for lively conversation and the adventure of choosing (and sharing) *tapas,* delicious and inventive appetizers or appetizer-size portions of Spanish origin. To do this right, order the traditional glass of sherry and make a meal from two or three of these (about $5 each), or order a dozen for the table to share. The kitchen closes at 11:00 P.M., so this is a great late-supper place après-theater. $$

Bangkok Garden 172 York Street (203–789–8684). You'll be glad you waited for a table at this charming Thai award-winner. Try for a table in the glass-enclosed sunroom in the front, so you can enjoy the extended ambiance of the Yale neighborhood. The entirely smoke-free environment allows you to fully savor the flavors and aroma of this delicious and authentic cuisine. Open for lunch and dinner daily from 11:30 A.M. to 10:00 P.M. $$–$$$

The Chart House 100 South Water Street (203–787–3466). For dinner on the water, this may be the best place in town. Reliable American menu of healthfully prepared seafood, excellent prime rib, a fair selection of chicken and pasta dishes, salads, oyster bar, and prizewinning clam chowder. Overlooking New Haven Harbor near the marinas in the City Point neighborhood, the restaurant has great views from its upper-deck lounge and its window tables; arrive early to get these highly prized front-row seats. Open for dinner only, daily year-round. $$–$$$

Places to Stay in New Haven

New Haven Hotel 229 George Street (203–498–3100). Elegant accommodations in the heart of downtown. The 92 units include balcony suites with wet bar, refrigerator, and deluxe amenities. Valet parking, dry cleaning services, fitness center, lap pool and therapeutic pool, access to adjacent Downtown Health and Racquet Club. Designated smoking rooms and nonsmoking floors. Templeton's Restaurant serves American cuisine; lounge open daily. $$$

The Colony Hotel 1157 Chapel Street (203–776–1234).

Sophisticated downtown landmark with 86 luxury units ranging from standard double rooms to two-bedroom suites. Association with the Downtown Health and Racquet Club; convenient to downtown and university sites. Valet dry cleaning, valet indoor parking, room service, courtesy van to Tweed airport, train, or bus terminal. Steakhouse on first level. $$$$

Three Chimneys Inn 1201 Chapel Street (203–789–1201). 1870 mansion located near Yale and the College and Chapel dining, shopping, and entertainment district. Ten guest rooms with private baths, canopied or four-poster beds, oriental carpets, and Georgian and Federal-style furnishings, plus cable television, voice mail, data port. Front veranda overlooking formal gardens, library, and club room. Complimentary buffet-style full breakfast and afternoon tea. On-site parking. No smoking except on veranda or in gardens. Young guests welcome over the age of 6; no pets allowed. Elevators provide full wheelchair accessibility. $$$$

Omni New Haven Hotel at Yale 155 Temple Street (203–772–6664 or 800–THE–OMNI). 306 deluxe rooms, including 6 luxury suites. Galileo's rooftop restaurant, lounge, health club, on-site garage parking. New incarnation of the old Park Plaza Hotel, fully renovated and greatly expanded, with a location right smack in the middle of New Haven's hub. $$$$

Holiday Inn New Haven at Yale 30 Whalley Avenue (203–777–6221). 160 units, restaurant, lounge, exercise facility, outdoor pool. $$$

Grand Chalet Inn and Suites at Long Wharf 400 Sargent Drive (203–562–1111 or 800–5–CHALET). 152 units including 55 suites. Complimentary continental breakfast. Restaurant, lounge, coffee shop, health club, sauna, outdoor pool. Near harbor sites and Long Wharf Theater; convenient to I-95. $$$

Residence Inn by Marriott 3 Long Wharf Drive (203–777–5337 or 800–331–3131). 112 suites (studios to two bedrooms), all with fully equipped kitchens and some with fireplace. Outdoor pool, Jacuzzi, sports court, access to Downtown Health and Racquet Club. Continental breakfast. Long-term rates for stays over five nights. $$$$

Public Boat Launch

Lighthouse Point Park Exit 50 off I–95, south on Townsend Avenue, right on Lighthouse Road to the park. Parking for 60 cars; seasonal weekend and holiday parking fee.

For Further Information

Greater New Haven Convention and Visitors Bureau 59 Elm Street, New Haven 06511 (800–332–7829 or 203–777–8550). Brochures, maps, and information on lodging and restaurants. Ask for a copy of their terrific *Guide to Greater New Haven.* Monday through Friday year-round 8:30 A.M. to 5:00 P.M.

Long Wharf Visitor Information Center 355 Long Wharf Drive, New Haven 06511 (800–332–7829 or 203–777–8550). Booth off I–95; stocked with maps and brochures from Memorial Day through Labor Day, Monday through Friday 10:00 A.M to 7:00 P.M. and weekends until 5:00 P.M.

SNET Access Hotline (203–498–5050). Call this number, then punch in the code 1315 to get information on the day's special events, theater performances, and more.

Yale University Free Events Hotline (203–432–9100). Information on all Yale events that the public may attend free of charge

Yale University Sports Hotline (203–432–YALE).

Arts Council of Greater New Haven (203–772–2788) Publishes the free monthly publication *Greater New Haven Arts! A Guide to Arts, Entertainment, and Culture* distributed at many locations in town.

 # East Haven

Even though East Haven was first settled in the mid-1600s in connection with an ironworks that had been established at the southern end of Lake Saltonstall, the real development of the town came much later as an outgrowth of New Haven's sprawl. Industry here centered on the ironworks that processed bog iron from North Haven, and farming and fishing supplemented the town's economic base. Life in East Haven remained relatively quiet for most of its early history, the high point being the British raid on the town during the Revolution and Lafayette's encampment on the town green.

Today the town is mostly residential with unremarkable support-ing commercial establishments seen mostly by travelers passing along I–95 through the shopping areas on Frontage Road. Few travel-ers slow down along this route to see what the town has to offer. Those who exit the highway in East Haven, however, will find one of Connecticut's most popular family attractions, the Shore Line Trolley Museum.

The Best of East Haven

Shore Line Trolley Museum

The mostly volunteer efforts of the Branford Electric Railway Association have kept alive and well one of Connecticut's oldest tourist attractions—the oldest continually operating suburban trolley line in the United States. The museum still offers the same sense of oldtime Connecticut that it did when it was part of the trolley system that carried thousands of visitors along the shoreline in the early years of the twentieth century. Beginning in 1900, this particular stretch ran from the East Haven Green to Branford's Short Beach; today it follows all but a few missing yards of that exact route through the woodlands, marshes, and meadows—and back to yesteryear.

Nearly 100 classic trolley cars are stored on the grounds along with the first electric freight locomotive, the country's oldest rapid

Shore Points
Battle on the Beach

The linear distance from Lighthouse Point in New Haven to Guilford Point in Guilford is only 12 miles, but the coves and bays of the coast-line create a shoreline distance of more than 34 miles. Of those, only about 7 miles are sandy beach, and of these, only 2.5 miles are owned by state or municipalities. Notwithstanding the small amount of beach, several projects of beach stabilization have been attempted along this corridor. Predictably, however, few have succeeded. The construction of seawalls, groins, and other types of jetties and the addition of trucked-in sand in a process called beach nourishment have done nothing to keep some of the cottages at Momauguin and Silver Sands from standing in water twice a day, even at normal high-water condi-tions. The sea wins the struggle, sweeping tons of sand off the beaches with each tide.

A Day at the Beach

A spin around the East Haven beach neighborhood of Momauguin is a worthwhile shoreline journey. Interestingly enough, conservationists might say that a drive along East Haven beaches provides a great example of improper and unwise building of houses and seawalls along the coast. To be fair, East Haven is far from the only community in which construction close to the water—in fact, well below the flood line of the 1938 hurricane—defies common sense as well as Mother Nature. Nevertheless, here, as in other towns, human attraction to the beauty of the beach often denies recognition of the Sound's power and fury.

Take Route 142 south from Route 1, which you can reach from either 51 or 52 off I-95. Follow Route 142 to Coe Avenue, which leads directly south from the point at which Route 142 swings eastwardly toward Branford. At the foot of Coe Avenue is Cosey Beach Avenue, which runs east-west, immediately parallel to the Sound. The **East Haven Town Beach,** with restrooms, showers, a pavilion, and snack bar concession, is almost exactly at this junction. As with most public beaches, off-season use of the East Haven Town Beach is unmonitored; thus, visitors are welcome to swim, beachcomb, or picnic here anytime from Labor Day through Memorial Day. A town park and playing fields also lie along Cosey Beach Avenue, as do a variety of restaurants and markets. In-season beach use and parking is limited to East Haven residents. Call the East Haven Town Beach (203–468–3800) or the Recreation Department (203–468–3367) for further information.

transit car, and a rare parlor car. The car barns house both restored and unrestored trolleys, and you may be able to see a restoration in process on the day you visit. Admission to the whole complex, which is listed on the National Register of Historic Places, buys you unlimited 3-mile round-trip rides on the trolleys, plus a self-guided tour of the car barns and display areas.

The trolley rides are great fun, especially for young children and adults with a nostalgic sense of romance. Some cars are closed and others are open to the air, briny with the tidal odors of the marshes, the East Haven and Farm Rivers, and the sea, which lies just a few hundred yards from the southernmost length of track on the Branford side of the line.

Special events are planned throughout the year: Laurel and Hardy Days in early June, Canada Days in early July, a Trolley Fair in

September, and New York Days in early October. Watch out on the "haunted" rides during the last week in October—not all the passengers are as alive and well as you are. If you haven't had the wits frightened out of you, return again on weekends in December for Santa Days, when the jolly saint himself rides the rails with you.

Enjoy the museum's picnic area, open from May through October, and check out the gift shop for souvenirs. You can arrange birthday parties, group picnics, and other special charters at a group discount for fifteen or more if booked in advance. For these special arrangements and charters, call (203) 467–7365. Restrooms and a soft drink machine are here, but there is no food concession or snack bar.

17 River Street (203–467–6927). Open daily from Memorial Day through Labor Day from 11:00 A.M. to 5:00 P.M. Also at the same hours in April on Sundays only, and in May on Saturdays and Sundays. In the fall, the museum is open on Saturdays and Sundays in September and October, plus Columbus Day and in November on Sundays only, prior to Thanksgiving. Call for a special events schedule for December. $5, seniors $4, ages 2 to 11 $2. Trolleys run at least every thirty minutes; last trolley leaves at 5:00 P.M.

Lake Saltonstall

Tucked into a narrow valley between the hills of East Haven and Branford, the crooked finger of Lake Saltonstall is one of Nature's gifts, partly used as a regional freshwater supply and partly as a recreation resource for all visitors. Because Lake Saltonstall is split in half by the boundaries of East Haven and Branford, activities on and around Lake Saltonstall seem well placed in this chapter.

One of the largest freshwater bodies near New Haven, Lake Saltonstall is open to anyone who would like to hike its surrounding trails and fish in its waters. Stocked each spring with brown and rainbow trout as well as largemouth bass, the lake is also home to native fish and waterfowl. Hiking the 10 miles of pretty trails of the 1,900 acres of woodland surrounding the lake is possible year-round, either with an annual $35 permit that also allows you to visit other water authority land throughout New Haven County or with a single-use permit ($5 per day). The recreation permits allow one adult plus one adult guest and any number of your children under the age of 21 to use the trails. Annual permits for disabled visitors or persons over the age of 60 are $20 (and also include their children and an adult guest).

Fishing season is from the third Saturday in April through

November 30, and fishing is also allowed with the purchase of that $35 annual permit or with a single-use daily permit, plus a state fishing license, which can be purchased at any Connecticut town clerk's office or from the state DEP fisheries licensing office (860-424-3105). Anglers are welcome to fish from the shore or from the 70-foot dock, the latter of which is wheelchair accessible. You might also enjoy searching for a quiet spot of your own by going out on the lake in a rental rowboat ($10 per day) or small powerboat with electric motors ($25 per day). Only these rental boats are allowed on the lake. Bring your own bait (worms are the only live bait allowed here) and tackle, plus anything you might want to eat or drink.

To reach the trails or the dock house, take Route 1 east from East Haven to a left turn on Hosley Avenue just over the Branford line. Follow Hosley Avenue to the turn-out for the lake. Purchases of annual permits can be made in person at the Water Authority office at 90 Sargent Drive in New Haven or by phone (203-624-6671). For a daily permit, come to the dock house anytime between 7:00 A.M. and 1:00 P.M. Monday through Friday or 7:00 A.M. to 7:00 P.M. Saturday and Sunday. Lake area open for hiking and fishing from sunrise to sunset.

Places to Eat in East Haven

The Beachhead Restaurant 3 Cosey Beach Avenue (203–469–5450). An East Haven tradition since the 1940s, this popular establishment was resuscitated a few years back by new owners who renewed old favorites with some innovative twists and a healthier spin on artery-clogging themes. Fresh fish, pastas, crisp salads, and veal and chicken dishes with an Italian background form the backbone of the menu. Casual ambiance across from the beach with outdoor patio dining in warm weather, but cottages chop up the water views. Lunch Tuesday through Friday 11:30 A.M. to 2:30 P.M.; dinner Tuesday through Sunday 5:00 to 10:00 P.M. Closed Mondays. $$–$$$

Sandpiper Restaurant 161 Cosey Beach Avenue on the corner across from Momauguin's park and town beach (203–469–7544). Very casual, very clean, very traditional shoreline seafood shack/diner cuisine. Fresh seafood platters with everything from fried clam strips to lobster, plus salads, house-made chowders, pasta specials, much more. Happy, busy dining room with great views of the water. Open daily year-round from 11:00 A.M. for lunch and dinner. $–$$

Antonio's 672 Main Street (203–469–2386). American and Italian fare that comes highly recommended after a quarter-century in business. Neapolitan favorites year-round at lunch Monday through Friday 11:30 A.M. to 2:30 P.M. and dinner Monday through Saturday

5:00 to 10:00 P.M. and Sunday noon to 9:00 P.M. $$-$$$

Ristorante Faustini 190 East Main Street (203–467–9498). Reservations are required in this 100 percent smoke-free establishment. Innovative contemporary and traditional Italian dishes, exquisitely seasoned, with a special section of the menu devoted to healthy selections with a low-fat content. Desserts are sublime. Open for dinner only, Tuesday through Sunday. $$$

Place to Stay in East Haven

Holiday Inn Express 30 Frontage Road (203–469–5321). 82 units, outdoor pool, shuttle service to New Haven; complimentary continental breakfast; senior citizen rates. Kids stay free. $$$-$$$$

For Further Information

East Haven Chamber of Commerce (203–467–4305). Maps, brochures on restaurants, lodging.

Cultural Arts Council of East Haven 1380 North High Street (203–486–2963). Ask for calendar of free Friday-night summer concerts near the gazebo on the town green, plus information on other cultural events.

East Haven Historical Society 133 Main Street (203–467–1766). Info on historic sites such as the Old Stone Church at Main and High Streets, but no tours. One-room collection in private 1790 home near the town green, open Wednesdays from 11:00 A.M. to 2:00 P.M.

Irish-American Community Center 9 Venice Place (203–469–3080). The New Haven Gaelic Players stages the works of well-known Irish playwrights; call for information.

Branford

The largest in population of the shoreline towns that lie between New Haven and New London, Branford is a thriving municipality with a history that blends the features of a summer resort, a suburban bedroom community, and a center of commerce and industry. Visitors who leave I-95 to travel only the Route 1 corridor through town will miss most of the pleasures of this dynamic and multifaceted area. Sadly for tourists, Branford's citizens cherish their precious links to the Sound so much that its public beaches are not opened to out-of-towners, and many stretches of waterfront property are in private hands. Luckily, however, Branford's roads and trails allow visitors ample opportunity to explore the wooded hills, the quiet coves, and the windswept peninsulas for a taste of the charms that have drawn settlers here for 350 years.

The Mattabesec were the first settlers of this land that they called *Totoket,* or *place of the tidal river.* Not surprisingly, when they sold their land to the English for twelve coats they reserved the Indian Neck peninsula for themselves. In addition to its value as a place of extraordinary beauty, the peninsula had been home to the Mattabesec tribe since at least 2500 B.C. because of its accessibility to the bountiful fish, fowl, and shellfish of the Sound. Archaeological research in Branford reveals that the Mattabesec had a well-developed way of life that relied upon an intimate understanding of the rhythms of the seasons and the fluctuations of natural supplies of food and shelter.

The English took a different approach to the land. Their aim was to subdue and control the environment, including its native inhabitants. Eventually the Mattabesec left the shores of Branford and the English pursued their own definition of progress in these ancient tribal lands. The seventeenth and eighteenth centuries brought the clearing of Branford's forests for farms and the construction of wharves for shipbuilding and the oystering industry. In the nineteenth and twentieth centuries came the stone quarries and the factories of such products as hardware, iron fittings, and wire.

During the latter two centuries of development, the shore remained a center for recreational pleasures and the stage, the railroad, and the trolley brought thousands of visitors to the Branford coastline for summer fun. In its heyday as a resort, Branford's shore and islands were dotted with twenty commodious hotels catering to the pleasures of folks from New York and Connecticut cities. Today private cottage rentals and chain hotels house the visitors who still come to tour the islands, ride the trolleys, launch their boats, and explore the woodlands.

This chapter focuses attention on Branford's center and its distinct enclaves of Stony Creek, Indian Neck, Pine Orchard, and Short Beach.

The Best of Stony Creek

One of the prettiest and most relaxing excursions on the Connecticut shore centers around Branford's Stony Creek, as quintessential a quaint New England fishing village as can be found this close to the more sophisticated port of New Haven. Only Stonington in New London County transports one more thoroughly to the nautical past.

Like Branford's other unique sections, Stony Creek has a long and lively history, complete with tales of pirate treasure and other romances of the sea and heart. Once home to farmers, fishers, and quarriers, the village is now famed for its quiet Yankee charm and its sprinkling of pink granite islands just offshore—the Thimbles.

Stony Creek Kayak

For an intimate experience with the Thimbles and the Sound, call Christopher Hauge, who offers guided sea kayaking trips around the islands for experienced as well as novice kayakers. Half-day trips last three hours and cost $45 per person; full-day trips take about 6 hours and cost $80 per person. Kayakers can be as young as 8 years old, with parental supervision and/or consent; groups of up to about ten paddlers can arrange to go on a single outing. Guided tours can also be arranged for the Connecticut River, Lake Quonnipaug in Guilford, Branford Harbor to East Haven's Farm River (featuring Kelsey Island and the Short Beach area), and Guilford's Lost Lake, Joshua Cove, and East and West Rivers. Stony Creek Kayak (203-481-6401) also offers sea kayaking instruction, including lessons devoted to safety and rescue.

In fact, the village's principal industry, if one can call it that, is the Thimble Islands sightseeing tour business. Three enterprising captains have updated the centuries-old trade of ferrying live-stock, groceries, visitors, and even the occasional piano from the town dock to the islands.

The largest group of islands on the Sound, the thirty-three Thimbles range in size from twenty acres to less than a quarter of an acre at high tide. Scattered in the waters around these are near-ly sixty other rocky mounds visible at least at low tide. Although their small size seems to provide a clue to their name, the islands actually are called the Thimbles after the native thimbleberries that once flourished here.

The islands are in private hands, used as summer hideaways for families and friends. High Island and Money Island enjoy the most thrilling reputations among the islands. None other than Captain Kidd took shelter here. Outer Island and Horse Island have the most honorable of reputations; the former is one of the eight units of the Stewart B. McKinney National Wildlife Refuge and is used by Southern Connecticut State University for an environmental educa-tion and research area; the latter is owned by Yale University and used as a marine biology research station.

Thimble Islands Cruises

Luckily for the touring public, cruises around this pretty archipelago at least allow a glimpse of the islands, a breath of bracing salt air, and a taste of the beauty of the Sound. To reach the Stony Creek Dock from I-95, take exit 56 and travel south on Leetes Island Road for 2 miles. At the first stop sign, go straight on Thimble Islands Road, and follow the signs to the dock. From Branford Center or Indian Neck, simply fol-low the signs for Route 146 west, taking a right onto Thimble Islands Road, and continuing to the dock.

Volsunga IV (203–488–9978 or 203–481–3345). From Captain Kidd to General Tom Thumb, the stories told by Stony Creek native Captain Bob Milne aboard the *Volsunga IV* are exceeded in quality only by his sure navigation of the reefs surrounding the islands. Milne's 40-foot vessel is rated for forty-nine passengers. Cruises every hour on the hour, weather permitting, daily from July 1 to the day before Labor Day, 10:00 A.M. to 4:00 P.M. From mid-May through June and from Labor Day through Columbus Day, the tour times differ somewhat, with fewer cruises daily and no operation on Mondays of several weeks at either end of the season. Adults $6, children $3. Groups of more than twelve should make reservations. Two-hour evening charters ($250 for 30 people) are also available.

Sea Mist II (203–488–8905). Captain Mike Infantino, Jr., offers stories that are an entertaining mix of myth and fact, along with the views of the sea, the birds, the islands, and the islanders. The 45-foot *Sea Mist II* carries forty-six passengers. Forty-five-minute cruises every hour on the quarter hour, from 10:15 A.M. to 4:15 P.M. daily except Tuesday, from June 1 through Labor Day, and in May and September (after Labor Day) through October on Friday through Sunday at 12:15, 2:15, and 4:15. Adults $6, children $3. Two-hour evening charters available ($275 for 30 people). Reservations suggested for large groups.

Islander (203–397–3921). Captain Dave Kusterer's 26-foot port launch carries about twenty-five passengers on a fifty-minute tour. The size of his boat allows exploration of a few spots the larger boats can't reach and also allows Captain Dave to be right there in the middle of the more intimately sized deck. His stories reflect his personal knowledge of the lifestyles and histories of the islanders. He shares a house on Kidd's Island with relatives who have owned the property. Cruises every hour leaving at twenty minutes before the hour, from 10:40 P.M. to 4:40 P.M. daily from mid-June through Labor Day. Adults $6, children $3. Reservations suggested for groups of more than twelve.

The Stony Creek Scene

On your ride down to the water, you may notice Stony Creek's other attractions. Just a hundred yards from the gazebo at the dock is **Stony Creek Marine and Tackle and Fish Market** (4 Indian Point Road; 203–488–7061). It masquerades as a quiet shop selling tackle and seafood along with deli sandwiches, but it's really the hoppin' domain of owner Mike McCleery and a Creeker community called the Sand Worms. Most of us would call this group a house band; Mike calls it "an eclectic aggregation of talented individuals." Among them are a former back-up musician for Dave Brubeck, a fellow who toured with the Monkees, and a Juilliard grad, and they bring mostly folk, blues, and Irish tunes to Stony Creek as they play here (usually) on weekends, often outside on the bulkhead in warm weather. And you won't be hungry while you listen to their magic. Year-round, the esteemed owner and short-order cook serves breakfast and lunch daily from

6:00 A.M. and dinner, in the warm season only, from Thursday through Sunday until 8:00 P.M. In summertime only, you can eat lunch (try the clam fritters) and dinner under a tent at the waterside. On the summer holiday weekends (Memorial Day, July 4, and Labor Day), the tent is the site of the market's famed Lobster Fests—from Thursday through Sunday on those weekends from noon to 8:00 P.M.

A bit farther back from the dock, at the curve of the road, is the **Stony Creek Market** (178 Thimble Islands Road; 203–488–0145; closed Monday), which is great for casual, day-tripping meals, soft drinks, and picnic fare. Come for breakfast from 8:00 to 11:00 A.M. For lunch, come between 11:00 A.M and 3:00 P.M. and take their overstuffed sandwiches and fresh salads out on the front deck for a great view of the harbor. For dinner, from 5:00 to 9:00 P.M. Tuesday through Sunday, the Market doubles as **Stony Creek Pizza**, serving thin-crust pies with a great reputation. Come early for dinner for a front-row sunset seat.

In the same building as the Market is **Stony Creek Antiques** (172 Thimble Islands Road; 203–488–4802), a place to browse for a one-of-a-kind memento. Directly across the street is a small beach with a swimming area, picnic shelter, and benches. Officially, it is open only to Branford residents, but guests are often here as well, especially between Labor Day and Memorial Day. Parking in this area, incidentally, is very limited, so be sure you have left your vehicle in a legal space before settling too comfortably in your sand chair, in the park, or over your plate of steamers.

A half block north of the beach, the small town park offers picnic spots, swings, and a sand-carpeted playscape with slides and such. At the nearest street corner adjacent to the park is a funky cafe-cum-antiques shop called **Island Tastes** (152 Thimble Islands Road; 203–483–0564). Stop here if specialty coffees, soothing chai tea, or deliciously fruity coolers are what your whistle needs to stay wet. Homebaked muffins, great salads, and a soup or two freshly made each day on the premises are perfect for a light lunch or early dinner.

Up the road just another little piece is the **Stony Creek General Store** (124 Thimble Islands Road; 203–488–1892). Along with sundries like film, sunblock, newspapers, and such, it carries great deli goods and breads for beach and cruise picnics, and its tidy green-and-white-themed ice cream parlor serves up malteds, shakes, sundaes, splits, and more.

Stony Creek Puppet House Theatre

One of the village's most notable establishments, despite its modest facade, is the Puppet House, site of theater productions and musical performances throughout the summer and sporadically during the year. Built as a silent movie house around 1900, this 90-seat playhouse was once the home of Orson Welles' Mercury Theater; today, community theater groups and local artists form the backbone of the lineup. Jazz concerts are usually offered the first and third Saturdays of the month; Christian rock groups play the last Saturday. Acoustic folk and bluegrass musicians also may appear on the schedule, and in the summer the Shakespeare Youth Theatre usually stages a production. Every Saturday and Sunday in the summer and possibly continuing through the winter are children's matinees at 2:00 P.M.; among these one-hour performances may be clown, puppet, or magic shows or educational demonstrations. Tickets are $5 for adults and children 5 and over, $3 for kids 4 and under, and free to parents escorting four or more children.

128 Thimble Islands Road (203–488–5752 or 203–931–6326). Seasonal children's shows; year-round calendar of productions for teens/adults. Call for calendar or ticket information.

Macri-Weil Sicilian Puppet Theatre

Brought to life by puppetmasters Jim Weil and Salvatore Macri, the puppets are extraordinary 4- to 5-foot figures with heads of hand-carved walnut and bodies of wood and steel covered with hemp and canvas. Beautifully painted and dressed in armors of hand-embossed brass, these 100-year veterans of the stage battle each other furiously in the enactment of tales of the Crusades, Charlemagne and his Paladins, and the Sicilian Knights. The Crusades productions are usually an eight-week series with a new episode each week, but the schedule is changeable and seasonal, so call ahead for information.

128 Thimble Island Road (203–488–8511; 203–488–3771; 203–488–5752).

The Best of Pine Orchard and Indian Neck

You won't have seen some of the prettiest parts of the Branford-area coastline unless you make the drive or bicycle ride along Route 146 through Pine Orchard and Indian Neck. These are mostly residential sections with little of the shore accessible to tourists, but the ride is so pretty and the views so striking that a journey past the houses most of us can only dream of owning is still a jaunt worth taking.

Follow Route 146 from its intersection with Thimble Islands Road; from that point, this designated scenic highway is called Stony Creek Road, but it will soon turn toward the south and you may notice that it is then called Totoket Road, then Blackstone Road, then Elizabeth Street, then Limewood Avenue, and finally, swinging northward from the shore, Montowese Street. Not to worry—it's all Route 146, so just follow the signs. When you reach the small commercial corner of Indian Neck, where Route 146 swings away from the Sound and Limewood Avenue becomes Montowese Street, take a brief detour to the left on Linden Avenue for some beautiful shoreline vistas. If you are walking or on a bicycle, you are free to stop along the route through Pine Orchard and Indian Neck to rest at whatever pretty view strikes your eye, but motorists will find no public areas and few good pull-outs in which to stop their cars. Even walkers and cyclists should keep in mind that the lawns, beaches, and beach association parks are private areas.

From 1850 and well past the turn of the twentieth century, Pine Orchard and Indian Neck were much more public than today. Summer hotels lined the shore, and the trolley brought city emigres by the scores to the clambakes and croquet games and tennis courts overlooking the boating and swimming in the Sound. Bad weather or bad finances led to the demise of these summer playgrounds, and today only one of Branford's famed summer hotels remains in operation.

The Indian Neck Scene

The Owenego Inn (203–488–3805) at 40 Linden Avenue in Indian Neck was opened in 1847 and includes an annex built in 1867 and a cottage from 1812. With a broad front lawn and sweeping views of the Sound from its 500-foot waterfront, it is the popular site of wedding receptions and other special parties from late April to early November. It also offers seasonal and overnight lodgings for individuals. A half-dozen or more spacious guest rooms in the main inn offer sinks in the room and a community bath—a truly old-fashioned charm that can't be found anywhere else on the Connecticut shoreline.

Retrace your route to Linden Avenue's intersection with Route 146 and stop for a while at this commercial junction. Here you will find **Lenny's Indian Head Inn,** a New England seafood favorite, and **Pasta Cosi,** popular for its contemporary Italian cuisine, fresh pasta, and house-made desserts. For fabulous seafood, premier lobster bisque, fresh breads, and every other gourmet treat you'd want in a picnic basket, stop at **Bud's Fish Market** (203–488–1019). They fly their lobsters in daily from Nova Scotia, and they'll steam any quantity for you to take home. If you need a crisp chardonnay to accompany your meal, stop at the **Indian Neck Liquor Store;** for other picnic needs, try the **Indian Neck Shore Market.**

The Best of Branford Center

Since early in Branford's history the area surrounding the town green has been a center of activity, and today that is no less true than in 1699 when the green property was bequeathed to the town. Site of free summer concerts, arts and craft festivals, and the like, the green is bordered by such important buildings as the town hall, the 1843 Congregational Church, and the 1851 Trinity Episcopal Church.

Come to Trinity Church for monthly concerts given from September through May by the **Branford Folk Music Society** (203–488–7715), which brings together local, national, and international performers for vocal and instrumental traditional folk music. A small tablet near the southeast corner of the green marks the former site of the Reverend Samuel Russell's house, where ten prominent clergymen met in 1701 to assemble their donated books as the beginning of the library for the newly founded Collegiate School, later known as Yale College and now the famed university. Also surrounding the green are shops, restaurants, an ice cream parlor, and other commercial establishments. Noteworthy among the restaurants are **Darbar of India, Webster's, Le Petit Cafe,** and **Cafe Bella Vita.** Among the structures in the center of Branford, the James Blackstone Memorial Library and the Harrison House are especially notable.

James Blackstone Memorial Library

Railroad magnate Timothy Beach Blackstone paid for construction of the library to honor his father, James Blackstone, born in Branford in 1793 and elected its first selectman as well as a member of both the Senate and House of Representatives of the Connecticut General Assembly. Constructed from 1893 to 1896 from Tennessee marble, the library's architecture was modeled after the Erectheum on the Acropolis in Athens. Ionic columns, marvelous bronze doors, and a domed rotunda are among the details that architect Solon Spencer Beman added to the building.

The focal points of the spacious rotunda are the eight murals, painted by Oliver D. Grover, that draw the eye toward the beautiful glass-ceilinged dome 50 feet above the marble floor. Called *The Evolution of the Book,* the 11- by 9-foot paintings depict Egyptians gathering papyrus reeds for the manufacture of paper, scenes from the *Iliad,* monks illuminating medieval manuscripts, and Gutenberg holding the first proof of the Bible printed in his press.

758 Main Street (203–488–1441). Open Monday through Thursday 9:00 A.M. to 8:00 P.M. and Friday and Saturday 9:00 A.M. to 5:00 P.M. Closed major holidays.

Harrison House

Home to the Branford Historical Society, this classic saltbox home was built in 1724 as the home of Nathaniel Harrison. With the typical post-and-beam construction of the time, the house features original paneling and clapboards. Period furnishings, early farm tools, kitchen implements, and historical memorabilia are among the Branford artifacts here. A barn, a privy, and an eighteenth-century flower and herb garden are also on the two-acre property.

124 Main Street (203–488–4828). Open June 1 through October 1, Thursday through Saturday from 2:00 to 5:00 P.M. and by appointment. Free; donations welcome.

The Best of Short Beach

The wide ribbon of roadway marked Route 142 curls south from Route 1 invitingly, coaxing the traveler toward the shore, past beautiful Granite Bay, and then westwardly to East Haven. Also called Short Beach Road and Shore Drive, Route 142 and the smaller avenues that splinter from it encompass the neighborhood called Short Beach. Mostly residential today, Short Beach still retains the summery character that it sported as a resort area in the golden days of the trolley.

Late Branford resident and poet Edna Wheeler Wilcox, most famed for her lines "Laugh, and the world laughs with you; Weep, and you weep alone," called Short Beach her "Earthly Eden"—no exaggeration considering the spectacular view of the Sound she enjoyed from her home at the edge of the bay. No less breathtaking now than it was a century ago, Granite Bay is the focus of the neighborhood, a cozy warren of small streets lined with modest homes and summer cottages, a handful of commercial establishments, and a few pocket-size parks.

The Short Beach Scene

At the East Haven River, Route 142 curves uphill across the East Haven line, so look for a place to park in the neighborhood before you cross that border. In any season, Short Beach is perfect for bicycle and pedestrian traffic, and because the public beaches in this area are closed to out-of-town visitors in the summer season, a tourist's best bet is to explore on foot. Find a place to park on one of the side streets, and lace up your sneakers or unclip your bikes for a tour better than any you could get by car alone. Remember that the off-season from Labor Day to Memorial Day is the time when walk-in visitors can use beaches and parks that are reserved for Branford residents in the summer. Parking prohibitions must be respected, all year long.

A nice place to start a walk is at **Judie's European Baked Goods** at 126 Shore Drive (203–488–2257). Just walk right in any time after 6:30 A.M. until 5:30 P.M (2:00 P.M. on Sunday) any day except Monday and indulge yourselves with butter-laminated pastries, crusty peasant breads, heavenly sandwiches, and a marvelous brunch made to order every Saturday (9:00 A.M. to noon) and Sunday (8:30 A.M. to 1:00 P.M.) year-round. If you prefer lunch or breakfast to go, ask the staff to pack up your treats and beverages then head across Route 142 and down to the water on one of the side streets.

If you'd like to head inland a tad, walk north from Judie's on Court Street and pass through the gate across the pathway that leads to the Branford end of the **Shore Line Trolley** line that originates in East Haven (203–469–6927). Bring your picnic aboard the trolley and take the 3-mile ride across the meadows to the ticket terminal and museum and then back to the Branford platform, where they'll let you debark. You'll pay the operator $5 per adult and $2 per child, and he or she will get you a ticket for the museum as well as the return trip when you arrive at the East Haven depot. Keep in mind that the museum opens in East Haven at 11:00 A.M. and the trolleys run every thirty minutes, with the last leaving East Haven at 5:00 P.M. You ought to be at the Branford end at about ten minutes past or twenty minutes before the hour to catch one of the twice-hourly trolleys.

To add to your perfect day, continue your tour of Short Beach by walking, cycling, or driving along Clark Avenue back out to Route 142 and following it back around Granite Bay to a right turn on Stannard Avenue. Take another right turn on Harbor Street and go to the town dock and Parker Memorial Park at Branford Point. (The distance from Clark Avenue to Parker Memorial Park is about 2.5 miles.) Parking is limited in summer to Branford vehicles but open during the off-season to out-of-towners. Walkers and cyclists can visit here year-round. The park offers a beach, picnic areas, swings, restrooms, grills, and other amenities for outdoor recreation, and the town dock at Branford Point offers a great place to fish, to watch the maritime traffic, or to enjoy the beautiful views at the Harborview overlook next to the dock.

The Best of Branford's Borders

The Branford area just won't give tourists a break. Something different is always just around the next bend in the road, and you won't want to miss it. If you've been in Short Beach, return on Route 142 to Route 1, take a right, and travel to the intersection with Cedar Street, where you'll take a left. If you've been in downtown Branford or south, take Cedar Street north from Route 146. From Cedar Street, hop on I–95 heading east (north) and exit at Leetes Island Road. Turn left at the top of the ramp to go north on Leetes Island Road. At Route 1, take a right and visit these favorite spots in Branford's northeast corner before heading east to Guilford.

Hilltop Orchards

When owner Wayne Cooke's great-great-grandfather came home from the Civil War, he bought the farm, so to speak, and for the next four generations he and his descendants tilled the soil, dissecting a hilltop with orchards of apples and other fruits of tree and shrub. Established in 1867, **Hilltop Orchards** is now Branford's oldest continuing business. Today the orchards still produce apples and pumpkins and such, but the principal focus is its country store. Famous for its fabulous pies and fresh-baked breads, it's also the place to buy honey and maple sugar, coffees and teas, candles, and old-fashioned toys and gifts.

Hilltop is gradually taking on a whole new aspect as a band of pirates stakes a claim on the peaceful knoll behind the store. By the summer of 1999, **Captain Kidd's Landing** will be operating alongside the country store. Designed to highlight Branford's legendary association with Captain William Kidd, who plied the waters of Long Island Sound during the seventeenth century and reputedly buried some of his treasure on the Thimble Islands, this living history museum will focus on the decidedly colorful lifeways of pirates.

616 East Main Street (Route 1) (203–488–0779). Open year-round daily, 9:30 A.M. to 5:30 P.M.

Branford Fine Art and Craft Village at Bittersweet Farm

If you continue east on Route 1 from Hilltop Orchards, you'll find this complex less than a mile away on the south side of the road. Twenty or so shops and restaurants have been established in an eclectic cluster of buildings on a former farm site. An antiques shop, a glassworks, a paper cutting studio, a rock/mineral/shell shop, a woodcarver's shop, a knitter's shop, an art gallery, a metal sculpture shop, a framing gallery, and several others open their doors to shoppers and browsers. Watch a glassblower make an oil lamp, a whittler carve a decoy, or the paper cutter create an amazing artwork.

Especially inviting is the **Nightingale's Nest** (203–483–5827), an herbary and tea room in the white clapboard homestead at the front of the property. Come here for tea and a little something sweetish, like fresh muffins, scones, or tea cakes. Its cozy tearoom is warmed by soft yellow walls and burnished woodwork as well as steaming pots of fine teas. In the warm months, the light-washed sunroom overlooking a pretty shade garden provides a summery alternative to the more traditional formality of the tea room—a perfect spot to sip herbal iced teas. The sunroom is also used for talks and workshops given year-round. Among recent events have been herbal craft workshops, cooking lessons, and holistic mental, spiritual, and physical health presentations on such topics as Reiki, meditation, communication in relationships, and simplification of stressful lives. Call for a calendar and register early; most workshop fees range from $12 to $20. The Nightingale's Nest also offers a retail area stocked with dried culinary and medicinal herbs and teas, everlasting flowers, candles, soaps, and locally crafted artworks and jewelry. The Nest is open Tuesday through Saturday from 11:00 A.M. to 5:00 P.M. and Sunday from noon to 5:00 P.M.

When you're ready for dinner, try **Nata's** in the rustic building set in the middle of the complex. It has excellent prix-fixe dinners that draw a colorful crowd to its creative cuisine.

The Village is at 779 East Main Street (Route 1) (203–488–4689). Open year-round Tuesday through Saturday from 11:00 A.M. to 5:00 P.M. and Sunday from noon to 5:00 P.M. Free.

Places to Eat in Branford

Lenny's Indian Head Inn 205 South Montowese Street in Indian Neck (203–488–1500). If you drive by here without turning in for dinner, you'll be missing a famed menu of New England seafood, epitomized in Lenny's Famous Shore Dinner of clam chowder, cherrystones, sweet corn on the cob, lobster, steamers, and watermelon. The casual ambiance of worn wood floors and wooden booths makes Lenny's a happy, noisy place perfect for families; great specialties like zuppa d'clams and house-made seafood bisque, and a wine list and beer on tap make it a fine place for adult tastes. Indoor seating year-round; patio in warm season. Open daily year-round for lunch and dinner. $–$$

Sam's Dockside At Bruce and Johnson's Marina, Block Island Road off South Montowese Avenue (203–488–3007). Views of this spacious marina and beautiful sunsets over the trees on the horizon draw crowds in the summertime, but it's the excellent seafood and grilled specials that cause an hour-long wait here some weekend nights. Indoor and outdoor dining. Grilled chicken, Caesar salads, and other favorites are offered along with fresh seafood fried, broiled, steamed, or sauteed. Great New England clam chowder. Open only from March through the end of October. $–$$$.

Le Petit Cafe 225 Montowese Street (203–483–9791). Tiny and charming, this diminutive establishment offers French bistro cuisine presented family-style in four-course, prix-fixe ($21.50) dinners of appetizer, soup, your choice of a half-dozen entrees, and dessert. Among the savory delights here are some perfect for seafood lovers and others for meat-eaters. You'll be glad the meal includes dessert so you won't feel the need to resist: the chocolate soufflé is decadently superb. Seatings are Wednesday through Saturday at 6:30 and 8:00 P.M. and on Sunday at 5:00 and 7:30 P.M. $$$

Cafe Bella Vita 2 East Main Street (203–483–5639). Overlooking a pretty twist of Main Street, Cafe Bella Vita offers a tantalizing contemporary angle on dishes with Northern Italian and continental roots. The chef's seasonings and sauces are especially intriguing and invariably delicious accompaniments to seafood, poultry, pastas, and fine cuts of meats. Persuasive desserts exert formidable pressure on the willpower at the end of the meal. Open year-round daily for dinner only. $$$

Darbar of India 1070 Main Street (203–481–8994). If you love Indian cuisine or if you would enjoy the adventure of experimenting, come to Darbar, right on the green downtown. Delicious traditional favorites plus a few Nepalese specialties delight the senses and tease the palate. Vegetarians will revel in the abundant and tasty choices perfect for them. Try the best bargain in town for lunch—the buffet special Friday through Sunday from noon to 2:45 for $7.95 per person. $–$$

Cibo Restaurant 126 Shore Drive in Short Beach (203–488–7437). Located next door to the wonderful Judie's Bakery, this off-the-beaten-path restaurant offers sophisticated fine dining with a contemporary continental flavor. Intimate and elegant, the candlelit dining room is redolent with the aromas of marvelous sauces, fresh seasonings, and crusty breads. If you walk in to make reservations at midday when chef John Swett is preparing for evening, you will wish you could be seated immediately. A perfect place for a special dinner near the shore. Open Tuesday through Saturday for dinner only. Also open some holiday weekends; call to inquire. $$–$$$

Nata's 777 East Main Street in the Branford Craft Village (203–315–0180). Prix-fixe menu with an alternative twist in a stripped-down setting where the food is the focus and the service an entertainment by itself. Delicious and astonishingly affordable at $12 for appetizers, salad, entree, and fresh-baked pies for dessert, this delightfully unpretentious eatery offers daily lunch (except for Monday) and dinner, with dinner seatings at 5:00, 7:00, and 9:00 P.M. on Friday and Saturday nights. (On weekends, come at 5 or 7 when the atmosphere is merely relaxed; at 9, it's positively heathen.) Don't even try to get in on weekends without a reservation. Traditional dishes like scampi and chicken Marsala are excellent; innovative pasta dishes are dressed with fresh produce, herbs, and seafood or poultry; and creative specials make imaginative use of the best the market offers that day. Bring your own wine or other beverages. $$

Places to Stay in Branford

Days Inn and Conference Center 375 East Main Street (203–488–8314 or 800–329–7466). 77 units with 3 suites and 2 mini-suites, outdoor pool and Jacuzzi, continental breakfast. $$$

Ramada Limited 3 Business Park Drive (203–488–4991 or 800–950–4991). 85 units including 1 efficiency and 30 suites. Rooms have king or two double beds; suites have a double bed, a convertible sofa/daybed, and a kitchenette with fridge and microwave. Health club includes small indoor pool, spa, weight room, and sauna. Continental breakfast. $$

Motel 6 320 East Main Street (203–483–5828). 99 nearly-new units well off the road. Pets okay; nonsmoking rooms. $

MacDonald's Motel 565 East Main Street (203–488–4381). 22 units, 1 suite. Senior citizen rates. $$

Owenego Inn 40 Linden Avenue, in Indian Neck (203–488–3805). The last of this area's shoreline hotels, overlooking the Sound with 550 feet of beachfront and all the charms of yesteryear paired with modern amenities. Seasonal, monthly, weekly, or nightly accommodations. Open April through early November. $$$$

Public Boat Launch

Branford River to Branford Harbor Turn south off Route 1 onto Route 142 (Short Beach Road); take left on Stannard Avenue to Goodsell Point Road, left into dirt access road and parking area; steep ramp; seasonal weekend and holiday parking fee.

For Further Information

Branford Chamber of Commerce 230 East Main Street (203–488–5500). Lodging and restaurant information, maps, and brochures.

Branford Land Trust (203–483–5263). 246 Pleasant Point Road, P. O. Box 254, Branford, CT 06405. Guides to hiking and cross-country ski trails.

Branford Recreation Department 46 Church Street (203–488–8304). Information on use of town parks and beaches.

Guilford

Guilford's wide, colonial green, crisscrossed by pathways that seem to lead back in time, encourages the visitor to pause a while to savor the town's agreeable setting on the Sound, its tranquil atmosphere, and its beautiful architecture. Busier now than in earlier decades, especially along commercialized sections of Route 1, Guilford is still considered one of the most pleasant places on the Connecticut shore.

Named for the town of Guildford in Surrey, England, Guilford was settled by the English in 1639. Led by the Reverend Henry Whitfield and lawyer William Leete, the mostly young and prosperous Puritan farmers and landowners purchased the land called Menuncatuck from the Menuncatuck people of the Mohegan nation. For a few coats, some hats, a couple of iron kettles, and a handful of hatchets, the Menuncatuck sachem squaw Shaumpishuh gave the English, a parcel at a time, land that includes present-day Guilford and Madison.

Earlier, in the summer of 1637, the Mohegan sachem Uncas and his people had helped the English hunt down the Pequots who had survived the massacre at Mystic only to be murdered in Guilford on the peninsula now called Sachem's Head. In that bloody battle, Uncas took the head of the slain Pequot sachem and placed it in the fork of a prominent oak tree, where it rested for many years as a reminder of the Mohegan victory. Perhaps Uncas failed to predict that if the English were anxious to decimate his enemies, the Pequots, they might not be too reluctant to break faith with his people as well.

Surely he didn't predict that the peaceful woodlands of Menuncatuck would ring with the sound of axes as the English cleared great swatches of land for their farms and for the four fortified stone houses they built as protection against the Dutch. As more English arrived, the Mohegans were pushed back from the shoreline to the settlements near the Thames River. By 1774 only twenty-three Menuncatuck natives remained in Guilford's boundaries

Today Guilford has an eclectic flavor that enriches the largely residential community. Charms of the country are still apparent in its orchards, farms, lakes, and nature preserves; the link to the sea is obvious in its scenic shoreline drives and busy marinas. Appealing in all seasons, Guilford is a shoreline gem.

The Best of Guilford

Henry Whitfield State Museum

The Henry Whitfield House is the oldest stone house in New England and the oldest house in Connecticut. Built in 1639 for Reverend Henry Whitfield, the post-medieval structure has stone walls three feet thick and is the last remaining of four such houses strategically placed in Guilford as strongholds for the citizens during threat of attack by of the Dutch.

Guilford's founder and first minister, Whitfield lived in the house and conducted community business and religious services here before he left his fellow settlers and returned to England in 1647. Now more a museum than a period house, the structure contains an outstanding collection of furniture, housekeeping implements, textiles, weapons, and other important Connecticut pieces. The entire house, including the attic, is open to the public, as are the gardens and lawns. Among the large collection of local artifacts displayed in the attic, you can see the 1726 Ebenezer Parmelee steeple clock, the first wooden works tower clock made in the colonies.

248 Old Whitfield Street, south of the green at the corner of Stone House Lane (203–453–2457 or 860–566–3005). Open for mostly self-guided tours Wednesday through Sunday from February 1 to December 14, from 10:00 A.M to 4:30 P.M., and from December 15 through January by appointment. Repairs may affect the public hours of the museum in the next few years; call ahead for information. Adults $3, children 6–17 $1.50.

Hyland House

On Boston Street, northward and around the corner from the stone Henry Whitfield house, is a red overhung saltbox frame house with leaded glass casement windows and hand-split clapboards. Originally the home of George Hyland and his family, it is believed to have been constructed in 1660. The museum's focus is on the fifty to seventy-five years before the Revolution, and everything that the family might have used during that period is displayed.

Here visitors step into the eighteenth century, especially in the wonderful kitchen in the 1720 lean-to addition at the back of the house. Little imagination is necessary to conjure visions of pre-Revolutionary family life in this marvelous space with its boards, bowls, and basins worn smooth by the fingertips and footfalls of generations of early Guilford homemakers. Be sure to have a look at the "gossip wheel"—a double spinning wheel that allowed two women to spin yarn together as they shared news and stories.

The architectural details and the collections in this house are among the finest in the state. Gorgeous paneling, wide-board floors, walk-in fireplaces, rare examples of Delftware, and artifacts of every sort are abundant throughout the house. Outside, the flower and herb garden at the back of the house is especially lovely in summer and fall.

84 Boston Street (203–453–9477). Open from early June to early September daily except Mondays from 10:00 A.M. to 4:30 P.M. and on weekends from Labor Day to Columbus Day. Adults $2, children 12 and older $1.50.

Thomas Griswold House

Greatly restored by the Guilford Keeping Society, this 1774 saltbox home just a few doors east of the Hyland House has an original Guilford cupboard and a 10-foot-wide fireplace with two beehive ovens. Home to five generations of Griswolds who changed the house to meet their needs, the house has been returned to its original saltbox shape. Now on the National Register of Historic Places, the home's period rooms are set with furnishings and implements in positions of use. Samplers, coverlets, costumes, dolls and toys, and a whimsical napkin ring collection are among the treasures here.

An antiques festival held annually on the last Saturday in July and an annual Civil War encampment are hosted on the museum's expansive grounds. On these special days the museum's blacksmith shop and barn are also open.

171 Boston Street, at the corner of Lovers Lane (203–453–3176 or 203–453–4666). Open from mid-June until mid-September, Tuesday through Sunday, 11:00 A.M. to 4:00 P.M. Adults $2, students $1.

Guilford Handcraft Center

Notable among the special shops *not* on the Green is the outstanding Guilford Handcraft Center. Comprised of a shop, a gallery, and a school, the Handcraft Center was founded by local artists in 1962. The center has pottery, weaving, painting, and metalsmithing studios, plus a variety of multi-use classrooms for instruction in such other arts as basketry, etching, printmaking, woodcarving, and much more. Visiting artists travel here to offer workshops in their areas of expertise.

Downtown Guilford

One of the most exceptional colonial greens in New England is at the core of downtown Guilford. Lying south of the Boston Post Road, its twelve acres are dissected by pathways and dotted with benches that make it a popular site to relax and to play. Once an unkempt and irregular sixteen-acre parcel of ponds, pasture, and gravel pits overrun by sheep and geese, the green is now tidy and rectangular, bordered by three churches and colonial, Federal, and Victorian structures that house restaurants, galleries, shops, and even a few private citizens.

Placed on the National Register of Historic Places in 1976 along with much of the rest of the town center, the green is the third largest in the Northeast. In summer, come here to listen to an outdoor concert or to browse at one of its frequent fairs or festivals. In winter, enjoy the lighted Christmas tree, the candlelight church services, and the old-fashioned trolley rides that make holiday shopping especially festive.

An excellent walking guide to the green and its surrounding streets has been published by the Guilford Preservation Alliance. Available at **Breakwater Books** (203-453-4141; 81 Whitfield Street on the green) or through the Guilford Keeping Society (203-453-3176), *Guilford: A Walking Guide* by Sarah Brown McCulloch is an informative and practical glimpse into Guilford's architectural importance. *Around the Green: A Children's Walking Guide,* adapted by Guilford educator Joann Carmody Corlett, is an excellent interpretation of the adult version.

Guilford's green is bounded on the north by Broad Street, on the east by Park Street, on the south by Boston Street, and on the west by Whitfield Street. Church, Fair, and State Streets lead from Broad Street north to the Boston Post Road. Many of Guilford's finest and most interesting shops and restaurants are on the green, but the Boston Post Road is home to many others. Whitfield Street continues south past the green toward Guilford Harbor and the beaches, so if it's a view of the Sound you're hoping to see, head down there.

Also known as Route 146, Water Street is a designated scenic highway. Officially, it begins at the eastern end of Boston Street, but visitors to the green will spot signs for it near its Water Street intersection with Whitfield Street. Be sure to include this 12-mile route back toward Branford on a driving or bicycling tour. Along the way, turn off at Mulberry Point Road or Sachem's Head Road for a ride through the scenic neighborhoods at the edge of the Sound. Parking is prohibited on most of the roads in this residential area, and the beaches are private, but the views are free and the roads are public.

The Mill Gallery hosts various small expositions and special events throughout the year. You can purchase the works of as many as 300 artisans, and the school offers classes and workshops for adults and children.

411 Church Street (Route 77), north of Route 1 and approximately 200 yards north of the I-95 overpass. (203–453–5947). Studios open year-round for classes and visitors; call for schedule and course catalog. Gallery and shop open year-round Monday through Saturday from 10:00 A.M. to 5:00 P.M. and Sunday from noon to 4:00 P.M. Extended hours for annual Holiday Exhibition and Sale in December. Closed Thanksgiving, Christmas, and New Year's Day. Free.

Westwoods Trails

Henry David Thoreau would have loved these pathways. In 1862 he wrote, "I think that I cannot preserve my health and spirits, unless I spend four hours a day at least . . . sauntering through the woods and over the hills and fields, absolutely free from all worldly engagements." Few of us are afforded the luxury of four-hour daily walks, but each of us should try this once a month on Connecticut's exceptional trails.

Westwoods is a great place to start. Thousand acres of forest and marshland are laced with 40 miles of trails that lead to waterfalls, rock cliffs, colonial and Indian caves, rock carvings, and vistas of the Sound and lake. The "G" Trail connects the Westwoods trails to the Stony Creek Quarry Preserve; here you can see the remains of old quarrying operations. A trail map is essential to a safe hike here; pick one up at the Guilford Free Library, the town hall on the green, the community center on Church Street, Bishop's Farm Market on the Boston Post Road, Breakwater Books on Whitfield Street, or from the Guilford Land Conservation Trust, P. O. Box 200, Guilford, CT 06437.

To reach Westwoods, take Route 146 west from the Guilford green for less than a mile to Sam Hill Road and park in the small unpaved lot right near that corner. Follow the white-blazed trail from that point and connect with any of the several other trails you will note on your map.

Trail entrance on Sam Hill Road near its junction with Route 146 (203–453–8068). Open year-round at no charge from dawn to dusk.

Jacobs Beach

Hikers and bikers may want a refreshing swim or at least a cool

Nathanael B. Greene Community Center

Just yards from the north end of the Guilford green at 32 Church Street is Guilford's public community center (203–453–8068). Open year-round Monday through Friday from 8:30 A.M. to 4:30 P.M. and on weekends seasonally, it has a tourist information desk in the front atrium of the building. Often staffed by helpful volunteers, this area is stocked with free brochures, maps, community newspapers, and other useful information. Upstairs are the offices of the Guilford Parks and Recreation Department (203–453–8168) from which visitors may obtain season passes to Lake Quonnipaug. Public restrooms are located on the center's first floor, and free public parking is available to visitors who would like to leave the car and walk through downtown.

wind through their hair after some trail exercise. Head down to the Sound for a rest on the sand at Jacobs Beach. Comb the sand for treasures swept in on the tide, listen to the rustling marsh reeds whisper a seaside serenade. You can swim if the lifeguards are on duty, but you can use the beach and volleyball court even if the guards are off duty. Restrooms and a pavilion with picnic tables and nearby grills are here. A playscape in a large grassy area makes the space fun for children. The beach itself is relatively small, but it's a pretty spot, and out-of-towners are welcome.

Seaside Avenue off Whitfield Street (Guilford Parks and Recreation, 203–453–8168). Park and playground area open year-round from 8:30 A.M. to 9:00 P.M. Swimming allowed only when lifeguards are present, from Memorial Day to Labor Day, on Monday through Saturday from 9:00 A.M. to 5:00 P.M. and on Sunday from 11:00 A.M. to 5:00 P.M. Out-of-town visitors pay $4 per vehicle on weekdays and $6 per vehicle on weekends from Memorial Day through Labor Day.

Chaffinch Island Park

If you'd like to enjoy a view of the water with a bit more privacy, head to Chaffinch Island Park. It's just across the harbor from Jacobs Beach, but you'll need to take Seaside Avenue back out to Whitfield Street, take a left on Whitfield and return to its intersection with beautiful Route 146 near the green. Hang a left onto Route 146, then another left onto Mulberry Point, and another left onto Chaffinch Island Road. At its end, past Brown's Boatyard, is a pretty park overlooking the Sound and the marshes at the mouth of the West River.

The land practically rolls into the sea at this point, as you'll see if you park the car or your bikes in the gravel lot near the huge boulders in the center of the park's circular drive. Climb the humped back of the grassy knoll that provides great picnicking sites and walk out to the edge of the water. Wave-worn rocks arch gently above the water at the southernmost tip of land; be sure to explore here and enjoy the views of Faulkner Island and its lighthouse. Picnic tables appear late in May and stay until autumn, but besides those the town provides only trash barrels. The gift is that most of the year the only visitors are you and the gulls.

At the foot of Chaffinch Island Road off Mulberry Point Road; open year-round daily, dawn to dusk; no facilities; no charge.

Lake Quonnipaug

Freshwater swimming may be more pleasing to you than the Sound. If so, head north to Guilford's mile-long Lake Quonnipaug for salt-free water play, boating, fishing, and picnicking. This pretty lake is in a beautifully rural area dotted with barns and pastures, stone walls and fences—the perfect setting for a New England day trip.

A good-sized beach and grassy area are open to the public there. Lifeguards are on duty whenever the swimming area is open. Restrooms with outdoor showers are also provided. Small cartop boats such as inflatables, canoes, kayaks, sailboards, or tubes may be launched from the grassy area, but no snorkeling or scuba div-

Guilford Handcrafts Exposition

Surely the most magical of all the events held on the Guilford green, this fabulous three-day festival, from Thursday to Saturday in the middle week of July, celebrates American handcrafts created by juried artists from all corners of the nation. Displayed under huge tents, the pieces demonstrate an astonishing array of talent in every medium. Basketry, woodcraft, weaving, jewelry, toys, clothing, candles, tinsmithing, leather goods, sculpture, pottery, paper crafts, glass, musical instruments, furniture—you name it, it's here.

Thousands of folks converge on the green for this beautiful event, which begins around midday and continues through the evening. Hands-on activities and demonstrations and a small variety of entertainments such as storytellers, face painters, or other performers help make the Expo a happy experience for all visitors. Adult admission $5; children under 12 free. Call for more information (203–453–5947).

ing is allowed. A state-owned public boat launch ramp is at the north end of the lake, outside of the Guilford property.

Route 77 in North Guilford, about 3 miles north of Route 80. Open Memorial Day through Labor Day (gated during remainder of year) Monday through Saturday 9:30 A.M. to 7:30 P.M., Sunday 11:00 A.M. to 7:30 P.M. Purchase day tickets at the lake for $4 per person on weekdays and $6 per person on weekends. Best buy for families is a season pass for $20 per adult 21–59 or $30 per adult couple, plus $5 per child under 12, and $10 per child 12 to 20. The pass allows unlimited visits per season and can only be purchased at the Guilford Parks and Recreation Department (203–453–8068) at 32 Church Street.

Dudley Farm

If you're exploring Route 77 (its total length from the Guilford green to its end in Durham is 11.56 miles), you may wish you could stop in to one of its appealing farmsteads—even the one called Insulting Manor has a kind of allure—but you might feel shy unless you're in immediate need of hay or manure. Lucky for you, one of Guilford's historic farms went public recently, hanging out a welcome sign for visitors with an appetite for country pleasures. Settled in the arms of nature, the eight standing buildings and nearly two dozen remnant structures at this peaceful ten-acre farm site are the legacy of the Dudley family, who tilled the soil and tended both crops and animals through two centuries in Guilford.

Under development as both an attraction and an education center, the farm offers guided and self-guided tours, activities, workshops, and demonstrations. Tours of the farm and adjoining mill site feature an 1840s farmhouse with some of its seventeen rooms restored to their turn-of-the-twentieth-century state, an enormous U-shaped barn that evolved through two centuries of farm life, a sugarhouse, a small barn restored for use as a schoolhouse for visiting classes, herb and flower gardens, a vegetable field, and beehives. Long-range plans include restoration of the entire farmhouse and the standing buildings, plus the creation or restoration of other areas in a style circa 1900.

Day-trippers may prefer to visit on Saturdays when the farm is at its busiest. In the morning it offers a farmers' market of its own produce as well as the produce of local farmers and crafters. Depending on the season, you may also see the farm staff demonstrating sheep-shearing, beekeeping, twig furniture construction, rag rug weaving, or barn chores and tool repair.

Faulkner Island Lighthouse

Slightly more than 3 miles off the coast of Guilford is a small island that rises steeply out of the water. From shore it sometimes resembles a long, flattish ship firmly at anchor, but its ever-changing shape is at the root of its current fame. Formed during the Ice Age when glaciers pushed rock and soil southward and scooped out Long Island Sound, Faulkner Island was well-known by the Menuncatucks. They called it Massancummock, or "place of the great fish hawks," and they frequented it in spring and summer in search of game and shellfish. Colonial farmers, on the philosophy that what's yours is mine, supplanted the Menuncatucks and grew crops and grazed livestock there. In 1802 the island began to serve its most useful purpose; in that year Thomas Jefferson commissioned a lighthouse on it to warn mariners of dangerous shoals.

Today, however, the white octagonal tower is itself at grave risk as erosion of the island's east embankment threatens the lighthouse's stability. In 1991 a committee formed to save the light, which is the second oldest in the state. Faulkner Light still operates as an aid to navigation and orientation, and the Faulkner's Light Brigade can't bear to see it slip into the Sound. Just 35 feet from the bluff face, the light is now protected by an erosion control plan and an initiative to restore both the tower and the island's wharf. The island itself is part of the Stewart B. McKinney National Wildlife Refuge. One of the world's largest breeding colonies of the roseate tern, Faulkner is also second home to more than 150 species of other migratory birds.

The Light Brigade sponsors an annual migration of humans to a sort of island open house. On the first Saturday after Labor Day, visitors can tour the tower and learn about the research on the terns from the biologists who set up house here during nesting season. (For information on visiting the island, call 203–453–8400 or 203–453–1111.)

2351 Durham Road (Route 77) north of Route 80 (203–457–0770). Open April 15 to October 15 on Saturday and Sunday from 10:00 A.M. to 2:00 P.M. Call for a schedule of events. Farmer's market on Saturday from 9:00 to noon. Suggested donation $3.

Bishop's Orchards

One of the many charms of the coastal towns to the east of New Haven is that farms and orchards still flourish right along Route 1. Established in 1871, Bishop's is perhaps Guilford's best-known and most popular of these, open to the public year-round for fresh-from-the-field shopping in its large market or pick-your-own pleasures in its many fields and orchards. Fresh produce of all kinds, eggs, breads, cheeses, and locally made jams, honey, cookies, pies, and cider help make Bishop's a great place to build either picnic or banquet. Look here in the fall for mums, gourds, and cornstalks for autumn decorating; come back in December for wreaths, garlands, and Christmas trees.

Call the infoline for the latest news on picking your own harvest throughout the summer and fall. Come for strawberries in June, blueberries in July, peaches and pears in August, raspberries in September, apples and pumpkins in October.

The Monastery of Our Lady of Grace

You won't come closer to Heaven than this secluded enclave preserved for the glory of God by the most devoted of servants—the Dominican nuns who seek the face of the Lord through their silent contemplation, their study, and their prayer. Within the confines of their beautiful enclosure, the sisters also observe other practices of simplicity and sacrifice, making candles and pottery, sewing liturgical vestments, creating artworks in praise of God, and growing vegetables and flowers.

Although their orchards and gardens are screened from view, their chapel is open daily and guests are welcome. The sisters' voices rise in prayerful song several times daily; those seeking peace and healing will surely find comfort here. Vespers, offered at the close of the afternoon on weekdays and on Saturday evenings, is especially moving. Visitors may also purchase the sisters' handiwork in the monastery gift shop. An area outside the cloister offers visitors a shaded pathway punctuated by the Stations of the Cross; it is accessible year-round at all times. An annual monastic fair is a small but merry celebration of the gifts of the harvest; call the gift shop to inquire as to its date this year.

To reach the monastery, go north from I-95 on Route 77 for about 5 miles; turn right on Race Hill Road, which is the first right after Route 77 crosses Route 80. The monastery is at the corner of Race Hill and Hoop Pole Roads. Daily Mass is at 7:00 A.M. on weekdays and 8:00 A.M. on Sunday; Vespers is at 4:40 p.m. on weekdays and 8:00 p.m. on Saturday. Additional Masses are scheduled on special holy days such as Christmas and Easter. The gift shop (203–457–0599) is open Monday through Saturday from 10:00 to 11:45 A.M. and from 1:00 to 4:00 p.m.; on Sunday, it opens at 9:00 P.M. A few guest rooms are available in the sister's retreat quarters for those who would like to join the sisters for a few days or a week of prayer, silence, and solitude.

1355 Boston Post Road (farm market 203-453-2338; pick-your-own infoline 203-453-6424). Open year-round Monday through Saturday from 8:00 A.M. to 6:00 P.M and from 9:00 A.M. on Sunday

Places to Eat in Guilford

Quattro 1300 Boston Post Road (203–453–6575). Delicious Italian cuisine elegantly presented. Popular with adult diners. Open for lunch and dinner daily. $$–$$$

Bistro on the Green 25 Whitfield Street (203–458–9059). Delicately seasoned soups, quiches, salads, pastas, and daily-special entrees in a casually sophisticated setting. Lovely for lunch; cozy for dinner; nice for breakfast and afternoon tea also. Divine pastries and cakes. Open daily for all meals. $–$$$

Sachem Country House 111 Goose Lane (203–453–5261). Colonial inn serving well-prepared American cuisine in charming period chambers. Dinner Tuesday through Saturday 5:00 to 9:00 P.M., Sunday brunch 11:00 A.M. to 2:30 P.M., Sunday dinner 3:00 to 8:00 P.M. Closed Monday. $$–$$$

Guilford Tavern 2455 Boston Post Road (203–453–2216). Top-quality poultry, ribs, prime rib, steaks, and seafood plus sandwiches, salads, and soups. Open for lunch and dinner and Sunday brunch. $$

Nata's of Guilford 63–R Whitfield Street in Whitfield Alley (203–453–3288). Innovative, fresh, and affordable prix-fixe lunches and dinners in tiny, crisply clean dining room. Seafood and pastas are especially delicious. Dinner includes appetizer, salad, entree, and dessert for $15.95. Lunch is $8.48. Open daily for lunch and dinner. $

The Place 901 Boston Post Road (203–453–9276). Seasonal dining in the rough, at one of Connecticut's most unusual eateries. Outside under tents, sit on rough-hewn seats at picnic tables and eat charcoal-grilled steak, pit-roasted corn on the cob, fresh seafood, and more. Open from May through October, depending on the weather, Monday though Thursday 5:00 to 10:00 P.M., Saturday 1:00 to 11:00 P.M., and Sunday noon to 10:00 P.M. $$

Places to Stay in Guilford

Guilford Corners B&B 133 State Street (203–453–4129). Romantic decor in a restored 1732 colonial in the center of town. Spacious rooms with private baths; a two-room suite great for families has a shared bath. Four-poster queen-size beds, sherry in the afternoon, home-baked treats in continental-plus breakfast. Open year-round. In season, May 1 to September 1, $$$$ (lower in off-season).

Cottage on Church Street B&B 190 Church Street (203–458–2598). Smack-dab in the center of everything, but a world away. A sunny soul-soother with charm to spare. A private cottage with king-size bed, sitting and dining area, full bath, and garden patio. Full breakfast of baked goodies and fruit delivered to your door in the morning. Smoke-free. $$$$

B&B on Boston Street 279 Boston Street (203–453–6490). Close to the green and set back from the road, this establishment provides a comfortable two-room suite with king-size bed, private bath, and full use of common areas on upper level of twentieth-century split-level home. Full breakfast, screened deck, large yard with a pool. Pets welcome. $$$

Guilford Suites Hotel 2300 Boston Post Road (203–453–0123 or 800–626–8604). 32 suites with bedroom, sitting room, bath, and kitchenettes; continental breakfast; open year-round. $$$–$$$$

Tower Motel 320 Boston Post Road (203–453–9069). 15 units with 13 efficiencies. Clean and affordable. Open year-round. $$

Public Boat Launch

Guilford Town Marina At Town Dock at foot of Whitfield Street (203–453–8092). One transient slip; boat launch ramp (nonresident day use $20). Phone, restrooms. Stone House restaurant nearby for adult dining; Steamers Grill and Bar for seafood and family fare (boaters welcome at Steamers' dock); Guilford Lobster Pound behind Steamers.

For Further Information

Guilford Chamber of Commerce 741 Boston Post Road, Suite 101 (203–453–9677). Maps, brochures, general information.

Guilford Web site: http://www.guilfordct.com.

Madison

Once called East Guilford and connected geographically and politically to the town of Guilford, Madison seemed at one time typical of the small English settlements along the coast. Farmers and fishermen kept Madison well-stocked with onions and potatoes and oysters; sawmills and shipyards used the natural resources of both forest and harbor to build Madison's reputation as manufacturer of oceangoing wooden vessels. Incorporated as a separate town in 1826 and renamed in tribute to President James Madison, the village eventually took a different course from that of other rapidly developing coastal towns.

The railroad and the steamship brought an end to the era of great wooden sailboats, and, by the late nineteenth century, the clamor and activity at Madison's shipbuilding wharves changed to a different kind of clatter. The shipyards closed, and the hotels opened, welcoming train passengers who fell in love with the natural beauty and healthy atmosphere of Madison's beaches. By 1904 Madison was an established seaside resort area, with more than three hundred cottages dotting the shoreline.

Today Madison is primarily a residential suburb populated by descendants of its original settlers, happy heirs of those pretty Victorian cottages, and families of professionals and executives who work in more developed towns within commuting distance. Early each June, Madison's population swells by several thousand as the "summer people" return to the shore and tourists double the sidewalk traffic past Madison's shops, galleries, and restaurants. Hammonasset State Park draws more visitors than any other park in the state, and Madison merchants, restaurateurs, and cultural arts folks work hard to coax travelers to linger. Pack a bicycle, a bathing suit, and a beach blanket, and come to enjoy the halcyon time warp that bewitches pretty Madison.

The Best of Madison

Deacon John Grave House

Close to four centuries have elapsed since European settlers brought new models of housing to the summer campgrounds of the native population. Concerned more with surviving the harsh New England winters than with adapting to the nomadic lifeways of the Algonkians, the colonists built sturdy shelters guaranteed by massive posts and beams to withstand the assault of severe weather. Have a look at the colossal central fireplace of Madison's Deacon John Grave House, and you'll be unsurprised that the house has stood on this spot since the settlement's earliest days.

Just a block east of the Madison green on a pretty two-acre parcel known in the past as Tuxis Farm, the Grave House was occupied for more than three hundred years by descendants of its original owner, Deacon John Grave. Adapted for use in the past as an ordinary, a school, a wartime infirmary and weapons depot, and even a courtroom, the house also was home to ten children at one time—and that was before its eighteenth-century additions were added! Come here to imagine the life of a farming family in pre-Revolutionary days, see the secret staircase that led to a room used for storing arms during the French and Indian War, hear the ghost stories associated with the house, and admire the pretty door-yard garden.

Call to inquire about special days when tours include demonstrations or costumed interpreters, often in association with other special events such as the Civil War reenactment and encampment that takes place in April or May at Hammonasset State Park. In some years during late October, the ghosts of the house are enlisted to help out with some haunted Halloween shenanigans. This dramatic event is very realistically staged and promises to send shivers up the spines of those brave enough to enter.

581 Boston Post Road (203–245–4798). Open in summer Wednesday through Friday from noon to 3:00 P.M., Saturday from 10:00 A.M. to 4:30 P.M. and Sunday from noon to 4:30 P.M. After Labor Day through Columbus Day, open Saturday and Sunday noon to 3:00 P.M.; in winter, by appointment. Adults $2, children $1.

Allis–Bushnell House

In Madison, large numbers of vintage homes still rest right along the Boston Post Road (Route 1). Along this thoroughfare are homes

Downtown Madison

Madison's centerpiece is its tree-shaded green surrounded by homes from three centuries. The stately, white First Congregational Church is a Greek Revival beauty capped with a gilded dome that once served as a landmark to guide returning seamen into Madison's harbors. Today the church seems to preside over the happy activity of weekend art festivals, antiques shows, and concerts that blossom on the green from April through October.

From late May through November 1, the Madison Visitors Information Center (6 Meetinghouse Lane; 203-245-5659) operates in a tiny yellow brick building called the Powder House, immediately to the east of the larger yellow-brick Memorial Hall at the east end of the green. Hours vary, but on weekends from 9:00 A.M. to 6:00 P.M. you can usually stop for brochures and a calendar of events or to obtain directions to local points of interest.

The relatively small area of downtown Madison makes it especially conducive to strolling. The business "hub" of Madison centers on the intersection of the Boston Post Road and Wall Street. Springtime brings a flourish of cherry blossoms to the trees that line the main sidewalks, but the town center is pretty in all seasons. In winter the center esplanade is adorned with a row of lighted Christmas trees in white-washed half-barrels that in summer overflow with colorful flowers.

If the scenery is not enough to urge visitors to slow their pace, Madison's shops provide a marvelous alternative to cookie-cutter chain stores and impersonal outlets. Many of the boutiques, galleries, antiques stores, cafes, and restaurants of Madison are located in vintage homes and historic commercial buildings on or near "Main Street" and Wall. Be sure to stop for coffee or cappuccino at the **Madison Gourmet Beanery** or have lunch at **Sweet and Savoury Deli** or **Perfect Parties,** then browse a while at **R. J. Julia Booksellers** (voted the best independent bookstore in the entire nation) or one of the score and more eclectic establishments offering clothes, jewelry, clothing, toys, handcrafts, and home furnishings. A stroll through the **P. Hastings Falk Fine Art Gallery** and a restorative cup of tea at the incomparable **British Shoppe** and its **Front Parlour Tea Room** may be just the right end to an afternoon in Madison. Don't skip town without stopping at **Marie's Sweet Shop.** This little pink storefront with the park bench out front has terrific homemade ice cream, great chocolates, and all the fountain treats you'd expect from an independent ice cream emporium.

that belonged to Madison's oldest families. Markers on the houses note their original owners—Scranton, Dudley, Wilcox, Bradley, Chittenden, Meigs—but travelers can admire only their exteriors. The stewardship of Madison residents with a respect for history has kept these homes in private hands that minister lovingly to their preservation.

To see an eighteenth-century interior that is open to the public, drive to the center of the village. Built exactly a century after Madison's Deacon John Grave House, the 1785 Allis-Bushnell House is headquarters of the Madison Historical Society. The house is notable for its unusual corner fireplaces and cupboards, its beautifully stenciled floors, the exceptional collection of tools and fishing and farming equipment and artifacts in its annex, and its pretty formation of eighteenth-century herbs in its lovely rear garden. Home of Cornelius Bushnell, a founder of the Union Pacific Railway and chief financier of the Civil War ironclad ship USS *Monitor*, it also has a collection of fascinating memorabilia regarding the famed vessel.

Costumed junior docents add a charming and authentic touch as they greet visitors and perform tasks throughout the house. Senior docents lead the one-hour tours that are willingly tailored to your interests and schedule. Children may particularly enjoy the home's small collection of toys, dolls, period costumes, and interesting medical implements.

853 Boston Post Road (203–245–4567). Open Memorial Day to October 1 on Wednesday, Friday, and Saturday, 1:00 to 4:00 P.M. Donation.

Madison Town Beaches

While Madison extends northward nearly 15 miles from the shore of the Sound to the border of Durham, it is primarily rural and nearly strictly residential north of I–95. A driving tour of the area south of the Boston Post Road gives the visitor a sense of the coastal flavor of Madison and also takes a route past or near its beautiful beaches. Open a map of Madison and discover the roads that lead to the shore. Along the route you choose, stop at Madison's wonderful beaches and historic wharves.

The **Surf Club** is the largest town beach, with playing fields, a nature trail, bocce, basketball, volleyball, and horseshoes courts, a large picnic grove with barbecue grills, and a pavilion with a first aid station, restrooms and showers, game room, and snack bar.

The tiny crescent of **West Wharf Beach** lies at the left side of the stone wharf at the foot of West Wharf Road. Stop at this point for a great view of Tuxis Island to the east near the shore and Faulkner's Island in the distance to the southwest. Anglers, photographers, and barefooted tidepool explorers are drawn to the area's famed rock outcroppings, once called Reuben's Rocks. Beautiful from dawn to sunset, this popular destination was the site of Madison's busiest and most profitable shipbuilding wharf in the nineteenth century.

At **East Wharf Beach**, tucked neatly in the heart of Madison's private beach community, a large wooden gazebo shelters visitors in all seasons; restrooms, a water fountain, and an outdoor shower add to the comfort of summer travelers. A public landing place since 1765, this site was home to Minor's Shipyard until 1890, when the yard and all of the tall ships in it burned to the ground.

Just yards from Hammonasset State Park at the place where tranquil Tom's Creek enters the Sound, **Webster Point Beach** presents a secluded alternative for folks who walk or bike in from the center of town. In exchange for its lack of parking, lifeguards, and facilities, visitors enjoy a wide sandbar, good snorkeling places, and lots of privacy.

Webster Point Beach at the foot of Pent Road off Webster Point Road (walk-in only; no street parking, even in the off-season), East Wharf Beach on Middle Beach Road, West Wharf Beach at the foot of West Wharf Road, and Surf Club Beach on Surf Club Road. Visitors are welcome to use Madison town-owned beaches in the off-season only. From Memorial Day through Labor Day, the beaches are restricted to Madison residents and visitors staying overnight at Madison inns and hotels. For further information, call the Madison Beach and Recreation Department (203-245-5623).

Hammonasset State Park and Meigs Point Nature Center

If you wander east from the center of Madison on the Boston Post Road, you will soon reach Hammonasset State Park. Enormously popular, this park offers nearly one thousand acres and its 2 miles of shorefront—Connecticut's longest stretch of public beach. Provided for your comfort and pleasure are pavilions and picnic shelters, a 550-site campground, playing fields, a nature center with walking trails, a bike path, a wide, wooden boardwalk, and sun, sand, rocks, and salty spray in abundance.

Come here to camp, swim, fish off the jetty, scuba dive, picnic, play ball, hike, sailboard, or boat on Long Island Sound. Day visitors and campers alike should stop at the **Meigs Point Nature Center.** An excellent small facility, it has fresh- and saltwater aquariums, a marine touch tank, dioramas, and a good variety of live amphibians and reptiles of the area. Outside is the Willard's Island walking trail that rambles through the salt meadow and onto Willard's Island, once farmed in colonial times and now home to the small mammals and birds of the marshlands.

The Nature Center rangers provide free bird walks, slide presentations, canoe trips, bike hikes, and nature workshops for all ages throughout the summer. Special activities such as the Junior Naturalist program and the Outdoor Explorer program are scheduled for children. Held midweek in July and August, the children's programs are open to drop-in visitors.

The parking lot immediately to the east of the Nature Center is a good place to stow the car if you'd like to set yourself up on the beach for a few hours to catch a few rays or watch the ospreys that nest here. Across the road from the lot is a long wooden walkway to one of the park's smaller, quieter pavilions. If you travel eastward from the Nature Center toward the boat launch site at Meigs Point, you'll stop at a dead-end parking area just before the lane to the beach reserved for boaters. Be sure to park and walk to the top of the rocky hill at the Point; its sandy paths lead to beautiful views of the Sound and shore. An expansive wooden deck at the summit provides a place to enjoy the broad sweep of seascape and the songs of the gulls and warblers.

For those unsatisfied by a mere few hours at the shore, Hammonasset's windswept campground is a great seaside vacation spot. Well-run and very clean, it is extremely popular in the summertime. The sites are almost all open, so if you like the hills and woods, you're in the wrong park. Bring a metal tub or fire ring if you want to sit or sing around a campfire; pack a grill or hibachi if you want to cook over a flame; the state provides no grills or firepits at this park, and campfires are permitted only in metal containers. Campfire programs, bingo, an occasional dance and a children's playground with swings and a great wooden ship ensure fun for all ages. A camp store rents fire rings and stocks firewood, a moderate variety of groceries, and essentials like marshmallows and chocolate.

Bring bikes and in-line skates—the campground has excellent

lanes for both sports. Biking and in-line skating are possible all year round, even though the campground closes; just park your vehicle outside the gate and enter the lanes with bikes or blades.

Off the Boston Post Road at exit 62 of I-95 Park (203–245–2785). Open daily year-round, 8:00 A.M. to sunset. Campground (203–245–1817) open mid-May to September 30. Nature Center (203–245–8743) open late April to September 30, Tuesday through Sunday, 10:00 A.M. to 5:00 P.M. Per-vehicle admission charge $5 for in-state license plates and $8 for out-of-state plates on weekdays from Memorial Day to Labor Day; $7 and $12, respectively, on weekends. Also $5 and $7 on weekends only from mid-April to Memorial Day and from Labor Day through mid-October; weekdays free to all during those weeks. No charge off-season. Campsites $12 nightly.

Places to Eat in Madison

Cafe Allegre 725 Boston Post Road (203–245–7773). By day, sunlit rooms and front-porch seating; at evening, an air of elegance in a vintage inn at the heart of downtown. In the main dining rooms, enjoy Italian cuisine with a gourmet flair, charming table lamps, and an atmosphere of casual elegance. Creatively presented seafood, pastas, freshly made sauces, tasty house-made soups, good salads. Open year-round for lunch and dinner. Full bar. $$$–$$$$

Chestnut Hill Concerts

A summer day spent in Madison can stretch well into the evening if you stay for one of the concerts of the acclaimed Chestnut Hill chamber music series. Produced for thirty summers, the series drew its early performers from the Yale Music School. Now the concerts, performed at Madison's First Congregational Church on the green, feature world-class performers from New York, Boston, and Europe. The acoustics in this spacious yet intimate setting are superb for the purpose. Classical chamber music with an emphasis on the Romantic period is the focus of the series, but the program may yield equally pleasant surprises.

Four concerts are offered each season on the first four Fridays in August at 8:00 P.M. Subscriptions are $55; individual tickets are $17.50. Senior and student discounts are available. For further information, call the box office (203–245–5736).

Many concertgoers picnic before the performances. Boxed picnic suppers can be ordered in advance ($13 per person) and picked up at the church after 6:00 P.M.

The Wharf Restaurant at the Madison Beach Hotel; 94 West Wharf Road (203–245–0005). The only restaurant on the Sound in Madison. Seafood, steaks, and pasta for lunch and dinner in the main dining rooms. Upstairs in the Crow's Nest lounge are sandwiches, chowders, and other light fare. Live music in the Crow's Nest on weekends after about 9:30. If you want to enjoy a quiet, leisurely dinner downstairs, make reservations for 7:00, not 8:00. Open late March through December. $$

Noodles Casual Cuisine 508 Old Toll Road (Route 80) (203–421–5606). Off the beaten path at the north end of town, this notably good restaurant is worth the 6-mile drive up Route 79. Its warm ambiance and excellent service are pleasing accompaniments to well-prepared dishes perfectly seasoned and freshly made. Casual, comfortable, and affordable enough for the whole family. Closed Monday. Open year-round for lunch and dinner and Sunday brunch $–$$

Lynch and Malone's Restaurant 56A Academy Street (203–245–1145). Smartly dressed salads and sandwiches, grilled seafood and steaks, terrific salads, innovative pasta dishes. Open year-round daily for lunch and dinner and Sunday brunch. $–$$

Friends and Company 11 Boston Post Road (203–245–0462). A busy local favorite on the banks of the East River. Casual and reasonable with good pastas, fresh fish, crisp salads, excellent herb bread. Best of all, smoke-free. Open year-round for dinner daily; lunch Wednesday through Saturday, Sunday brunch. $–$$

Lenny and Joe's Fish Tale 1301 Boston Post Road (203–245–7289). A busy, favorite on the Hammonasset end of town. Casual eat-in or take-out atmosphere with indoor, porch, or outdoor picnic-table seating. Heaping plates of fresh fish, corn on the cob, salt potatoes, good rings, lobster, chowder, and much more. Open year-round for lunch and dinner daily. $

Red Tomato Pizzeria 37 Boston Post Road (203–245–6948). Order out or eat in at this cheery eatery that makes excellent thin-crust New Haven–style pizza baked right on the bricks. Fresh vegetable and meat toppings make it easy to design your own tasty creation—even the clams are freshly shucked. Calzones, a house salad, and antipasto are also on the menu. Open daily from 3:00 P.M. $–$$

The Clam Castle 1324 Boston Post Road (203–245–4911). Serving the shoreline since 1967, this classic seafood drive-in shack is owned by two cheerful brothers who take pride in upholding the tradition of fresh fish, terrific New England and Rhode Island clam chowder, famed onion rings, chili, a huge breakfast menu, and much more. Lobster rolls, soft shell crabs, clams nearly any way you can eat 'em (including clam fritters). Eat inside or out. Open daily. $

The Front Parlour Tea Room at the British Shoppe; 45 Wall Street (203-245-4521). Enter the 1690 Meigs Bishop House and enter another world—one you'll want to linger in well past teatime. Perfect crumpets and scones, delicate finger sandwiches, delicious pot pies and homemade soups, and, of course, the finest of teas and tea cakes, served exquisitely in the most romantic of settings by the most gracious of hosts. It's hard to leave the table, but be sure to save time to shop for teapots, bone china, English toiletries, and other British treasures in the marvelous store. Luncheon Monday through Saturday 11:30 A.M. to 1:30 P.M.; afternoon tea Monday through Saturday 2:00 to 4:00 P.M. and Sunday 12:30 to 4:00 P.M. $

Places to Stay in Madison

The Madison Beach Hotel 94 West Wharf Road (203-245-1404). Directly on the beach, this restored 1800 hotel offers a taste of Madison's history as a Victorian seaside resort. Add to that charm the best possible views of Madison's beautiful shoreline. You'll find 35 charmingly decorated units with 6 suites and some units with balconies overlooking the Sound. Continental breakfast served on porch, in Victorian lobby, or on your balcony. Beach chairs and towels provided. Open March 1 to January 1. $$$

Dolly Madison Inn 73 West Wharf Road (203-245-7377). In total, 13 rooms in traditional New England inn and "Tiltin' Hilton" out back. Several of these are large enough for families. Just a

The Legend of Tuxis Island

The small island just offshore Madison is Tuxis Island. Algonkian legend says that a great giant scooped up a handful of rocks and soil and flung it into the Sound, creating in one action the island and Tuxis Pond, which formed in the hollow left in the earth by the giant's hand. Today the island is uninhabited; it once was the site of a YMCA camp and has had at least one cottage on it. A nesting platform has recently been raised on the island to attract ospreys. As for the pond, it lies behind the firehouse in the center of town. A wooden boardwalk traces its western edge, and a small park with benches overlooking the pond's aeration fountain is accessible from the public parking area off Wall Street behind the post office.

block from the beach. Restaurant. $$–$$$

The Inn at Lafayette 725 Boston Post Road (203–245–7773). Includes 5 elegant, comfortable guest rooms with private marbled baths, gracious antique furnishings, and attention to detail apparent in every corner. Continental breakfast, fruit, and champagne. Open year-round. $$$$

Tidewater Inn 949 Boston Post Road (203–245–8457). Elegant nonsmoking inn with pretty gardens and a romantic ambiance. Total of 9 guest rooms with private baths; full breakfast; complimentary wine in late afternoon; beach passes, beach chairs, and beach towels in summer. Children over the age of 7 only. $$$$

Honeysuckle Hill Bed and Breakfast 116 Yankee Peddler Path (203–245–4574). Spacious bedroom suite in a private twentieth-century home in a quiet neighborhood near the center of town. Queen-size bed, fireplace, full bath, hearty breakfast, beach passes. Extra single room available. Families welcome. Open mid-May through mid-January. $$$–$$$$

Madison Post Road Bed and Breakfast 318 Boston Post Road (203–245–2866). You'll feel like you've lived here forever in this nineteenth-century treasure with twentieth-century comforts.

Shore Points

Osprey!

The cry of the female osprey and the spiraling air ballet of her mate during the courting season have to be among the most dramatic events to occur on the Connecticut shoreline each year. With the support of the public and the work of the biologists involved with the Long Island Sound Program of the Connecticut Department of Environmental Protection, the osprey population on the eastern shore has risen to new heights. Decimated in past decades by the effects of the pesticide DDT on the shells of their young, the ospreys have experienced such a hopeful comeback in recent years that they have been removed from the category of Special Concerns on the Connecticut endangered species list. In the summer of 1997, more than 110 nesting pairs fledged nearly 245 youngsters from the nesting platforms and natural nesting cavities along the coast. Now Connecticut residents and visitors look forward each spring to the return of the osprey from their winter digs in South America. Still protected under the U.S. Migratory Bird Act, the ospreys have no rivals as the most majestic residents of the Connecticut shore. Hammonasset State Park in Madison is home to several pairs of nesting ospreys.

There are 3 rooms with private bath, 2 with shared bath, and a welcoming common rooms. Full breakfast; deeded beach rights in walking distance; beach chairs and towels. Families welcome; children under 12 stay free. $10 extra for portacrib or rollaway bed. Nonsmoking. Open year-round; rates lower from January 1 to May 15. $$$–$$$$

Morning Glory Bed and Breakfast 395 Boston Post Road (203–245–9196). Offers 3 cheerfully decorated guest rooms with private baths, country antiques, and a private entrance to this lovely Federal home. Flowered patios and cutting garden. Full breakfast. Beach passes. Nonsmoking. Families with children over the age of 8 are welcome. Open year–round. $$$

Public Boat Launches

Hammonasset State Park at Meigs Point. One mile south of exit 62 from I–95. Cartop or carry-in access only. Launching over sandy beach; shallow at low tide. No docking or anchoring. No launch fee; parking fee on weekends and holidays in season.

East River State Boat Launch. On the east bank of the East River. From Boston Post Road, travel south for approximately 2 miles on Neck Road, Ridgewood Avenue, and Circle Beach Road to right turn on gravel drive to riverbank. No fees. Ramp only; no slips or moorings, no fuel or services.

For Further Information

Madison Chamber of Commerce 22 Scotland Avenue (203–245–7394 or 888–342–7394). Maps and brochures.

Madison Web site: http://madisonct.com.

Madison Land Trust P.O. Box 561, Madison CT 06443. Trail guide to thirteen hiking trails on conservation trust land.

Clinton

Any traveler approaching Clinton along the Boston Post Road at its western boundary with Madison will get an instant sense of the town's close connection with the Sound. The Hammonasset River cuts a swath through golden salt marshes; twisted junipers along the road bend permanently from the effect of the sea breeze; marine supply stores and boatyards advertise the latest deals for sailboarders and yachters alike. Heavy with salt and briny mud smells of the sea and shore and marsh, the air carries the sounds of screeching gulls, slapping rigging, and bellowing foghorns.

Halfway between New York and Boston, halfway between New Haven and New London, and situated on the land that in colonial days lay between the colony of Guilford and the colony of Saybrook, Clinton enjoys a central location that adds to its appeal to travelers. Once called Homonoscitt, Clinton's colonial settlement began in 1633 when Hartford Colony appointed a committee to lay out the Homonoscitt land as a plantation.

As was true in most settlements along the Sound, Clinton's early economy focused on farming, fishing, and shipbuilding. Its earliest claim to fame is that the first classes of what later became Yale College were held in the parsonage of its minister, the Reverend Abraham Pierson, also appointed first rector of the school. Later the town became known for its manufacture of Pond's Extract, distilled from native witch hazel cut from the Clinton woodlands. The Chesebrough-Pond's factory is still a noticeable presence along Route 1. By the end of the nineteenth century Clinton, like her shoreline sisters, had developed a summer colony as steamships, the railroad, and improved highways encouraged the influx of visitors from the city. Today Clinton maintains its centered position between the busy cities to its east and west, still offering residents and travelers a respite from the hubbub and a link to the sea.

Very, very low in true tourist attractions, Clinton is a perfect town for skipping stones off the jetty, hitching a ride on a fishing charter, combing antiques stores for some old-fashioned treasures, and topping off the day with a shore dinner and an ice cream cone.

Downtown Clinton, Antiques Capital of the Shore

The center of downtown Clinton stretches along Route 1 for quite a distance, with the highest concentration of commercial buildings starting somewhat west of Route 81 and ending somewhat east of Route 145. The strip immediately east of Route 81 is where visitors will find the Andrews Memorial Town Hall, the information center, the Chamber of Commerce, the Vece Gazebo, and most of Clinton's historic sites. Along this thoroughfare visitors will also find one of Connecticut's highest concentrations of antiques shops. The following shops are a partial list:

The Loft at Cramer's Corner 57 West Main Street (860–669–4583). Open daily 11:00 A.M. to 5:00 P.M. This landmark shop has a congenial owner and an eclectic collection; great lamps, bottles, household tools, writing implements.

Clinton Antique Center 78 East Main Street (860–669–3839). Open daily 10:00 A.M. to 5:00 P.M. except New Year's, Easter, Thanksgiving, and Christmas. Seventy-five dealers in an enormous group shop.

Claire A. Anderson Antique and Art Center 89 East Main Street (860–669–1936). Nine rooms of artwork and antiques in 1797 farmhouse.

Barker & Chambers Antiques on Main Street 100 East Main Street (860–664–9163). Open Thursday through Saturday 10:00 A.M. to 5:00 P.M. and often on Tuesday and Wednesday. Nineteenth- and twentieth-century goods exhibited in an eighteenth-century home. Wicker, books, fine porcelain and glass, decorative accessories.

Carlson Collection 101 East Main Street (860–669–2275). Open Wednesday through Saturday 10:00 A.M. to 5:00 P.M., Sunday 11:00 A.M. to 4:00 P.M. Antiques, consignments, new home furnishings, and fine gifts in the yellow Federal residence at the roadside.

Reflections 104 East Main Street (860–660–3301). Period furniture, small collectibles, decorative arts displayed in 1763 home.

Waterside Antiques 109 East Main Street (860–669–0809). Open Thursday through Sunday 11:00 A.M. to 4:00 P.M. Primitive furniture, textiles, woodenware, redware, folk art and lighting reproductions, baskets, glass, small collectibles.

Shops at Clinton Village 327 East Main Street (860–669–3350). Open daily 10:00 A.M. to 5:00 P.M. Six rooms of primitive and country furniture, books, jewelry, and china at the Wooden Wheelbarrow shop, plus a handful of diminutive cottages offering treasures old and new.

Square Rigger Antique Center 350 East Main Street (860–664–9001). Close to the Westbrook line, this large shop offers furniture, jewelry, glassware, small accessories, ephemera.

The Best of Clinton

Adam Stanton House and Store

Every Connecticut town has a noteworthy house open to the public, and Clinton is no exception. Owned and maintained as a museum of American antiquities by Connecticut National Bank, it was built in 1789 by Adam Stanton, a Rhode Islander who came to Connecticut during the Revolutionary War. Stanton operated a general store and a salt distillery on the property. Preserved with both store and home portions, the house contains almost all original furnishings. Along with an excellent collection of china and furniture, the house has some interesting features such as hinged wall paneling that allows the panels to be fastened to hooks in the ceiling so as to expand two rooms into one.

Stanton's store has been restored to its earliest condition, with its original counter, shelves, accountant's desk, and even labeled drawers. Behind the house is the original well of the Reverend Pierson, who owned an earlier house built on the site in 1694. It was in that first house that Pierson, from 1701 to 1707, taught the first classes of the new collegiate school later known as Yale.

63 East Main Street (860–669–2132). Open June 1 to September 30, Tuesday through Sunday from 2:00 to 5:00 P.M. Free; donations welcome. Ages 6 and older.

Captain Elisha White House

More commonly known as the Old Brick House, this 1850 home is owned by the Clinton Historical Society. The oldest brick house on the shoreline from New Haven to New London as well as the only brick house in Clinton, the house was built from handmade English brick brought to America as ballast in the ship of prosperous sea captain Elisha White. Today the property includes eighteenth- and nineteenth-century furnishings, portraits, and landscapes as well as a genealogical library inside and a colonial garden outside.

The Clinton Historical Society also maintains a local history room in the Andrews Memorial Town Hall (room 107). Its collections include dolls, china, silver, clothing, household implements, pressed glass and tin, and nautical items. The room is open on weekdays in July and August from 2:00 to 4:00 P.M., on Wednesdays only from September through June, or by appointment.

Elisha White House, 103 East Main Street (860–669–6059). Open

1630 House Visitor's Information Center

In front of the firehouse at 49 East Main Street is a small brown cabin that houses Clinton's Visitor's Information Center. From its handhewn boards to its wooden pegs, the structure is an exact reproduction of a typical 1630 house of the New England colonies. Staffed in the warm seasons by helpful volunteers, the center is stocked with maps, brochures, and other information to aid the traveler's enjoyment of the town. Hours are seasonal, but generally they are weekends from 9:00 A.M. to 3:00 P.M. from late May though Labor Day and on weekdays from 12:30 to 5:00 P.M. from late June through late August. Should the cabin be closed, stop by the Chamber of Commerce, directly across the street, on weekdays from 9:00 A.M. to 3:00 P.M.

on Wednesday year-round from 9:00 to 11:00 A.M. and in July and August on weekends from 2:00 to 4:00 P.M. or by appointment. Free.

Clinton Town Beach

If it is the sea that has beckoned you here, then you must be sure to sink your toes in the sand at Clinton's pretty town beach. Out-of-town visitors can use this crescent-shaped parcel for a reasonable day fee. From the center of town, turn south off the Boston Post Road onto charming Waterside Lane. This narrow avenue leads past lovely ancient houses and crosses a wooden bridge at the edge of the shore. Within the beach area are a children's playground, restrooms and an outside shower, volleyball courts, barbecue grills, and a snack bar that provides simple summer fare. This small, quiet beach is perfect for families with very young children and couples in search of some solitude.

At the foot of Waterside Lane off Route 1 Open year-round. Concession and restrooms in season only. Day-use fee, $7 per car.

Chamard Vineyard

Established in 1983 on a sun-kissed forty-acre property just 2 miles from the shore, Chamard has twenty acres of vines used to make premium table wines from such classic European grapes as chardonnay, cabernet sauvignon, pinot noir, merlot, and cabernet Franc. Winemaker Larry McCulloch and owner William Chaney credit Clinton's moderate microclimate and rich, stony soil for the success of the vineyard. Surely their own expertise and dedicated hard labor have something to do with the growing reputation of the beautiful wine-making operation here.

Even the brief distance through the vineyard from the gate to the winery reveals the painstaking work of pruning, trellising, and hedging the vines. A visit to the magnificent winery includes a walk through the underground wine cellar and barrel aging rooms. Throughout the tour, the wine-making process and its technology are clearly explained. In crisp weather a cheerful fire adds to the relaxing ambiance of the tasting room; in spring and summer the doors to its spacious deck overlooking the pond and vineyards are swung open so visitors can savor the wine samples in the open air.

The tours and tastings are complimentary, but you may be tempted to purchase a bottle or two. The purchase of a case buys you an invitation to return to the vineyard for special events such as barrel-tastings. Be sure to buy a bottle of Chamard's prize-winning chardonnay for your picnic dinner or a spicy cabernet Franc to accompany pasta with Thai or Cajun shrimp. Superb!

115 Cow Hill Road (860-664–0299 or 800–371–1609). Tastings and tours Wednesday through Saturday 11:00 A.M. to 4:00 P.M. Call ahead to confirm hours, especially during winter or on holiday weekends.

Shore Points
Pretty as a Picture

A visit to the **Clinton Town Dock** could be the perfect close to your day. Take Grove Street south from Route 1 at the weathered blue sign that lists the harbor sites. This quiet, residential avenue reaches the water about a half-mile down, then turns onto Riverside Drive, where you will find marinas, restaurants, a great old lobster shack, a public boat ramp, and tiny Esposito Beach. (You can also come south on Commerce Street from Route 1.)

Strolling the dock area on foot is the best way to see the sights. Park in the large public lot between the boat launch and the Cedar Island Marina and order an ice cream at the dockside snack shack. Sit a spell at Esposito Beach. No lifeguard supervises here and only a few benches on a pretty brick patio provide a resting spot on this diminutive pier-side patch of sand, but it's a great place to watch the boats go by. The view just before sunset across the boats and water to Cedar Island is the sort that artists come to paint. Savor it yourself in living color.

Shoreline Pitch and Putt

If you're looking for some quintessential shore-style recreation, a game of miniature golf should be added to your itinerary. Nineteen holes ensure fun for putters of all ages. Kids play free on their birthdays, and a hole-in-one on the last hole wins a free game. Six batting cages are also here for those who want to practice a different sort of swing. Picnic tables make it easy to pack in a snack or some dinner from a nearby eatery.

141 West Main Street (860–669–1848). Open seasonally, usually mid-May through October. Open daily 10:00 A.M. to 11:00 P.M. Admission is charged.

Boat Charter

***Early Bird* Charters** Captain Tony Barone; Clinton Town Dock, Riverside Drive (860–664–4540). The 34-foot twin diesel *Early Bird* takes up to six passengers on a sportfishing cruise (striped bass, bluefish, bottomfish; all bait and tackle supplied) or a Long Island Sound cruise; half- or full-day charters.

Places to Eat in Clinton

Aqua Restaurant 34 Riverside Drive (860–664–3788). Near Cedar Island Marina with great views and a friendly ambiance for families as well as adult diners, this is the place for perfectly prepared seafood. Its excellent chef ensures that it remains a cut well above the typical shoreline fish house, but traditional favorites like fish and chips are also on the menu for shore dinner diehards or hungry children. There's no better place to watch the sailboats return to the marina. Open nearly year-round for lunch and dinner. $–$$$

The Log Cabin Restaurant 232 Boston Post Road (860–669–6253). In a real log cabin with lace at the windows, choose from a large menu of steaks, chicken, seafood, salads, and much more, all served in very generous portions with a huge bowl of steaming pasta for the whole table. Delicious lobster ravioli; lots of daily specials. Open year-round daily for lunch and dinner. $$

Chip's Pub III 24 West Main Street (860–669–3463). Casual pub fare, typical but tasty. Burgers, sandwiches, salads, soups, ribs, steaks, chops, pasta; children's menu. Open year-round daily for lunch, dinner, Sunday brunch. $–$$

Nine East Main Dockside 32 Riverside Drive (860–669–6649). This seafood shack/snack bar has been here for years as the famed

Holiday Dock. New ownership brought a new name, but the fare's the same. Open daily from Memorial Day to Labor Day, plus weekends in September and October. Breakfast, lunch, and dinner in the form of pancakes, egg sandwiches, traditionally fried seafoods, grilled sandwiches, and more. Dine alfresco on picnic tables overlooking the boats. $

Mom's Country Muffins At Harborside Marina; 131 Grove Street (860-664-1693 or 860–664–1701). Nothing could be finer than breakfast by the sea with Mom. Except maybe lunch. Gourmet coffee, egg sandwiches, fresh bagels, enormous muffins, cinnamon buns, overstuffed sandwiches, fresh soups, stews, chili, salads, and more. Open year-round on weekdays 7:00 A.M. to 2:00 P.M. and on weekends 8:00 A.M. to 2:00 P.M. $

BB&G Lobster 152 Commerce Street (203–669–2005). Fresh live lobster for those with a pot to cook it in, or steamed lobsters for a small extra fee. Bait, ice. Open late spring to early fall, Tuesday through Saturday from 9:00 A.M. to 5:00 P.M. and Sunday until 3:00 P.M. In early spring, Wednesday through Sunday at the same hours. $

Places to Stay in Clinton

Captain Dibbell House B&B 21 Commerce Street (860–669–1646). If you are traveling without children under 14, this is the best place in town to stay. Every detail in this 1866 Victorian beauty has been attended to by your gracious hosts, Helen and Ellis Adams, from down pillows on antique beds to fluffy robes, fresh flowers, and gourmet coffees. Crackling fires in winter and breakfast in the gazebo in summer. You'll find 4 uniquely decorated but equally charming rooms, all with private bath. Bicycles, beach chairs and towels, and much more. Nonsmoking. Open April through December. $$$

Marina Cottages 345 East Main Street (860–669–3009). New owners have made this little complex sparkle. Fully furnished studio and one-bedroom cottages with private baths, phone, cable TV, kitchenettes, and some fireplaces. Landscaped common area with shade trees and roses galore in summertime. Passes to nearby beach; weekly rates available. Open year-round. $$$

Clinton Motel 163 East Main Street (860–669–8850). Clean, comfortable, basic lodging; air-conditioned double rooms with refrigerators, phones, televisions, baths; outdoor swimming pool. Open year-round. $$

Riverdale Farm Campground 111 River Road

(860–669–5388). At the edge of the pretty Hammonasset River on a twisting country road not far from town. Provides 250 wooded or riverfront sites. Spring-fed pond for swimming, fishing, canoeing. Restrooms, showers, launderette, camp store. Water, electric, and three-way hookups. Recreation hall with billiards and Ping-Pong; outside courts for tennis, horseshoes, shuffleboard, basketball, and softball. Open April 15 to October 1. AAA-approved; Woodall-rated. Daily, weekly, and monthly rates. $

Public Boat Launch

Clinton Town Dock and Ramp Riverside Drive (860–669–2611). Four transient berths; public boat ramp (day use $15, seasonal nonresident $70); fuel.

For Further Information

Clinton Chamber of Commerce 50 East Main Street (860–669–3889). E-mail: chamber@clintonct.com

Clinton Web site: http://www.clintonct.com.

Clinton Park and Recreation Department Killingworth Turnpike (Route 81) (860–669–6901). Information on the Ethel C. Peters Recreation Complex (bocce courts, horseshoes pits, picnic area, concession stand, kiddie park, and fields and courts for softball, soccer, football, tennis, and basketball), the Indian River Recreational Complex (nature trail, in-line skating area, pond and river fishing, ballfields, and pavilion), and Deane Haag Nature Trail.

Westbrook

Anchored to the sea by its twin rivers, the Menunketesuck to the west and the Patchogue to the east, Westbrook makes the most of its 4 miles of shorefront. A good stretch of this prime real estate is publicly owned and/or protected, so human as well as furred and feathered creatures can enjoy a taste of the sea in this quiet community.

Settled in 1638 as the Pochaug, or Patchogue, section of Saybrook Plantation, Westbrook was renamed in 1810 and incorporated as a separate town in 1840. Shipbuilding was the primary industry here until the age of the steamship and the railroad, and the manufacture of staves and heads for use in hogshead barrels made sure that colonial goods bound for the West Indies arrived safely.

It was through the genius of one of her native sons that Westbrook contributed most to maritime history. David Bushnell, born in Westbrook about 1742, set aside his wages until he had saved enough to enroll in Yale College at the age of thirty-one. During his last year as a student there, he invented the submarine and brought it back to Saybrook to test it. Completed in 1776, Bushnell's wood-and-steel *American Turtle* was a hand-powered one-man ship that submerged when its ballast tanks were filled with water. Used in an unsuccessful attempt to attach a torpedo mine to the belly of the sixty-four-gun British man-of-war *Eagle* in New York Harbor during the Revolution, the submersible vessel was the forerunner of the modern-day submarine.

Today the United States center of submarine production has moved eastward to Groton, and the vessels plying the waters of Westbrook are mostly pleasure craft and fishing boats. The ripple of sails and the chatter of lines teasing at spars are the sounds to steer by if you want to find Westbrook.

The Best of Westbrook

Westbrook Town Beach

Even if you are not a sun worshipper, a drive along Westbrook's beaches may do wonders for your soul. From the Boston Post Road, turn south onto Seaview Avenue. Highlighted by one of the prettiest views of the water and the offshore islands, this drive also takes you to what might very well be the best public beach from Clinton to Old Saybrook. For a small day fee that nonresidents pay only in summer, you can spend the day on the sand or stroll the long seawalk past the cottages that line the roadway across from the shoreline.

Officially called West Beach, this town-owned property is clean and well maintained. In the summer, lifeguards help to ensure

Westbrook Fife and Drum Muster

When the Ancient Mariners march down the Boston Post Road with their fifes trilling and their cannon booming, you'll swear you've awakened in an earlier century. Colonial flags wave and the boots of the drummers in tri-cornered hats hit the pavement in exact unison. Songs of the Revolution pierce the thick salt air of late summer, drowning out the usual cries of the gulls over Westbrook center. An annual event since 1959, the Westbrook Fife and Drum Muster brings thousands of visitors to town the fourth weekend of every August. Approximately fifty fife and drum corps from the East Coast meet for a two-day encampment that includes an opening tattoo on Friday evening, a Saturday parade, a muster that lasts throughout Saturday afternoon, and informal jam sessions on both evenings.

The tattoo, beginning on Friday at 7:00 P.M. in the Ted Lane Field behind the Westbrook Town Hall, features just a half dozen corps; the jam session following the formal portion is a casual affair open to musicians from any corps. On Saturday the two-hour parade begins at 11:00 A.M. on Route 1 in the center of town and ends at the encampment in Ted Lane Field, where the muster, in which the corps perform separately, lasts until about 6:00 P.M.

The whole event is free unless you buy a trinket or two on Saturday at the flea market where vendors display wares related to the music and culture of the corps. Here's the place to find a tri-cornered hat or a handcrafted fife. A food concession at the field offers burgers and dogs and the like, or you can pack in a picnic. Parking is available at the back of the Town Hall or in the back lot of the Wilcox Fuel Company; be here by 9:30 A.M. on Saturday to be sure of a spot. This popular event is a shoreline classic.

public safety, and the restrooms, showers, and concessions make the beach a good destination for a daylong visit to the seaside. Perfect for young children and reluctant swimmers, its swimming area has an extraordinarily sandy bottom that slopes very gradually toward deeper water. A small playground provides entertainment for the young and the young at heart.

Seaview Avenue. Open 8:00 A.M to 10:00 P.M. Day-use vehicle fee from Memorial Day through Labor Day. Restrooms, concession, and outdoor showers in summer only; lifeguards in summer only. Call the Westbrook Park and Recreation Department (860–399–3095).

Salt Island Road and Middle Beach

Diminutive Middle Beach is located at the southern end of Salt Island Road off Route 1, a short distance east of Route 153. The road turns toward the left as you reach its end, and the beach lies across the road from private cottages. Limited parking is available here, and there are no facilities such as changing areas or restrooms. The swimming area is not lifeguarded, and signs state that no fires, dogs, flotation devices, or ball-playing are allowed. All of these factors conspire to make Middle Beach a perfect spot for a peaceful swim or a quiet picnic. The larger of the two small islands directly opposite the beach is Salt Island, the site of early salt works, oil works, and warehouses where fishing and trading ships once loaded their cargoes.

Open all year; no fee; no facilities

Salt Meadow National Wildlife Refuge

Comprised of salt marsh, grassland, and forest habitats, this beautiful spot is the headquarters for the Stewart B. McKinney National Wildlife Refuge, which also includes seven other Connecticut shore sanctuaries (including Chimon, Sheffield, and Goose Islands in Norwalk and Faulkner Island in Guilford). Sliced into northern and southern parcels by railroad tracks, Salt Meadow begins, at its southernmost tip, at the confluence of the Menunketesuck and Patchogue Rivers, just yards before the two rivers meet the Sound. This southern parcel is still mostly inaccessible; the best way to enjoy the southern parcel is over a plate of whole clams at Bill's Seafood Restaurant (see Places to Eat), which affords great views of the marsh and its osprey platform.

The northern portion of the 192-acre refuge has nearly 3 miles of public trails through all three habitats, from the salt marsh at the rim of the Sound, through shrubland and grassland, and upward to the woodland as much as 110 feet above sea level. Bring binoculars; more than 200 species of birds have been observed at Salt Meadow. Migrating warblers stop to vacation here in springtime. Be sure to wear long pants and socks and/or tick repellent, and please leave bicycles and pets at home.

A trail map is posted on a kiosk near the main entrance headquarters building. If you are packing in snacks or sandwiches, be a thoughtful guest. Garbage of all kinds endangers the lives of the migratory and resident birds and mammals who are sharing their space with you. Your attention to proper trash disposal assures that you and other humans will be invited back. An area especially for picnicking has been created near the main office building, and restrooms are also located at these headquarters.

Old Clinton Road. From I-95 exit 64, go south on Route 145 to blinking red light at first intersection, then left on Old Clinton Road to refuge entrance and trailhead 1 mile on right. Or, from Route 1, head north on Old Clinton Road, which lies just west of the town green; refuge will be on your left. Open year-round daily, half an hour before dawn to half an hour past dusk. Call for more information (860–399–2513).

Military Historians Museum

The Company of Military Historians Museum to the east of the town green houses the nation's largest collection of American military uniforms. Completely restored and operable military vehicles from World War II and other late twentieth-century conflicts plus other memorabilia such as Army crests and books and videos about American military involvements are also a part of the collection.

Westbrook Place on North Main Street (860–399–0460). Open year-round Tuesday through Friday 8:00 A.M. to 3:30 P.M. and by appointment on evenings and weekends. Free.

Westbrook Factory Stores

The Westbrook Factory Stores complex includes seventy stores open for year-round bargain-hunting. Clothing, footwear, home furnishings and accessories, books, music, housewares, luggage, vitamins, and cosmetics are among the categories of merchandise you will find here. Timberland, J. Crew, Nine West, Levis/Dockers, Corning/Revere, Pfaltzgraff, Black and Decker, Bugle Boy, American Tourister, Rockport, Reebok, Carters, London Fog, OshKosh B'Gosh, Nordic Track, and Oneida are just some of this center's big-name manufacturers.

Restrooms and a food court help to make the complex comfortable, and an ATM helps you indulge in bargain after bargain. Just keep in mind that Westbrook's best bargains are its pretty backroads, its charming country inns, and its sea and sand and salty breeze.

Flat Rock Place off Route 153 just south of exit 65 on I-95 or north on Route 153 from the Boston Post Road (Route 1). January through March: Monday through Wednesday 10:00 A.M. to 6:00 P.M.,

Thursday through Saturday 10:00 A.M. to 9:00 P.M., Sunday 11:00 A.M. to 6:00 P.M. April through December: Monday through Saturday 10:00 A.M. to 9:00 P.M., Sunday 11:00 A.M. to 6:00 P.M. Call for further information (888–SHOP333 or 860–399–8656).

The Pink Sleigh

Head north, appropriately, from exit 65 off I-95 to see a little bit of magic. Best seen in the twilight when the air is crisp is a haven of peace and beauty for anyone who delights in the wonder of Christmas. Housed in an old barn, this store is breathtakingly beautiful—a place where every small child (and not a few adults) will suck in his or her breath in awe of all its glitter and gold. Dazzling displays of every color and material fill the two-story 1830s rustic barn, which is in itself beautiful.

Stepping into this place is like stepping into an elfin workshop hidden in the hills. Tucked into every corner and hung from the highest rafters are thousands of ornaments recalling the Spirit of Christmas and the loving message of one Jolly Old Elf. Whether you prefer designs made in America or imported from the finest manufacturers in Europe, you will find treasures here for every taste and style.

For the crafter, the store stocks materials for autumn and Thanksgiving wreaths and centerpieces: candles, silk and other everlasting flowers and greenery, and an extensive stock of tassels, garlands, and ribbons. As far as Christmas is concerned, the Pink Sleigh can't go wrong. As an independent emporium, it's a symbol of what's right with Westbrook.

512 Essex Road (Route 153), half a mile north of I-95 (860–399–6926). Open from early July until Christmas Eve, Tuesday through Saturday from 10:00 A.M. to 5:00 P.M. and Sunday from noon to 5:00 P.M. Also open 10:00 A.M. to 5:00 P.M. on Mondays from Columbus Day to December 24, and until 8:00 P.M. on Thursday, Friday, and Saturday in December.

Boat Excursions and Charters

Catch 'Em Charters Captain Richard Siedzik; Pilot's Point Marina, North Yard (860–223–1876 or 860–399–5853). Five-hour sportfishing cruises for one to six passengers. Bait and tackle provided; mate will clean and fillet your catch. Bring your own lunch and soft drinks.

Sail Westbrook 629 Boston Post Road (860–399–5515). Yacht

sales and brokerage; yachting instruction for teens
cruising under power and sail aboard 30- to 35-foc
charter management for cruises to such destinat
Fisher's Island, Newport, Narragansett Bay, Block Is
Martha's Vineyard.

Places to Eat in Westbrook

Westbrook Lobster Restaurant and Market 346 East Main
Street (860–664–9464). Right on the Clinton/Westbrook line, this
spic-and-span Route 1 eatery has served up great broiled, grilled,
and fried seafood for forty years. Steamers, steamed lobsters,
quarter-pound lobster rolls, crab cakes, New England clam chowder, lobster bisque, famous clam chili, and much more, including
choices for those who eschew gifts from the sea. Open daily for
lunch and dinner year-round. Smoke-free. Fish market has fresh
seafood, plus oven-ready treats. $–$$

Lenny and Joe's Fish Tale 86 Boston Post Road
(860–669–0767). At the Clinton line, this shoreline classic is more
refined than its sister in Madison. Here table service and a more
formal decor make the Westbrook Fish Tale a restaurant rather
than a counter-service drive-in. Window-dressing aside, it features
the same fresh fish, delicious salt potatoes, tasty homemade chowders, and other typical shoreline fare. Open year-round for lunch
and dinner daily. $–$$

Marty's Seafood Restaurant 110 Boston Post Road
(860–669–1269). You might think this corner's getting too crowded
with competing establishments, but the supply barely meets the
demand. Marty's is a good bet on the nights when Lenny's line
stretches out the door, especially since Marty's is serving up similar fare practically right next door. The chowder's great, the fish is
fresh, and the ambiance is pure Cape Cod. Marty's also does breakfast—the best deal in town. Open year-round. $

Bill's Seafood Restaurant 548 Boston Post Road at the Singing
Bridge (860–399–7224). Coming from the Westbrook green, cross the
Patchogue River on the metal deck of the 1925 steel bridge that has
its name on the National Register of Historic Places. Listen carefully
for the happy hum of your car wheels as you turn right into the dusty
parking lot of a conglomeration of structures known as Bill's. This is
a local favorite for more than a few reasons. The food is good, the
prices are reasonable, and the setting couldn't be more picturesque.
Watch the swallows swoop and chatter; look for the ospreys nesting

bove the tidal marsh. The moon rises nicely over the boats in the marina, and the clientele is much more colorful and interesting than in fancier places. If you're going to eat chowder and steamers and clam strips, you might as well do it here. The place hums most nights with live jazz, Dixieland, rock 'n' roll, and banjo/oldtime played by locally famed combos. $–$$

Westbrook Deli on the Green 27 Essex Road (Route 153) (860–399–5090). You can't beat this cheerful enterprise for great take-out sandwiches, coffee, muffins, and other tasty treats perfect for the beach or hiking. You can eat in, too, for breakfast and lunch, year-round, from Monday through Saturday, 7:00 A.M. to 3:00 P.M. Closed Sunday. $

Water's Edge 1525 Boston Post Road (860–399–5901). In the luxury resort of the same name, have an elegant breakfast, lunch, dinner, or Sunday brunch overlooking the shore. The *New York Times* gave the restaurant a "Very Good" rating; the *Hartford Courant* gives it three stars. Reservations are a must for Sunday brunch, voted the best brunch in the state by readers of *Connecticut* magazine. Offered year-round, this sold-out affair begins at 10:00 A.M., last seating at 2:30 P.M. $$$–$$$$

Places to Stay in Westbrook

Welcome Inn B&B 433 Essex Road (Route 153) (860–399–2500). Built in the 1890s, this comfortable homestead benefits from the unique talents of its owners, she a graphic artist, he a furniture maker and restorer. Lovingly and beautifully decorated and furnished, this smoke-free home offers guests 3 equally charming rooms, plus extras like complimentary sherry in the afternoon and a delicious home-cooked full breakfast by the fire in winter or on the deck in summer. Though best suited to adults, the inn welcomes family groups that may want to share the house for a reunion or special event. Open year-round. $$$–$$$

Westbrook Inn B&B 976 Boston Post Road (860–399–4777). This 1878 Victorian home is often booked solid in summer and fall. Restored to its original colors and decor, it has 9 rooms, plus 1 suite and a two-bedroom cottage perfect for families or couples looking for extra privacy and some elbow room. Air-conditioning, color televisions, and refrigerators in all rooms. On the river with a dock and fishing; three minutes to beach. Continental breakfast daily; full breakfast on Sundays, on the wraparound porch in fair weather. Gear available for boating, biking, and fishing. $$$

Angel's Watch Inn 902 Boston Post Road (860–399–8846). This establishment aims to give its guests their own private heaven in an 1880 Federal just a block and a half from West Beach. Its 5 air-conditioned guest rooms beautifully evoke the Victorian or Art Deco periods. Three rooms have private baths; two share a bath or can be booked as a private suite or single. Full gourmet breakfasts fuel guests until dinnertime. Beach blankets and towels are in every guest room; barbecue grills are in the backyard if you'd like to make a dinner here. Strawberries dipped in chocolate may tease you to relax in the afternoon with a complimentary glass of wine or iced tea. The house sleeps fifteen easily, and reunions and wedding parties are welcome. $$$–$$$$

Captain Stannard House 138 South Main Street (860–399–4634). The worst complaint about this establishment is that it's closed to guests from November through March. In season, the 6 spacious guest rooms in this enormous nineteenth-century sea-captain's mansion offer visitors the comfort of private baths and the charm of pretty, antique furnishings. Close to the beach and the center of the village, the house and its eclectic additions total an amazing 10,000 square feet. Not surprisingly, the gracious host says he's never had an unpleasant guest—the pleasing accommodations and delicious breakfasts can't fail to keep moodiness at bay. $$$$

Talcott House 161 Seaside Avenue (860–399–5020). With an unobstructed view of the Sound and a private bath in each of its 4 waterfront guest rooms, this expansive cottage is a summer dreamhouse. A hearty continental breakfast is served in the fresh and sunny common room each morning, perfect for energizing guests for a walk on the beach or an invigorating swim. One first-floor room has its own private porch overlooking the water. Open most of the year, except for a month or so in winter when repairs and alterations are done. $$$$

Water's Edge Inn and Resort 1525 Boston Post Road (860–399–5901 or 800–222–5901). If you have the budget and a desire for something posh, this resort offers fifteen acres on the Sound, 33 plush rooms in the main inn, and 68 luxury two-bedroom villa units in time-share buildings. A private beach, terraced gardens, tennis courts, indoor and outdoor pools, health spa and fitness center, and a public restaurant with gorgeous views are all part of the package. Nightly entertainment and planned activities for all ages are on the resort's active schedule. Have fun on the

Sound in a paddleboat, relax in the Jacuzzi, have a massage and a facial, and then have dinner overlooking the sea. Open year-round. $$$$

Maples Motel 1935 Boston Post Road (860–399–9345). Offers 18 immaculate, air-conditioned, and nicely decorated units, including some with efficiencies and some separate cottages. Playground, heated outdoor pool, picnic area with grills, five-minute walk to private Chapman Beach, beach passes to public town beach. Refrigerators, color cable TVs, and modern baths in every unit. Nightly and weekly rentals. Owned and operated by the congenial Crawford family, this is a shoreline best buy: Cottages are $500 per week; nightly rentals on motel units are $55–$70 for one or two people; add $5 per night for each additional person. Open year-round. $$

For Further Information

Westbrook Chamber of Commerce P. O. Box 267, Westbrook CT 06498 (860–395–0445).

Westbrook Web site: http://www.westbrookct.com.

Westbrook Parks and Recreation: 860–399–3095.

Westbrook State Welcome Center on I–95 northbound between exits 65 and 66. Staffed Memorial Day to Labor Day daily from 8:00 A.M. to 6:00 P.M. and on some spring and fall weekends. Maps, brochures, information on lodgings, restaurants, attractions. Restrooms, picnic area. Closed in midwinter.

 # Old Saybrook

Nowhere else on Connecticut's 253–mile coastline has human progress been more obviously outwitted by the sea than in Old Saybrook. In this case, however, the supremacy of the sea against human interference has, ironically, been a gift to the 410-mile Connecticut River. At the shallow mouth of New England's longest waterway, Nature provided the Connecticut River Valley her first big break: a big old sandbar. Located right near Fort Saybrook at Saybrook Point, the sandbar impeded colonial navigation, prevented large oceangoing vessels from entering the river, and thus arrested the development of a deepwater port. Thanks to the tides and currents that create the shoals and sandbars, the Connecticut is the largest river in America without a port. Consequently, despite pollution that entered the waterway from upriver factory waste, the river has stayed healthier than many others and her towns have retained many of their oldtime characteristics. While much more developed commercially than her peaceful sister, Old Lyme, across the river, Old Saybrook has managed to protect its prettiest parts south of the Boston Post Road.

Founded by a group of high-falutin' Englishmen of Puritan descent, Saybrook Colony was first seen in 1614 by Dutchman Adriaen Block, who explored and charted the river past what is now Hartford. Not until Block had long sailed away from the pesky Saybrook Bar did the English arrive in 1635 to ready the place for the building of their fort. Viscount Saye and Lord Brooke were among the fifteen lords who were granted this land by the Earl of Warwick, and they gave their names to the colony. Surprisingly, however, neither of these two ever lived in the settlement. John Winthrop was the gentleman actually responsible for the establishment of the town, and Lion Gardiner was its first engineer.

In its early years, the Saybrook Colony also included the settlements of Chester, Deep River, Essex, Lyme, Old Lyme, and Westbrook. Today it is the most populated and most commercially developed of these now-separate towns, but its location on the river, its providential sandbar, and its 16 miles of shoreline ensure that it remains a popular recreational destination for travelers.

Saybrook Visitor Information

At the south end of the town green near the Old Saybrook Town Hall is a visitor information booth that operates in the summertime. Volunteers can help you find your way to beaches, attractions, restaurants, and lodgings, and they can give you a walking tour pamphlet to nearly forty nearby historic sites and structures. Stop here from Memorial Day to Labor Day, Monday through Friday from 9:00 A.M. to 2:00 P.M. Throughout the year, you can visit the Chamber of Commerce offices at 146 Main Street, Monday through Friday. from 9:00 A.M. to 3:00 P.M.

Begin a driving tour of Old Saybrook by taking Route 154 south from I-95, bearing left on Main Street and continuing basically straight on College Street (both of which are Route 154) toward the water. Stop to see the following sites along the way, and feel free to wander the side roads, too, especially North and South Cove Roads, where you will have views of both marsh and sea and historic homes. Cyclists may want to rent a bicycle to explore these sights. Call the Saybrook Point Inn (860–395–2000) or the Saybrook Cycle Works (860–388–1534) for rental information.

The Best of Old Saybrook

General Hart House

Today the home of the Old Saybrook Historical Society, this structure was originally the home of General William Hart, who retired here after leading Patriot troops against the British in the American Revolution. Many members of the Hart family lived in town for many years, and the house still contains Hart family furnishings. Built in 1767, it bears the marks of an affluent owner; besides being a general, William Hart owned a fleet of trade ships. Fine wood paneling covers many first-floor walls, and Staffordshire tiles with scenes from Aesop's Fables decorate the library fireplace. Docents give guided tours of the fully restored house. Outdoors, visitors are free to explore a beautiful and extensive eighteenth-century herb garden and award-winning rose garden. Call for a calendar of events like demonstrations of colonial crafts and activities or special tours.

350 Main Street (860–388–2622). Open from May through mid-September, Friday to Sunday, 1:00 to 4:00 P.M. Free; donation suggested.

James Gallery and Soda Fountain

Not far from the Hart House as you drive out of the main business area toward the section of Route 154 called College Street, your eye may be caught by a sign marking a curious combination of enterprises. True to its label, the large white house on the right is both old-fashioned ice cream parlor and marine art gallery.

Built in 1790 as the general store for the Humphrey Pratt Tavern, this clapboard building with the red and white awnings operated as a pharmacy (and later also as a soda fountain) from

1877 to 1994. Originally owned by Peter Lane, the business was turned over to Miss Anna Louise James in 1917. The first black woman pharmacist in Connecticut, the well-loved Miss James ran the store for fifty years, and it is due to her maintenance of the house and her own historical importance that the house was added to the National Register of Historic Places in 1994.

When the pharmacy closed in 1994, marine artist Yves Parent added a twist to the historic business. Retaining the original wooden display cases and the 1896 soda fountain complete with a gray marble bar, oak Coke tables and chairs, and its old black and white floor tiles, Parent modified the pharmacy space to display marine art by painters from all over the country.

Now new owner Paula Palmieri has whipped the neglected ice cream parlor back into shape and has set the gallery in the back two rooms to give browsers a quiet spot to shop. Among the artworks are oils, watercolors, photography, and limited prints, plus a selection of pottery, handpainted woodenware, and handcrafted Nantucket lightship baskets.

The new design has created a spacious "front parlor" that gives visitors more room in which to linger over ice cream and other treats. Just like back in the good old days, the parlor serves ice

The Windmill of Saybrook

Lion Gardiner, the first architect of Old Saybrook, built a windmill at Fort Saybrook in 1636. Similar to Dutch designs, the windmill was perfectly functional as a grinding mill, but its principal purpose was as a lookout tower from which sentries could detect raiding Pequots during the war that terrorized the settlers in 1636–1637. Before the Pequots attacked, Lion Gardiner barricaded the windmill site with a sort of old-fangled land mine system: long, sharp nails driven into long pieces of wood that were left on the ground in front of the advancing natives. As the Pequots landed at Saybrook Point, they stepped onto the boards and screamed as the nails pierced their feet. Alerted by their cries to the direction of their approach, the colonists successfully defended the fort from attack. The windmill as well as the settlers survived the war, but the windmill finally burned to the ground 175 years later. Its millstones can be seen near the shore on the left side of College Street, past the Hart House and the James Gallery and Soda Fountain, but a good distance before you reach Fort Saybrook Monument Park. Right in front of a private home, the stones are surrounded by a low iron fence with a sign.

cream, floats, frappes, sundaes, milkshakes, and specialty teas and coffees. Baked goods, jars of old-fashioned candies, and all sorts of creative fountain treats are served in a spotless setting.

Making matters even better is the occasional live music offered at no extra charge on Friday or Saturday evenings from 7:30 to 9:30 P.M.

2 Pennywise Lane, right at the edge of Route 154 (860–395–1406). Open daily from Memorial Day through Labor Day, noon to 10:00 P.M.; weekends only from Labor Day to Memorial Day, Friday and Saturday from noon to 10:00 P.M., Sunday from noon to 6:00 P.M.

Saybrook Point Park and Fort Saybrook Monument Park

Proceed down Route 154 to its end to enjoy the pleasures of **Saybrook Point Park.** Stop for a while in the big parking lot to your left as you approach the dead end in the roadway here, and walk to the seawall along the Connecticut River. You'll find great fishing spots on the seawall, long-range binoculars to help you get a better view of the boats and lighthouse, and benches and picnic tables.

You can play eighteen holes here at the **Saybrook Point Mini-Golf Course** (203–388–2407); it's an affordable and well-maintained course with traditional designs that hark back to simpler times. Be sure to flip a coin into the Wishing Pond near the Brooklyn Bridge. Picnic tables add to your comfort. The course is open daily from Memorial Day through Labor Day.

You can also have lunch or dinner inside the **Dock & Dine** restaurant overlooking the river or outside on its patio. Outside, you can choose from the full menu or from the lighter fare on their Quick Bites menu. However long you dally over the table, leave time to see the artwork of the wonderful **Saybrook Colony Artists** at their gallery on the walkway near the river.

Just a few yards back up Route 154, **Fort Saybrook Monument Park** covers eighteen acres and has storyboards that depict the history of Saybrook Colony and the fort that Lion Gardiner built here in 1635. Today, the site is a great place for enjoying the views of the marshes and the shorebirds that inhabit the area. In or near the site are other historic points of interest such as a statue of Lion Gardiner, the Cypress Cemetery with its tomb of Lady Fenwick (wife of Saybrook Colony Governor George Fenwick) and other Saybrook notables, and a stone monument marking the location of Yale College in its early years. The park and these ancillary exhibits are open daily year-round at no charge.

When you've soaked up the sights, follow Route 154 across the causeway and all the way around the peninsula. Enjoy the water views as you drive along this wide-open-to-the-Sound coast road, usually called Maple Avenue along this stretch. Cyclists may rest along the way to enjoy the sights, but motorists won't find too many places to stop along this route. It's a mostly residential neighborhood with private beach associations, but a town beach awaits you if you follow Route 154 toward the left onto Indianola Road, which becomes Great Hammock Road after the coast turns northward at Cornfield Point.

Follow College Street (Route 154) to its end at Saybrook Point Park (860–395–3123). Open sunrise to sunset daily year-round. Free.

Harvey's Beach

One hundred yards of sandy shore greet the feet at Harvey's Beach, a town-owned property tucked between the picturesque marshes and rows of cottages along Route 154. Available throughout the year for diehard beachcombers, it officially opens on Memorial Day weekend for summer activities. A bathhouse with restroom facilities, outdoor showers, and a concession is the only structure here, at least outside of the tiny entrance booth that collects a daily fee from nonresidents only and in season only. A swing set provides simple entertainment for the youngsters.

Lifeguards are on duty on weekends only from Memorial Day through June, then daily through Labor Day. Check to be sure that a food vendor has been given the contract for the snack bar/concession before you decide *not* to bring a picnic or refreshments from home or market. Also confirm beach hours of operation. Lifeguards leave at 4:30 P.M., and it is believed but not certain that beach-lovers may stay on the sand until sundown.

Great Hammock Road, Route 154 (Parks and Recreation, 860–395–3152). Free to residents; nonresidents pay daily charge from Memorial Day to Labor Day only: $6 per vehicle and driver, 50 cents per additional passenger, walk-ins 50 cents each. Seasonal passes $65 (available from Parks and Recreation).

Boat Excursions and Charters

Deep River Navigation Company (860–526–4954). The M/V *Aunt Polly* departs Saybrook Point near the Dock and Dine restaurant

Take a Trolley

Summer visitors may enjoy a tour of Old Saybrook on its seasonal trolley. It runs on the hour on weekends in June and September and daily throughout July and August. Among the points of interest are historic landmarks like Fort Saybrook Monument Park at Saybrook Point, the private area called Fenwick (home of Katharine Hepburn), the marinas, the railroad station, and downtown commercial areas. Stay on for the full one-hour loop tour and listen to the commentary from the driver, which makes the ride of interest to tourists. Rides are $1, or $3 for a full-day pass.

and sails downriver for a two-hour cruise of Long Island Sound. Daily, mid-June to early September; $10 per person. Also cruise options to Essex Harbor (two hours, $10) or late afternoon lighthouse cruise (one hour, $6). Lively narration about flora, fauna, local history and lore on every cruise. Children 3 to 11 half price, children under 3 free, senior discounts. No reservations necessary; free parking. Restrooms, snack bar on board.

Captain John's Sport Fishing Center (860–443–7259). Departs Saybrook Point for winter wildlife cruises to see bald eagles upriver; February and March. Naturalist on board.

African Queen (860–388–2007). The original 30-foot steam launch made famous by Kate and Bogey. Departs from the Saybrook Yacht Basin at 142 Ferry Road for forty-five-minute narrated tour on the Connecticut River, carrying fourteen passengers. July through October, Tuesday through Sunday from 11:00 A.M. to 6:00 P.M.

Eden **Charters** Captain Paul Retano (860–388–5897). Customized sportfishing cruises for one to six passengers on 31-foot twin-engine sportfisher for "less time travelin', more time fishin'." Inshore bottomfishing, offshore, and deep sea off Montauk, from flounder to tuna. Bait and tackle provided.

Sea Sprite Captain Peter Wheeler (860–669–9613). Saybrook Point Marina. Twenty-two years doing deep-sea charters; all kinds of fish in their respective seasons, May 1 to December 1. Plum Gut, the Race, Block Island Sound, Montauk; $525 full day/$425 half day, by reservation only, on 42-foot Hatteras Sportfisherman; up to six passengers. Bait and tackle provided.

Odyssey Saybrook Point Marina (860–388–0897). On a beautiful sailboat, book half-day and full-day outings or overnight to one-week adventures. All meals included in fare. Up to six passengers.

North Cove Outfitters 75 Main Street (860–388–6585). Call for info on special trips planned by naturalists from this great outfitters store: hawk-watching, bird walks, meteor-watching, kayaking clinics, paddlesport rally, slide lectures, and more. Ask for wonderful Explorer newsletter.

Places to Eat in Old Saybrook

Saybrook Fish House 99 Essex Road (860–388–4836). A classic tucked away from the main drag, this establishment is a sure bet for dozens of traditional favorites like clams casino, shrimp scampi, and crab cakes, plus plenty of innovative daily specials featuring the freshest of fin and shellfish. Open year-round, lunch Monday through Saturday; dinner Monday through Sunday. $$

Cafe Routier, The Truck Stop Cafe; 1080 Boston Post Road (860–388–6270). French and American favorites with a homespun flair. Call it bistro cuisine, peasant fare, or comfort food—in any case, it's a simple menu of traditional dishes properly prepared. Open for dinner Monday through Saturday 5:00 to 9:00 P.M.; summer hours 5:30 to 11:00 P.M. $$–$$$

Terra Mar Grille At Saybrook Point Inn; 2 Bridge Street (860–388–1111). Overlooking the inn's marina, enjoy American and northern Italian cuisine with views of Long Island Sound at the mouth of the Connecticut River. Elegant ambiance for special occasions; fresh seafood, creative pastas, exquisite house-made desserts. Open year-round daily for breakfast, lunch, and dinner and Sunday brunch. $$$

Summer Arts on the Green

Old Saybrook offers two more ways you can linger downtown in the summertime. On Wednesdays from late June through late August a series of outdoor concerts is held at the gazebo on the town green on Main Street. Bring chairs or a blanket and a picnic or dessert and soak up the sounds of a different group each week from 7:00 to 8:00 P.M. All concerts are free of charge.

You won't be able to leave the Annual Old Saybrook Art and Craft Show quite so inexpensively. The arts here are sure to lure your checkbook right from your pocket. Held on the last weekend in July, the show brings more than 200 artisans to the green from 10:00 A.M. to 5:00 P.M. on Saturday and Sunday. Painters, photographers, potters, metalsmiths, jewelry-makers, sculptors, and doll-makers are among the artists exhibiting here. Admission is free.

Shore Points
Lynde Point Lighthouse

The Old Saybrook Inner Light at Lynde Point was honored by the State of Connecticut when it chose the image of the lighthouse by local artist J. H. Torrance Downs for its commemorative Long Island Sound license plates. Originally built in 1803, the first lighthouse here was only 35 feet high and constructed from wood. The present 71-foot structure is the second incarnation, completed in 1839. Painted white and made from brownstone blocks, it was first fueled by whale oil but later received an electric 500-watt lightbulb, visible as much as 13 miles away. Beginning in 1852 one of its keepers, James Rankin, kept meticulous logbooks, recording not only the maritime traffic but the weather and the migration of birds. Today his records are in the Smithsonian Institution.

Saigon City 1355 Boston Post Road (860–388–6888). Beautifully presented and graciously served Vietnamese cuisine in, surprisingly, an eighteenth-century farmhouse setting. It works!—and it's delicious. Open year-round for lunch and dinner. $–$$

Gateway of India 1333 Boston Post Road (860-388-9627). An unpretentious setting in a modest shopping area, but a fine dining experience, say aficionados of Indian cuisine. Vegetarian, chicken, seafood, and lamb specialties, curries, tandoori, and biryani, wonderfully seasoned and fun to share. The all–you–can–eat lunch buffet is a best buy from noon to 3:00 P.M. on Friday, Saturday, and Sunday. Open year–round for lunch and dinner daily. $-$$

The Cuckoo's Nest 1712 Boston Post Road (860-399-9060). Voted Connecticut's best Mexican restaurant, this definitively casual eatery offers tasty Mexican, Cajun, and Creole cuisine. Live music on weekends and outside patio seating in summer. Open daily year-round for lunch and dinner, plus Southwestern Sunday brunch buffet from 11:30 A.M. to 2:30 P.M. $–$$

Dock & Dine At Saybrook Point (860–388–4665 or 800–362–DOCK). Right on the Connecticut River, grab a picture-window seat for good, fresh seafood, chicken, pastas, surf and turf, or, in warm season, eat outside on the patio near the river; choose full or Quick Bites menu. Open year-round daily for lunch and dinner. $$

Aleia's 1687 Boston Post Road (860–399–5050). Recently moved from its former home in Westbrook, Aleia's still offers a contemporary twist on Italian cuisine. Freshly prepared, light sauces, vegetarian choices, and tempting house-made desserts draw the dinner crowd indoors in this new facility. Bakery open Wednesday through Friday 9:00 A.M. to 5:00 P.M. and Saturday 9:00 A.M. to 4:00 P.M. Dinner served Tuesday through Sunday from 5:30 to 10:00 P.M. $$–$$$

Pat's Kountry Kitchen 70 Mill Rock Road East (Route 154) (860-388-4784). Pat's has a clear reputation as the best place for families in the whole darned state. She's not resting on those laurels, though; daily specials are always added to the already extensive menu that pleases everyone from infancy to grandparenthood. Decorated from top to bottom with toys and dolls and bears galore, the large dining room is a casual and friendly place that goes all out to satisfy. Open daily year-round from 7:00 A.M. $

Johnny Ad's 910 Boston Post Road (860-388-4032). Can't do Saybrook without a visit to Johnny Ad's. Forty years of incomparable drive-in seafood. Have the perfect fish sandwich, an order of rings, and a real milkshake. Open all year in case you need a midwinter fix. $

Places to Stay in Old Saybrook

Saybrook Point Inn and Spa 2 Bridge Street (860-395-2000 or 800-243-0212). Put yourselves in the lap of luxury and wait for the pampering to begin; 62 elegant rooms decorated in English country style and overlooking river, Sound, and marina; 7 suites in the inn and 1 lighthouse room with kitchenette. Spa, steam room, and fitness room; indoor and outdoor pools, bicycles, restaurant and lounge. $$$$

Deacon Timothy Pratt House B&B 325 Main Street (860-395-1229). Offers 2 rooms with private bath and fireplace and a two-room suite with private bath in restored 1746 center-chimney colonial on the National Register. Four-poster beds; air conditioning; lovely common rooms and pretty property with tree swing, hammock, gardens. Full homestyle breakfasts with treats like Belgian waffles or eggs Benedict served by candlelight in the dining room on fine china. Beach passes. Open year-round and lovely in all seasons. $$$$

Days Inn 1430 Boston Post Road (860-388-3453 or 800-329-7466). 52 units with 6 suites, rooftop indoor pool, continental breakfast. $$–$$$

Comfort Inn 100 Essex Road (860-395-1414). Suites and double rooms, indoor pool, sauna, exercise room, laundry, restaurant. $$$–$$$$

Sandpiper Inn 1750 Boston Post Road (860–399–7973 or 800–323–7973). 45 units, outdoor pool, beach passes. Basic, but nicely kept and popular with families. $$–$$$

Public Boat Launch

Baldwin Bridge I–95 to Route 9 north; take either exit 1 or 2, turn right and follow Ferry Road to the launch area under the Baldwin Bridge. Daily fee; room for 75 cars.

For Further Information

Old Saybrook Chamber of Commerce 146 Main Street (860–388–3266). Information, brochures, walking tour map. Open Monday through Friday, 9:00 A.M. to 5:00 P.M. Tourist Information Booth on the town green open from Memorial Day to Labor Day, 9:00 A.M. to 2:00 P.M.

Old Saybrook Web site: http://www.oldsaybrookct.com.

Old Saybrook Parks and Recreation 308 Main Street; actually facing Sheffield Street, in Old Main Street School Building behind Old Saybrook Town Hall (860–395–3152). Purchase seasonal beach passes here, Monday through Friday 9:00 A.M. to 5:00 P.M.

Old Lyme

A curious mix of authors, painters, and mariners inhabits Old Lyme, a lovely village that revels in its artsy reputation as well as its nautical one. It's no surprise that Old Lyme can employ the phrase "colony" to describe itself—it has long attracted residents who fall neatly into one or more of these three categories.

One of the earliest and most permanent of these groups were the artists who gathered at the home of Florence Griswold from 1899 until nearly four decades past the turn of the century. Known as the Lyme Art Colony, the folks who lived at Miss Florence's beautiful late-Georgian mansion played with light, color, and tex-

Old Lyme Treasures

The influence of the American Impressionists on Old Lyme culture is clearly seen in its art school and in the galleries and shops that pepper the village center. Most notable among these is the **Lyme Academy of Fine Arts** (84 Lyme Street; 860–434–5232). This nationally accredited school offers a bachelor's degree program in fine arts plus part-time study in drawing, painting, and sculpture. The school's gallery features the work of its renowned faculty and its students. Visitors are asked for a small donation and are welcome to stop by Tuesday through Saturday from 10:00 A.M. to 4:00 P.M. or Sunday from 1:00 to 4:00 P.M.

The Lyme Art Association (90 Lyme Street; 860–434–7802) also has a gallery displaying the work of regional artists. Five major shows are hung each year, and demonstrations, workshops, and lectures may also be of interest to visitors. The association's hours are roughly the same as the Academy's. A suggested donation of $3 is appreciated at the gallery. Call for schedules and hours.

Other shops and small galleries on Lyme Street allow visitors to see and purchase the work of talented local contemporary artists as well as past masters. The best of these is the **Cooley Gallery** (25 Lyme Street (860–434–8807), which offers fine American paintings of the nineteenth and twentieth centuries. Excellent, too, is the **Shippee Gallery** (Mile Creek Road; 860–434–5108); it had a wonderful recent show featuring American Impressionist Roger Dennis. **The Old Lyme Frame Shop** (91 Halls Road; 860–434–1004) offers antique maps, old and new etchings, nautical art, and new posters. **Morelock Antiques** (860–434–6333) and **Antiques on Lyme** (860–434–3901), both at the Village Shops on Lyme Street, offer eighteenth- and nineteenth-century furniture and home furnishings plus other decorative objects, drawings, and prints. English, European, and American fine collectibles are among the eclectic selection in both shops.

ture until they successfully settled upon characteristics later to become known as American Impressionism.

Long before Old Lyme caught the attention of artists, it had been an enclave of mariners. Back in 1665 when the town's first thirty families split off from the colony at Saybrook to form their own union, many citizens were farmers and a few were merchants. The water and the rivers bordering their land caught their attention, too, but for more practical reasons than light and shadow. Maritime trade and shipbuilding became the principal industries during the eighteenth and nineteenth centuries.

At the end of the clipper ship era, the wharves went silent, and the docks were filled with passengers from the steamships. Outsiders, like the artists, came from the cities to the shore, and the character of the still very small town shifted toward tamer adventures. Summer cottages sprang up along the Sound, and a resort atmosphere settled upon the village. Life in Old Lyme (population 6,500) is fairly quiet these days. The population nearly doubles in summer when the cottagers return, and the principal industry seems to be getting the family boat in the water.

The Best of Old Lyme

Florence Griswold Museum

Located on eleven beautifully landscaped acres next to the lovely Lieutenant River, this National Historic Landmark built in 1817 holds a magnificent collection of the works of the first American Impressionist artists. Beginning in 1899, these creative spirits brought their paints and brushes to Old Lyme and accepted the gracious hospitality of Miss Florence Griswold, sea captain's daughter and owner of the house. Setting their easels on the sand, at the edges of marshes, and on the banks of the rivers, they endeavored to capture the marvelous summer lights and shadows, the colors and movements of the sea, and sky, and shore.

As much a history museum as an art museum, the house features period rooms as well as galleries of Impressionist works, contemporary works, and changing exhibitions that celebrate other artistry throughout the year. You may wander the upper gallery rooms of the museum unescorted, but a guided tour of the downstairs period rooms is given first. Visitors of all ages will enjoy the tales of Miss Florence and the talented houseguests who came to re-create the beauty of Old Lyme. Especially wonderful are the original paintings these artists left directly on the wall panels in the dining room.

Outside of the main house is the restored studio of William Chadwick, re-created to represent its appearance during his lifetime. Also on the grounds are several gardens showcasing perennial herbs and flowers.

Every December the mansion is decorated with trees for the Christmas Tree Festival. Story readings and special tours of interest to children are offered to families who visit during this time, but this festival has appeal to guests of all ages. Call for the exact dates of this year's fete, then plan to do some holiday shopping at the wonderful gift shop offering books, prints, posters, stationery, and other items related to American art, architecture, and regional history and culture.

96 Lyme Street (860–434–5542). Web site is http://www.flogris.org. Open year-round: June through December, Tuesday through Saturday from 10:00 A.M. to 5:00 P.M. and Sunday from 1:00 to 5:00 P.M.; January through May, Wednesday through Sunday from 1:00 to 5:00

Lords Cove and Hamburg Cove

To fully immerse yourself in the beauty of Old Lyme it seems necessary to gain at least a modest understanding of the relationship between the sea and the river, the salt marshes and the tides that influence the ecology within them. Quiet waters and softly rustling cordgrasses and phragmites belie the steady miracle constantly at work in the salt marsh. As the fresh river waters rush to the Sound at each low tide and the salty sediments sweep upriver with each high tide, a rich and unique ecosystem is created. Even the black muck that impedes human foot traffic and threatens boat props is alive with microorganisms and redolent with the aroma of the plant nutrients chopped and whisked and stirred into a fine stew by the moving waters. Feeding on that stew are the snails and the frogs, the mud worms and the fiddler crabs—even the mosquitoes and their microscopic larva—and feeding on them are the sandpipers and the mummichogs and the marsh hawks, and on and on upward through the estuarine food web—to the raccoons and the muskrats, the meadow mice and the minks, the white-tailed deer and their loathsome passengers—the ticks that made Lyme a household word.

A good route for contemplation of the salt marsh begins at the edge of the Sound at **Griswold Point**, either at **White Sands Beach** off Route 156 or Smith's Neck Road off Route 156. Then leave the marsh at Griswold Point and travel north on Route 156 under the I-95 overpass and past Route 1. By car or bicycle, travel to the ends of any of the small roads at the left of Route 156 (Binney Road, Pilgrim's Landing, Tantummaheag Road) for views of **Calves Island, Goose Island, Lords Cove,** and **Nott Island**. Return to Route 156 and drive north through the pretty countryside bordering the Nehantic State Forest until you reach the village of Hamburg, which lies at the edge of Hamburg Cove at the mouth of the tiny **Eight-Mile River**. Take the left fork in the road after you pass the Congregational Church and follow Old Hamburg Road to the river's edge. Picnic here if you'd like to rest and refuel as you process the amazing impact of the sea and the river.

P.M. *Adults $4; seniors and students $3; children under 12 free. Only the first floor is wheelchair accessible. Guided tours generally on the half hour.*

First Congregational Church of Old Lyme

Considered one of the most beautiful churches in all of New England, the First Congregational Church was designed by Samuel Belcher, also the architect of the Florence Griswold mansion. Built in 1817, the original building burned to the ground in 1907, but the congregation agreed to replace the church with a new structure that would be an exact replica of the first. The builders achieved their goal in 1910. Its graceful Ionic columns lead the eye upward to its soaring steeple, and its simple but elegant interior is a tribute to Belcher's artistry. Walking tours featuring this church and other Lyme Street landmarks are scheduled from time to time; call the Lyme Historical Society (860–434–5542) for information.

The church is at 2 Ferry Road (860–434–8686) in the center of Old Lyme. Visitors are welcome; call for information.

McCulloch Farm

One of Connecticut's hidden treasures is the oldest continually operating and largest Morgan horse breeding farm in the state. Visitors are more than welcome, but a call ahead ensures that someone here is able to give you a tour. Half a dozen or more foals are born here each spring, and you can see them and their elegant parents nearly any day year-round. The farm itself is a Connecticut pearl—four hundred acres are yours to explore. While it's not at all laid out as a tourist attraction, its bridle paths lead through its quiet corners, where you may enjoy the wildlife of the eastern woodlands. The owners kindly ask that you enjoy the property respectfully. They prefer no pets and no picnicking, and there is no hand-feeding of their magnificent Whippoorwill Morgans.

Come in the spring for Open Barn Day, when visitors are welcomed into the barns for a close-up look at the newborn animals and how the farm operates. Come in early fall (sometimes the first weekend in September) for Versatility Day, which is a daylong demonstration of the talents and tasks performed by the horses. Morgans from all over the country arrive for this eye-opening show. Both events are free.

100 Whippoorwill Road (860–434–7355). Open daily from 10:00 A.M. to 4:00 P.M. but advance calls are appreciated.

Griswold Point and Great Island

A walk to Griswold Point will be a highlight of anyone's exploration of the Connecticut shore. This area is accessible by canoe and car, by foot and bicycle. In the off-season, when White Sands Beach is not restricted to Old Lyme residents only, nonresidents may park at the beach. From its parking lot, walk westward below the high-tide mark for about a half-mile to Griswold Point. Motorists may also enjoy views of the area by following the route the canoeists would take to the boat launch ramp. To reach that point, take Route 156 south for three-tenths of a mile from exit 70 on I-95 and take a right on Smith's Neck Road.

This beautiful twisting road, lined with stone walls and the stunted flora of the shoreline, leads to a parking area near the state-owned landing at the end of the road. No foot trails provide access to the area at this point, but a large observation deck with wonderful signage provides a sense of the area's diversity and prepares visitors for bird-watching opportunities. Crowds of snowy egrets decorate the gently shifting grasses of the salt marsh. Herons rise gracefully from the mudflats and ospreys draw the eyes skyward.

The hike around the perimeter of the Point is about 2 miles; should you decide to *cross* the spit, do so only on one of the two trails across the protected dunes. Pets should be left at home or at least kept out of this area, because the Point is a nesting site of piping plovers and least terns. The Nature Conservancy usually fences areas where nests have been noted; please respect these boundaries should you come in the nesting season between mid-May and early July. Connecticut's largest colony of ospreys can be observed from late March through the fall.

Access to Griswold Point is from White Sands Beach or Smith's Neck Road, both off Route 156. Open year-round, dawn to dusk; no overnight camping; no charge. Access from White Sands Beach is limited; from Memorial Day to Labor Day, parking at the beach is reserved exclusively for Old Lyme residents with windshield beach stickers. Walkers and bicyclists may enter the beach at any time. Be aware that White Sands Beach has two parts, a public town beach and a private beach association. If you are on foot or bicycling, do not cross private property to gain access to the beach. At the public beach, restrooms are open in season only; there are no concessions or other facilities.

Shore Points
Island in the Stream

Accessible by water only, **Selden Neck State Park** offers one of the best opportunities in the state to develop an appreciation for the power and impact of the mighty Connecticut River. The largest island in the Connecticut River, Selden Neck was sold to Joseph Selden of Hadley, Massachusetts, in 1695, thus giving it its name. Originally part of the mainland, the island is believed to have been separated in the 1850s by an exceptionally high spring freshet that cut a shallow channel across the low meadows at the island's northern end. To this day, especially at low tide, little water covers the bar that still remains at the north side of the island.

Visitors with canoes or kayaks can paddle to the island on their own, or they can contact **North American Canoe Tours** (860–739–0791), which offers guided overnight canoe/camping trips to this interesting site from July through October. Primitive riverside campsites are available at Selden Neck State Park from May 1 through September 30, for one-night stays only. The park provides tent ground sites, outhouses, fireplaces, drinking water, and hiking trails, but no concessions, lodgings, or mooring or docking facilities, and open fires aren't allowed. For a permit to camp at Selden Neck ($4 per person), write at least two weeks ahead to Manager, Gillette Castle State Park, 67 River Road, East Haddam CT 06423, or call for further information (860–526–2336).

Sound View Beach

A wide, popular beach in the midst of a busy beach colony that looks like a throwback to earlier decades is great for playing or relaxing on a summer day or for strolling in autumn or winter. No coolers are allowed on the beach, there are no changing facilities and no lifeguards, and the only restrooms are nearby portable toilets. Even so, tons of sunbathers come here, and on warm weekends the joint is hopping as the delightfully summery and slightly seedy arcades, amusements, and snack bars along Hartford Avenue are crowded with visitors.

The Carousel Shop, loaded with beach needs from ice cream to sunscreen, also rents and sells inflatable boats, sand chairs, and beach toys. (The boats and floats are allowed in the water at Sound View Beach—unlike in other lifeguarded public swimming areas where the lifeguards forbid such equipment.) The Carousel Shop also operates a brightly painted 1925 carousel, which runs nightly from 7:00 to 9:00 all summer. One ride is $1, twelve rides are $10, and so on up to one hundred rides for $65 for parties or merry-go-round fanatics. This small, carnival-style ride offers every young rider a chance to grab the brass ring.

For food, try the limited but beachy fare at whatever restaurants and snack bars may be open along the beach and on Hartford Avenue. Be sure to have an Italian ice from **Vecchitto's** or an old-fashioned bakery treat from the famed **Beach Doughnut Shop**. Keep in mind that most of these businesses are seasonal, often opening in late June after school gets out.

Hartford Avenue off Shore Road (Route 156) (860–434–2760, Parks and Recreation, in summer only). Open 8:00 A.M. to 9:00 P.M. Free street parking or parking fee ($4 to $8 at public and private off-street lots). No coolers, no pets, and no alcohol allowed on beach.

Places to Eat in Old Lyme

Old Lyme Inn 85 Lyme Street (860–434–2600). In an 1865 farmhouse converted to inn and restaurant are five dining rooms serving some of the best meals in the state. The Grill Room, a smoking area near the bar and fireplace, evokes the clubby atmosphere of a tavern and offers live entertainment on weekend evenings. The gracefully decorated Empire Room creates an aura of romance; candlelight and sparkling tableware are the perfect backdrop for a marriage proposal or anniversary celebration. Serving an award-winning menu for lunch and dinner, the chef's specialty is probably the outstanding seafood. Veal, chicken, prime rib, and many more choices are available, with seasonal changes reliably superb. Open daily year-round except for December 24; lunch is served noon to 2:00 P.M., dinner 6:00 to 9:00 P.M., and Sunday brunch 11:00 A.M. to 3:00 P.M. $$$$

Bee and Thistle Inn 100 Lyme Street (860–434–1667 or 800–622–4946). Dine in airy, flower-filled sunporches or a candlelit parlor with a flickering fireplace on a delicious ever-changing menu of award-winning American and continental cuisine. Stenciled walls, wide-board floors, and an eclectic array of well-loved antiques are among the many alluring features of this beautiful inn. *Connecticut* magazine readers consistently vote this restaurant the most romantic place to dine in the state and aver that its gourmet cuisine is outstanding among its peers. Every dish is finished to perfection and beautifully presented. A harpist on Sunday evenings and the soft touch of other musicians on other weekend evenings add to an idyllic setting. Open for lunch, afternoon tea, dinner, and Sunday brunch, year-round, except for the first two weeks in January, Christmas Eve, and Christmas Day. Jackets are required for gentleman at dinner. $$$$

Anne's Bistro Route 1 (Halls Road) at the Old Lyme Marketplace (860–434–9837). Comfortable for both adults dining alone and families hoping to have a tasty meal in a place without golden arches, Anne's is a friendly establishment with a perfect menu for seafood lovers and vegetarians as well as meat-eaters. Along with seafood, poultry, and pasta dishes are salads, soups, sandwiches, and delicious house-baked breads, breakfast treats, pastries, and desserts. Open year-round Monday through Saturday for breakfast 8:00 to 11:00 A.M. and lunch 11:30 A.M. to 2:00 P.M., and Wednesday through Saturday for dinner 5:30 to 9:30 P.M. Walk through the interior French doors of the bistro to the **Happy Carrot Bookshop** (860–434–0380)—a cheerful pairing for folks who like to read and eat at the same time. $–$$

Hideaway Restaurant and Pub Halls Road (Route 1) in the Old Lyme Shopping Center (860–434–3335). Similar in focus to Anne's, this casual restaurant in a village shopping area provides a wide range of choices for adults as well as children. Family-friendly but still refined enough for a quiet meal for adults alone, this establishment seems devoted to pleasing every taste. With a few ethnic dishes—a little Italian, a little Tex-Mex—and tasty desserts, patrons should find plenty to satisfy lunch and dinner cravings. Full bar. Open daily 11:00 A.M. to 9:30 P.M.; pub closes at 10:30 P.M. $–$$.

HallMark Drive-in Route 156 (860–434–1998). An Old Lyme tradition, this is another classic shoreline shack specializing in fresh seafood, clam chowder, chicken, all kinds of favorite American sandwiches, rings, chili, premium house-made ice cream and yogurt, and much more. Ten umbrella-shaded tables are outside overlooking the marsh so you can savor the salt air. The lobster rolls and fried seafood are excellent—whole belly clams, clam strips, scallops, shrimp, fish and chips, you name it. Open from late March or early April until the day before Thanksgiving. $

Places to Stay in Old Lyme

Old Lyme Inn 85 Lyme Street (860–434–2600 or 800–434–5352). Known for its fine dining as well as its genteel accommodations, this charming inn has 13 antiques-filled guest rooms as comfortable as an old quilt, as exquisite as the flowers that scent every room in the house. Rest on the front porch in white wicker chairs or explore the gardens in summer; in winter, enjoy the fireplace in the grill room or go for a bracing walk on pretty Lyme Street. Sink into down pillows under a lacy canopy when you close your eyes at night; rise for a continental breakfast of home-cooked goodness in the morning. All rooms have private baths; all are air-conditioned and have telephones, queen- or king-size beds, and televisions. Open year-round except December 24. $$$$

Bee and Thistle Inn 100 Lyme Street (860–434–1667 or 800–622–4946). On five-plus acres bordering the Lieutenant River, this 1756 homestead is both gracious hostelry and award-winning restaurant. The 11 guest rooms (and ten private baths) provide an old-fashioned and cozy ambiance perfect for romance and restful relaxation. Lovely gardens surround the house, six fireplaces add to the homey colonial atmosphere, and the standard of discreetly attentive service is unsurpassed. The inn also offers a cottage with a bedroom, kitchen, sitting room with fireplace, bath, and deck. Breakfast is not included in the price of the guest rooms, but it is served and is absolutely worth every extra penny. Like its restaurant, this inn is closed during the first two weeks in January. $$$–$$$$

Bayberry Motor Inn 436 Shore Road (Route 156) (860–434–3024). Not far from Rocky Neck State Park is this spotless motel with 10 spacious rooms perfect for families and wonderful for couples and seniors seeking quiet relaxation near the shore. Each room has two double beds and kitchenettes complete with fridge, stove, sink, microwave, toaster, and cookware. Although not directly on the water, the Bayberry can still provide a beachy getaway; passes to private nearby beach associations can be arranged, and for a small day fee, guests can enjoy the beautiful state park. Children under 12 are free. $$–$$$

Public Boat Launches

Four Mile River Boat Launch Access on the west side of the river. Take Route 156 to Oak Ridge Drive, then first right to launch area. Shallow launch conditions at low tide; clearance a problem at high tide. Parking for 55 cars. No fee.

Great Island Route 156 south to Smith Neck Road and Great Island Wildlife area. Sand ramp; shallow at low tide. Parking for 35 cars. Seasonal fee.

Lieutenant River Route 156, west side, south of Ferry Road. Carry-in or cartop access only. Parking for 3 cars. No fee.

East Lyme/Niantic

No matter how the traveler enters East Lyme—from the east along Route 156, from the west along Route 1 or Route 156, or from the north on Route 161—he or she can quickly sense that East Lyme is one of Connecticut's shore playgrounds. Motels provide more than 500 rooms for vacationers, restaurants advertise shore dinners and homemade ice cream, bait and tackle shops sit shoulder to shoulder with boatyards, and fishermen share the Sound with yachters and sunburned kids in Sunfish. Modestly suburban and even downright rural in parts, this town is *the* place in Connecticut to sit on a seaside patio and savor some native broiled scallops while you watch the boats and listen to the gulls.

Originally settled by Europeans in the 1640s, East Lyme was at first a village of just a few hundred people living between Lyme and New London. Primarily a farming community, East Lyme gained some fame for its cottage textile industry (hence the name Flanders for one of its hamlets, after its similarities to Belgian villages and their home-made textiles) and later for its superior fishing grounds.

Today Flanders centers on Route 1 where it bumps north of I–95. While a nice reminder of how the Boston Post Road looked before mile upon mile of gas stations and fast-food joints overtook most sections of it, Flanders itself offers limited activities and attractions for visitors—a few antiques shops, an art gallery, and its outstanding fish market and seafood restaurant. North of the village are Pattagansett Lake, Powers Lake, and the Nehantic State Forest, which offer real but little-publicized opportunities for outdoor recreation.

Pattagansett Lake and Powers Lake

Some native East Lymers say they've never heard of Powers Lake and have never been to Pattagansett. That's great news for folks who would love nothing better than slipping their canoes into quiet waters for a day of serene paddling with the mergansers and mallards. Surrounded by the beauty of the New England woodlands, both lakes are owned and managed by the state, and both offer public boat launches at no charge.

Pattagansett is in general the busier of the two lakes and is stocked with largemouth and smallmouth bass, rainbow trout, and perch. Waterskiing is allowed only between June 15 and the Sunday after Labor Day and is restricted to 11:00 A.M. to 6:00 P.M. To reach 123-acre Pattagansett Lake, take Route 1 in Flanders one mile west of its junction with Route 161. The launch is on the north side of Route 1, and a parking area provides room for about fifteen cars. No concessions or other facilities are here, but the lake is close to the stores and delis in Flanders. Be sure to bring sunscreen, drinking water, and bug repellent out on the lake with you; be sure, too, to pack out whatever you bring in.

At 152-acre Powers Lake, which lies within the boundaries of the Nehantic State Forest, you are likely to be entirely alone on any given day. Pristine and beautiful in all seasons, it is a great fishing spot for largemouth bass, yellow perch, pickerel, and sunfish. No waterskiing or surfboard towing is allowed. For access to the state dock at Powers, take Upper Pattagansett Road north from Route 1 in Flanders to a right on Whistletown Road, and a left at about the half-mile point to the gravel ramp at the lakeside. No facilities, except for a parking area for about twenty cars. For more information, call the State Department of Environmental Protection, Boating Division (860–434–8638).

Niantic, East Lyme's second village, south of both Route 1 and the interstate, is the center of East Lyme activity. Take Route 161 south and explore it and the east-west Route 156 to gain a perspective on this shoreline gem of private homes and beaches, marinas and fishing piers, and small shops and restaurants. Like most of the smaller shore towns, Niantic is most alive in summer, when concerts on the green, arts and crafts shows, farmer's markets, and festivals celebrating strawberries and lobsters add to the simple pleasures of the sand and the sun and the sky.

Niantic is undoubtedly a summer paradise of the New England variety. The air is so salty it stiffens your hair, the water so clear

Pattagansett Marshes

Boaters may want to explore the diversity of the Long Island Sound shore with an up-close look at the marsh habitats at the mouth of the Pattagansett River. Richly productive from an ecological perspective, the marshes of Watts Island and Long Ledge are protected both through the efforts of the Nature Conservancy and by a primary sand dune that is safeguarded from erosion by the rocky outcroppings of Black Point. This environment supports a wide variety of plant and marine life that attracts an equally diverse population of birds and animals. Ospreys, herons, terns, migratory warblers, and many other bird species are easily observed.

The marshes are accessible only by boat, preferably motorized since boaters must enter the Sound to reach the marshes at Watts Island. Neither Watts Island or nearby Griswold Island to its southwest or Huntley Island to its west are open to the public, so your exploration is limited to the waterways that lace through these areas. The nearest public boat launch is at the Four Mile River, opposite Rocky Neck State Park. From I-95, take exit 71 and head south on Four Mile River Road. Take a left on Route 156 and go seven-tenths of a mile. Take a left to the boat launch. Motor south to the Sound, then eastward toward Black Point. Be sure to bring drinking water, snacks, sunscreen, bug repellent, and a tide chart, and pack out all trash and disposable supplies.

you won't think it could possibly be the same Sound you swam in nearer to New York. Gulls and ospreys circle over the marshes, boaters circle among the bellbuoys and lobster pots, tourists circle for parking spots closest to the seafood shacks and ice cream vendors. Don't neglect East Lyme in the fall, however; that's when it's at its finest. The crowds leave, the rates go down, and the water's still warm.

The Best of East Lyme/Niantic

Rocky Neck State Park

Few better places exist for beachcombing and shore camping than Rocky Neck State Park. Its full mile of sandy beach frontage on Long Island Sound provides swimming, saltwater fishing, and scuba diving opportunities; its 150-plus campsites provide a home away from home for professional beach bums, amateur naturalists, and the children thereof.

Like other state parks, Rocky Neck is safe and clean, but its windswept bluffs and gorgeous views of the Sound and offshore islands clearly create a special attraction. Its crescent-shaped beach has exceptionally clean, fine sand, and the extremely gentle slope of the shore creates an unusually safe swimming area for young children. Play areas, picnic tables, benches, and dressing rooms add to visitor comfort and convenience.

Some campers say Rocky Neck's facility is the best campground in the state. Interpretive programs, junior naturalist activities, and a full summer calendar of nature lectures, walks, and slide shows are offered for campers as well as day visitors. The state provides picnic shelters, bathhouses, food concessions, lifeguards, first aid, and telephones for the use of all visitors. Campers have drinking water and bathrooms with showers and toilets. Most of the campsites are in wooded areas and will accommodate RVs (but no hookups) as well as tents. Other campsites are designated for tents only and have pit toilets.

A wooden observation deck provides a wonderful view of the salt marsh bordering the beach, and recent improvements have resulted in wheelchair access to a great little deck across Bride's Brook, perfect for fishing and crabbing. Fishing for winter flounder and striped bass is popular from the stone jetty that abuts the beach. Elsewhere in the park an interpretive nature trail points out shore flora and fauna.

The park is open year-round. From dawn to dusk in winter, the park's trails and open spaces can be used for cross-country skiing, and, in the fall, there is simply no better place to enjoy a crisp afternoon.

Route 156 or exit 72 from I-95 (860–739–5471). Open year-round 8:00 A.M. to 8:30 P.M. From Memorial Day to Labor Day, the weekday parking fee is $5 per Connecticut vehicle, $8 per out-of-state vehicle; weekend rates are $7 and $12 respectively. Off-season visitors pay a weekends-only fee or no fee at all. Campground open from April through September 30; $12 nightly for a party of four, $2 for each additional camper. Reservations are a must in summertime. No pets; campfires are restricted; call for information on cooking fires.

Camp Niantic by the Atlantic

Recently recommended by *Connecticut* magazine as one of the top twenty campgrounds in the state, this friendly, clean, family vacation spot is actually about a twenty-minute walk from the beach. The family that owns this property has created such a happy environment right here, however, that you may never leave to find the source of the salt breezes that stir the trees in this merry glade. Diehard beach-lovers will be glad to know that their campsite fee includes a pass to the beach at McCook Point Park and a map of the pathways that lead to the shore. At the beach, a great playground, picnic spots, and restrooms with showers will help you spend a comfortable day in the sand.

Back at camp, the mostly shady sites are temporary homes for 125 RVs, pop-up campers, and tents. Some folks love this place so much they rent for the season, but monthly, weekly, and daily accommodations can also be arranged. Hot showers, restrooms, a laundry room, a playground, a camp store, and a game room are just some of the amenities here.

A full program of activities is planned to keep youngsters entertained;among the special events are a Christmas in July celebration when Santa himself arrives. On at least four weekends each summer the owners bring in a 100-foot water slide for wet and wacky fun for all ages. Notable among all the events are the totally free dinners planned for all campers on several weekends during the season. On Sunday mornings the owners start the fresh coffee, then head out early to get complimentary doughnuts from the famed Flanders Bake Shop. These generous gestures are the owners' gifts to all the guests who contribute to the wholesome atmosphere apparent here.

271 West Main Street (Route 156) (860–739–9308). Open April through October. Campsites are $20 per night at the beginning and end of the season; $25 per night from late June through Labor Day. Pets are allowed if they are kept on a leash, cats included.

Smith–Harris House

Built around 1845, this white clapboard Greek Revival home has a sort of whimsical personal history that stands out from other more famous Connecticut historic homes. It was once owned by a farmer named Herman Smith and his nephew Francis Harris, who married two sisters named Florence and Lula Munger. The four lived together in the house for sixty years, the husbands farming the property then surrounding the house and the wives selling the produce, the eggs from their chickens, and their sweet-cream home-churned butter right from the home's back porch.

A tour here is an oddly charming introduction to mid-nineteenth-century life. The imagination is certainly sparked by the idea of the industrious foursome who lived here. Throughout the house are their personal effects, domestic utensils, textiles, a lovely collection of yellow-ware pottery, and many original furnishings and items on local history. Outside are a barn with a two-seater outhouse, and pretty plantings in the tree-shaded yard.

33 Society Road (860–739–0761). Open April through June and September through December on Saturday and Sunday from 1:00 to 5:00 P.M. Open in July and August, Wednesday through Monday from 1:00 to 5:00 P.M. Open January through March by appointment. Donation.

Thomas Lee House and Little Boston School

The 1660 Thomas Lee House has been touted as one of the best preserved seventeenth-century houses in the region, and its condition is indeed striking. Almost completely unaltered since late in the eighteenth century when a lean-to addition was built, the two-story, four-room house boasts one of the few remaining medieval-style casement window frames remaining in the state. Docents point out

Shopping in Niantic

The shops and galleries of Niantic provide a nice relief from the summer sun or winter wind. Some favorites are **The Silver Skate Christmas Shop** (488 Main Street; 860–739–8913), the **East Lyme Art League Gallery** (6 Grand Street; 860–739–3263), **Main Street Antiques** (413 Main Street; 860–739–9101), the **Made to Be Loved Doll Shop and Hospital** (Route 156; 860–739–7756), and **Sugarplum's II** (235 Main Street; 860–691–2255), the town's new sweet shop. Book lovers should plan at least half a day at the 4,000–square-foot **Book Barn** (41 West Main Street; 860–739–5715), which has 75,000-plus used books shelved in several buildings linked by pathways and gardens.

Folks who love the sun and the shore breezes may prefer to spend some time at **Mackey's Bait and Tackle** (Route 156; 860–739–2677), picking out gear for crabbing or for fresh- and saltwater fishing, or at **Scott's Yankee Farmer** (436 Boston Post Road; 860–739–5209), picking strawberries, blueberries, peaches, or apples right from the fields, and pies, cider, jams, milk, and produce from the farm stand open seven days a week all year-round.

the house's finest English furnishings and colonial artifacts and tell a bit about its early history. Right next door is a 1734 schoolhouse that was the first district school to be built in the colonies between New York and Boston; it is curated to represent a turn of the twentieth-century classroom.

230 West Main Street (Route 156) (860–739–6070). Open Memorial Day to Labor Day, Tuesday through Sunday 1:00 to 4:00 P.M. and by appointment. Adults $2, children 6 to 15 $1.

Children's Museum of Southeastern Connecticut

More a play area and experience center than a traditional museum, this very popular attraction provides a fantastic opportunity to develop young imaginations. In the hands-on area called Kidsville, youngsters can role-play in a kids-size hospital, fire station, grocery store, and three other businesses. Toddlers can be set free among the slides and building toys in the Nursery Rhyme Land play area. Outdoor explorers can go to the garden area and dig for fossils, play with the wondrous bubble table, or scale the climbing wall. Parents may even be tempted to push a button and make the trains go in a model railroad exhibit that depicts the real sights of the Connecticut shoreline and countryside.

Shore Points
The Legend of Bride's Brook

As the name implies, modest Bride's Brook is associated with a bit of East Lyme romance. It seems that in the depths of winter back in 1646, a young couple wishing to be wed were desperately disappointed when a bitter snowstorm prevented the usual magistrate from reaching them at the agreed-upon site. Standing together instead beside the icy waters of the swollen brook that then separated their colony of Old Saybrook in Connecticut from the next colony of New London (which was then part of Massachusetts), they called upon the services of the other colony's magistrate. This cooperative fellow was apparently Governor Winthrop himself, and, with all the grace and dignity that could be mustered under the difficult circumstances, he supposedly shouted the vows across the raging torrent. The relieved couple called back their pledges, and the happy pair and the governor parted company at the riverbank. Thereafter, the estuary—which you can visit today at Rocky Neck State Park—was known as Bride's Brook.

Activities and exhibits explore the sciences, the arts, safety and health, and culture and history in various centers such as an arts and crafts area, a computer lab, and a Discovery Room with a live bee colony, a glow-in-the-dark-room, an ant farm, and many other features. Changing exhibitions help to keep folks coming to see what's new.

409 Main Street (860–691–1255). Open year-round, Tuesday through Saturday, plus Monday in the summer or when school is closed, from 9:30 A.M. to 4:30 P.M., and on Sunday from noon to 4:00 P.M. Admission is $3 for each person 2 and up. Ages 1 to 10.

Millstone Information and Science Center

At this science center in downtown Niantic not far from the Millstone Nuclear Power Plant in Waterford, hands-on and interactive exhibits explain nuclear science and energy, show how reactors and power plants operate, and demonstrate the production of electrical energy. Exhibits on conservation and the marine environment of Long Island Sound include aquariums and touch tanks. You can enjoy all of these by yourself or request a guided tour.

A 1-mile self-guided nature trail is on the grounds of the power plant itself, which is located in neighboring Waterford on Millstone Access Road; park in the lot outside the protected power-plant area and look for osprey, herons, foxes, and more. Pick up one of the excellent trail guides at the science center before you go out to hike.

278 Main Street, East Lyme (860–691–4670 or 800–428–4234). Open year-round Monday and Tuesday 9:00 A.M. to 4:00 P.M., Wednesday through Friday to 7:00 P.M., and Saturday and Sunday noon to 7:00 P.M.; closed holidays. Free.

Boat Excursions and Charters

Black Hawk II East Main Street (exit 72, left at Route 156, go about 7 miles, drive under the bridge, turn into parking lot), at Niantic Beach Marina (860–443–3662 or 800–382–2824). Fishing trips out on the Sound are the specialty of this boat, which caters to adult anglers as well as to families. *Black Hawk II*'s crew and captain handle the driving, supply bait and set-up, rent rod and reel at $5 each if you don't bring your own gear, and turn burgers and dogs at the snack bar if you don't bring your own picnic. Free instruction is available for beginners. They stay out five to six hours in the sun and wind and even in light rain. It's first come, first served; arrive forty-five minutes before sail time on weekends and thirty-five minutes before on weekdays. From June through October, daily sails are at 6:00 A.M. and 1:00 P.M. Fare is $28, children under 12 half price; no reservations necessary.

Chartered fishing trips. All of the following boats hold up to six passengers and have captains licensed by the U. S. Coast Guard and registered by the State of Connecticut. *After You, Too:* Captain Frank Blume (860–537–5004), Harbor Hill Marina. *Atlantic Flyway:* Captain Dan Wood (860–442–6343), Port Niantic. *Dot-E-Dee:* Captain Jack Douton (860–739–7419 or 860–739–0156), Niantic Sportfishing Dock, Waterford side of the river. *Fly Guy:* Captain Kerry Douton (860–739–7419 or 860–739–0156), Niantic Sportfishing Dock, Waterford side of the river. *Osprey:* Captain Joseph Wysocki (860–739–4129), Niantic Sportfishing Dock, Waterford side of the river.

Ask at **Mackey's Bait and Tackle** (860–739–2677), **Hillyer's Tackle Shop** (860–443–7615), or **J & B Bait and Tackle** (860–739–7419) for information on local scuba diving and shellfishing opportunities and tips for great fishing spots. These details change seasonally, and these fisherfolk are the ones closest to the best and latest news. No license is needed for shore fishing, but inland freshwater angling requires a license for anyone 16 or older.

Places to Eat in East Lyme/Niantic

Flanders Fish Market and Restaurant 22 Chesterfield Road (Route 161) in Flanders (860–739–8866). This cheerful, busy establishment serves the best fish in town. Fried, broiled, baked, steamed, blackened, or raw, the fish are so fresh they're nearly jumping from the market to your table, inside or out. Bring your own wine if you plan to eat here; you can also take out anything on the menu. The sweet potato fries are a must, no matter what else you have ordered. Open year-round Sunday through Thursday 8:00 A.M. to 9:00 P.M. and Friday and Saturday until 10:00 P.M. $–$$

Mangia! Mangia! 215 Main Street (860–739–9074). This new restaurant at the old shoreline hotel Morton House offers Italian specialties, Alaskan king crab, Black Angus beef, and baked stuffed lobster. The outside patio evokes possibilities of moonlit dinners and a background of soothing beach music as the waves wash the shore, but my hunch is the place is a bit too popular for a romantic tête-à-tête. Open daily for lunch and dinner. $$

Constantine's 252 Main Street (860–739–2848). Specializing in tasty American cuisine since 1929, this clean, friendly eatery has fresh seafood, steaks and chops, pasta and salads, homemade soups, chicken and veal dishes, great overstuffed sandwiches and platters, and a children's menu. Open for lunch and dinner Tuesday through Sunday, plus Mondays only in the summertime for dinner only. $$–$$$

Dad's Restaurant 147 Main Street (Route 156) (860–739–2113). Overlooking Niantic Bay, this place is ultra-friendly, ultra-casual, very tasty, and has eleven flavors of gourmet soft-serve ice cream for dessert. Open daily for lunch and dinner. $

Village Bake House 289 Pennsylvania Avenue (860–739–9638). Perfect for beach picnic foods or a quick bite at the small tables inside or outside on the wide sidewalk of this shopping center storefront. Baked goods, crusty rolls, excellent soups, chowders, chili, inventive sandwiches, teas, coffees, and gourmet food gifts. Open Monday through Saturday 7:00 A.M. to 5:30 P.M. $

Places to Stay in East Lyme/Niantic

Holiday Inn Express Hotel and Suites Route 161 at I-95 exit 74 (860–739–5483 or (800–HOLIDAY). 87 units, including 37 suites, some with kitchens. Outdoor pool, fitness and sauna center; complimentary continental breakfast and passes to beaches. Senior citizen rates. $$$

Connecticut Yankee Motor Inn Exit 74, Route 161 (860–739–5485 or 800–942–8466). 50 units, outdoor pool, sauna, beach passes, in-room fridge, continental breakfast. Children stay free; senior discounts. $$–$$$

Best Western Hilltop Inn 239 Flanders Road (860–739–3951). 89 recently renovated units with television, in-room fridge. Outdoor pool, beach passes, continental breakfast. Senior citizen rates. $$$

Niantic Inn 345 Main Street (860–739–5451). 24 roomy studios with dining and living areas and in-room television, fridge, microwave, and coffeepot. Complimentary continental breakfast. Air-conditioned. Beach practically out the door. $$$$

Rocky Neck Motor Inn 237 West Main Street (860–739–6268). Offers 30-plus rooms, including 26 efficiencies, with passes to the state park, television, and air-conditioning. $$–$$$.

Elms Hotel 27–37 Ocean Avenue (860–739–5545). Just a stone's throw from Crescent Beach, this century-old waterfront classic offers totally renovated, spotless rooms with private and shared baths, continental breakfast, picnic area with outdoor games, and private beach association passes. Seniors and military get discounts; children under 12 free. $$

The Island 20 Islanda Court (P.O. Box 2) on Lake Pattagansett (860–739–8316). Provides 4 large and 2 small cottages with kitchenettes. Weekly rentals only: $375 or $250. Boating, fishing, and swimming in the lake. Also campsites $18 and $20 nightly.

The Inn at Harbor Hill Marina 60 Grand Street (860–739–0331). This waterside bed and breakfast offers 8 guest rooms with private baths, queen-size or twin beds, and water views from every room and every wicker rocker. Enjoy their deluxe continental breakfast on the wraparound porch overlooking the marina or linger instead on your private balcony with views of the Niantic River and the busy boat traffic. Accessible by boat or automobile; transient boaters welcome. Smoke-free inn open year-round. $$$$

Public Boat Launches

East Lyme Town Ramp On Niantic River at Grand Street, one block north of and parallel to Main Street (Route 156). Ramp for trailered or cartop boats; transients welcome to pull ashore here with small boats or dinghies.

Niantic River State Boat Launch Located approximately a quarter-mile northeast of the Route 156 bridge across the Niantic River. From the Waterford side of the bridge, take the first left-hand turn onto West Street; take another left at the stop sign, and then a quick right, which will lead you down to Mago Point Park. Parking for 100 cars is at the river edge straight ahead. Fee in summer. Access to both the Sound and the Niantic River and Bay.

For Further Information

East Lyme Tourism Information Center I–95 exit 74 (860–739–0208). On the right side of Route 161 near the Connecticut Yankee Motor Inn. Open daily July 1 to Labor Day from 9:00 A.M. to 6:00 P.M.; spring and fall hours daily 10:00 A.M. to 4:00 P.M. Maps, brochures, guidance to restaurants and lodgings.

East Lyme Parks and Recreation (860–739–5828). Information on in-season use of the beaches and parks. Use of the town beach at McCook Point Park on Columbus Avenue and Hole in the Wall on Baptist Lane is limited to residents, renters, and overnight guests at local lodgings, plus walk-ins and bicyclists. Nonresidents cannot park at this beach. Amtrak Beach near the Niantic River at the bascule railroad bridge is on Amtrak property and usable on an at-your-own-risk basis (which many folks do). It has no parking lot.

Waterford

Across the Niantic River from East Lyme is the town of Waterford—a community of 18,000 citizens whose livelihoods are often earned from the Millstone Nuclear Power Plant, Electric Boat in nearby Groton, the naval submarine base in New London, or from the Sound itself, as commercial fishermen or sportfishing captains. In any case, their lives are often as closely linked to the sea as those of earlier citizens who built ships, sailed ships, and fished in the nearby waters.

Originally home to the Nehantic people, who also lived in what is now East Lyme, Waterford was settled by the English in about 1651 and was once most important for its rope ferry that took travelers across the Niantic River. Massachusetts Governor John Winthrop and his family lived out on the small peninsula now called Millstone Point, operating a 600-acre farm that remained in the Winthrop family for three generations. In 1723 part of the Millstone property was sold to Peter Buor, who quarried millstones there. The property changed hands several times during the next century, but the quarrying operation continued, and by 1910 eight hundred men were employed as quarriers.

Quarrying stopped in 1963, and construction of the power plant began in 1966. Today the plant is a prominent sight on the Waterford shore. Lots of folks feel uncomfortable about the looming presence of the vast complex that dominates the point, but the plant is undergoing thorough scrutiny and the area surrounding the plant provides important osprey nesting sites and other protected areas for wildlife. In fact, conservation and water and soil monitoring at the Waterford shore is probably stricter than at any other point along the Connecticut coastline. Come here to explore the flora and fauna and enjoy the shoreline scenery. Though not as widely known as other shoreline maritime centers, Waterford is one of the best places in Connecticut for recreational boating and fishing. And it is also one of the best places for theater and musical performances. Let Waterford surprise you.

The Best of Waterford

Harkness Memorial State Park

On the gorgeous seaside site of a former private estate, 234-acre Harkness State Park is a feast for the eyes, drawing thousands of visitors each year. Bring a picnic to the lovely grounds surrounding Eolia, a 42-room Italianate mansion built in 1906 by Jessie Stillman Taylor, who sold the house and its property to her sister Mary Stillman Harkness for a cool $8 million in 1908. This summer home of Mary and her husband (oil tycoon and philanthropist Edward S. Harkness) had grass and clay tennis courts, extensive gardens and greenhouses, an eleven-hole golf course, a bowling alley, and squash courts among its many outstanding features, but it was also a working farm where prize-winning Guernsey cattle were raised.

Bequeathed to the State of Connecticut in 1952, the house has recently undergone a magnificent restoration as a museum and is now open to the public from May 1 through Columbus Day. Visitors can explore the mansion at no extra charge beyond the park entrance fee. Take a self-guided tour on any day or come for a guided tour given on weekends only. Outside the mansion, beautiful gardens are delightful places to wander on a spring or summer day.

Plenty of picnic tables help to make meals by the shore comfortable for folks who enjoy leisurely pursuits like watching the sailboats. Visitors who enjoy more active recreation may appreciate the opportunity to fish from the beach or the promontory for the winter flounder, bluefish, and sea bass that make Waterford a mecca for anglers. Swimming and boating are not allowed from the fine white fringe of beach at Harkness, but picnicking and beachcombing are encouraged. The beach is not guarded, however, and waders should be especially cautious if temptation overcomes discretion: The lovely tidal inlet that connects Goshen Cove with the Sound at the park boundary has a powerful current that is of real danger even to strong swimmers.

Harkness Memorial State Park, 275 Great Neck Road (Route 213). Call for park information (860–443–5725) or for concert information (800–969–3400). Open daily year-round from 8:00 A.M. to sunset. Daily parking fee from Memorial Day to Labor Day: weekdays $4 for Connecticut license plates and $5 for out-of-state plates; weekends $5 and $8, respectively; free after Labor Day

Summer Music at Harkness

If Harkness Memorial State Park is a feast for the eyes, the summer concert series held there in July and August is food for the soul. Internationally and nationally known performing artists, from B. B. King to Itzhak Perlman, entertain crowds of music lovers seated or sprawled on the lawn overlooking the sea. There couldn't be a better way to spend a summer night at the shore in Connecticut than to buy tickets for one of these Summer Music at Harkness performances (860–442–9199 or 800–969–3400; office at 57 Boston Post Road, Waterford). Concerts are Saturday evenings at 8:00 P.M., rain or shine; concert-goers are welcome to enter the grounds at 275 Great Neck Road (Route 213) any time after 6:00 P.M. without paying the usual day-use fee for the park.

Subscriptions are available to the whole ten-concert series, or, depending on the performer, you can choose lawn seats for $14 to $26 (bring your own chairs or blankets) or tent seats for $21 to $51 (900 white wooden folding chairs are provided). Children's tickets range from $5 to $13. If you bring your own dinner, you might want to go all out to try to win the prize for most elegant picnic. The only items prohibited are beer kegs and open grills or hibachis. You can purchase sandwiches and salads from the specially catered concession or snacks and beverages from the nonprofit-organization vendors who arrive at about 6:00 P.M., or you can order an exquisite gourmet picnic dinner ($13.50 per person) in advance by calling by noon of the day before the concert (800–969–3400). Call this number also for a calendar of this year's lineup and the complete summer menu.

until Memorial Day weekend. Mansion open from May 1 through Columbus Day, 10:00 A.M. to 3:00 P.M. on weekends only in May, June, September, and October and daily in July and August. No swimming; no campfires; no glass or kegs on the beach; all pets must be leashed.

Eugene O'Neill Theater Center

One of the most exciting places in the nation to see live dramatic performances is this theater center overlooking the Sound not terribly far from the cottage where its Nobel and Pulitzer Prize-winning namesake playwright spent the summers of his youth. Every summer for the past forty or so, students and masters of theater have met in Waterford for intensive workshops that lead to the development of some of the brightest new talents in the field. Nine distinct programs attract writers, actors, directors, musicians, even puppeteers each season, offering these artists an opportunity to sharpen their skills under the tutelage of an outstanding faculty and with the support of their peers.

The National Theater Institute, the National Puppetry Conference, the National Music Theater Conference, and the Cabaret Symposium provide an opportunity to be in the audience when the embryonic works of the artists are brought to the stage for the first time. The evening performances held either in or out of doors may be finished or nearly finished works honed over several weeks of intense evolution; others may be readings of works-still-in-process with minimal staging or costuming. Ticket prices vary from $8 to $25. Call for a schedule of the public performances of the current season. Ask about picnicking and/or boxed suppers that can be ordered for pre-show dining.

305 Great Neck Road (information and schedule 860–443–5378; box office 860–443–1238). Public performances are planned for each program of studies. The Puppetry Conference begins the season in June; National Playwrights Conference performances usually begin in July and run nearly nightly, plus Saturday matinees; Cabaret programs are generally two weekends in August; Music Theater programs are two to three weeks in August; the National Theater Institute has performances during its September to December and January through April sessions.

Colonial Village at Historic Jordan Green

Close to the docks and water is the Jordan green and its replica colonial village with the 1740 Jordan schoolhouse, the 1840 Beebe-Phillips farmhouse, a blacksmith shop with a working forge and smithing tools, a corn crib, and a barn with farm implements, equipment such as horse-drawn farm vehicles, and other historical artifacts. Two small apple orchards and an authentic colonial herb garden complete the historical exhibits; a few other buildings house offices and an education center. Tours include details of home, hearth, agriculture, and local history.

The "Sheep to Shawl" festival is held for one day each May, focusing on the shearing of sheep, the processing of their fleece, and activities related to creating the finished woolen thread and cloth. Traditional arts and crafts are demonstrated. Hearth cooking, food preservation, candle-dipping, carpentry, and blacksmithing are among the activities you might see.

Rope Ferry Road and Avery Lane (off Route 156)
(860–442–2707). Open June 30 through September 30, Wednesday
through Friday from 1:00 to 4:00 P.M. or by appointment, plus one
festival day in May. Free.

Waterford Speedbowl

Your attention will be a million miles from the sea at the exciting
stock-car races that may be of appeal to travelers weary of boat
rides and seafood shacks. The one-third-mile oval track offers
Saturday evening races in many categories, including strictly-
stocks, late models, mini-stocks, and modifieds. Special events
such as national championships, ladies' races, and stunt shows are
also scheduled throughout the season. Call for a schedule of events
and ticket prices. Regular Saturday races begin at 6:00 P.M. A concession offers simple American fast-food fare and snacks and beverages.

1080 Hartford Road (Route 85) (860–442–1585). Mid-April
through mid-October. Adult tickets usually range from $9 to $13,
depending on the event. Children 6 to 12 pay about $2 (or are
admitted free with a paying adult, depending on the event); chil-
dren 5 and under are always free. Parking is free.

Parasail USA

Parasailing from Diane and Jim Keller's boat is an amazing experience—quiet, peaceful, relaxing, and safe. Although the captain is
licensed by the U.S. Coast Guard, no training or special skill is
required of the passengers. Even two-year-olds can go up with an
adult or sibling on these wonderful rides up to 1,200 feet above
Long Island Sound. The winchboat has a sophisticated launch and
recovery system in which all takeoffs and landings are done
directly from the boat so there's no chance of being dragged
through the water. In fact, there is hardly a chance of getting wet!
Every rider wears a life preserver and is harnessed after the sail is
inflated. You'll be amazed at the gentleness of your ascent above
the boat and water. Soon you may forget you are tethered safely to
earth as you sail like the seabirds above the waves.

Jim and Diane also rent kayaks and inflatable boats to folks who
would like to explore Niantic Bay on their own. These are available
during the summer and at other varying times, weather permitting.
Two-person kayak rentals are $25 for a four-hour period and $40
for an eight-hour day. The inflatables, which have an 8 horsepower

motor, rent for $35 half-day or $60 full-day. No boating license is required.

Captain John's Sportfishing Dock, 15 First Street (860–444–7272). Daily 10:00 A.M. to 6:00 P.M (weather permitting) from Memorial Day weekend to the weekend after Labor Day; weekends only from the next September weekend through Columbus Day. The ten- to twelve-minute ride costs $45 per person for altitudes up to 600 feet, $60 for altitudes up to 900 feet, and $75 for the up-to-1,200-foot ride. Half- and full-day charters range from $736 to $1,656.

Boat Excursions and Charters

Sunbeam Express Nature Cruise Center

Down at the docks on the Niantic River between Niantic and Waterford at Captain John's Sport Fishing Center, you can catch Captain John Wadsworth's **whale-watching excursions** every Sunday, Tuesday, and Thursday in July and August at 9:00 A.M. A naturalist is aboard for each voyage of the *Sunbeam Express,* providing a narration on the animals, the ecology, and the environment. You cruise the 22 miles to Montauk Point and then search the waters in a 10- to 20-mile radius of Montauk and Block Island for fin whales, minke whales, humpbacks, and the occasional sei or right whale. The *Sunbeam Express* returns to Waterford at 4:00 to 5:00 P.M.

From mid-March to mid-May, Captain John offers **seal-watching trips.** The boat cruises Fishers Island Sound and other areas of eastern Long Island Sound in search of harbor seals and harp seals as well as waterfowl and other wildlife. From February through mid-March, the boat leaves for **bald eagle cruises** from the Dock 'N Dine Restaurant in Old Saybrook and heads up the Connecticut River. The naturalist-guided seal and eagle cruises depart at 9:00 A.M. and return around noon. Throughout the summer are eight to ten **lighthouse cruises,** all or most on Saturdays. Crossing the Sound through Plum Gut and across the Race, the five-hour cruise that highlights eleven lighthouses departs Waterford at 10:00 A.M. and 3:00 P.M.

On every cruise, the crew brings lunch food, snacks, and soft drinks aboard for sale in the galley, or you can pack a lunch (no alcoholic beverages). Dress appropriately for the weather. Wear sunblock and a hat and bring a sweatshirt even in summer. Winter gear will be necessary at other times. The heated cabin of this 100-

foot boat helps to keep you toasty, but despite the large windows the best viewing is still outside at the rail, so be prepared.

The Sunbeam fleet also includes charter and party boats for **deep sea fishing cruises** in the eastern end of Long Island Sound. Trips for bass and blues depart at 6:00 A.M. and 1:00 P.M. daily except Wednesday from July 1 through Labor Day and Friday through Sunday in June. Other trips for other fish and in other seasons are also on the schedule, as are night bass fishing and fluke fishing. Adults pay $25 plus $5 rod rental; children are $13 plus $5 rod rental. Boats hold 6 to 149 passengers.

Captain John's Sportfishing Center, 15 First Street (860–443–7259). Whale watch: adults $35, children 12 and under $20. Seal and eagle watch: adults $25; children $15. Lighthouse cruise: adults $30, children $20. Children under 4 are free. Family or other groups of ten or more get a discount. Reservations recommended. Boats leave promptly; plan to arrive 30 to 45 minutes prior to departure.

Dot-E-Dee Captain Jack Douton, Niantic Sportfishing Dock (J & B Tackle Shop), 15 First Street (860–739–7419). Fishing charters for up to six people. Reservations required.

Good Company II Captain Joe Garafano, Jr., Waddy's Dock (860–443–0269 or 860–443–0581). Fishing charters for up to six passengers. Reservations required.

Mijoy 747 Captain Paul Brockett, Mijoy Dock, 12 River Street (860–443–0663). Party boat that sails from May through October; two trips daily in midsummer, at 6:00 A.M. and 1:00 P.M. Reservations not necessary, but be at the dock a half-hour before sailing time for these first-come, first served trips for striped bass and bluefish. Cost is $28 for the transportation and the bait; rod and tackle rental is $5 extra. Inquire about children's rates.

Osprey Captain Joseph Wysocki, Niantic Sportfishing Dock, 15 First Street (860–739–4129). Fishing charters for up to six passengers. Reservations required.

Hillyer's Bait and Tackle Shop 371 Rope Ferry Road (860–443–7615). Offers the largest and best selection in the area, if not in the whole state. Located near the Niantic River Bridge at Mago Point, convenient to the Sunbeam fleet and other charters as well as the state boat launch. Come here for expert advice and good to superior equipment for saltwater and freshwater fishing. Huge selection of live bait, from Arkansas shiners to waxworms. Open Monday through Thursday 6:00 A.M. to 7:00 P.M. and on Friday until

8:00 P.M.; on Saturday and Sunday, they open at 5:00 A.M. and close at 7:00 and 5:00 P.M., respectively.

Places to Eat in Waterford

Unk's on the Bay 361 Rope Ferry Road (Route 156) (860–443–2717). Close to the banks of the Niantic River just north of the bridge, Unk's offers good food at fair prices. Nearly anyone around here will direct you to Unk's if you ask for the best casual place for a seafood dinner. It's also well recommended for steak, pasta dinners, and other basic American fare. Children's menu. Outside seating in warm weather. Open daily year-round for lunch and dinner. $–$$$

Sunset Rib Company 378 Rope Ferry Road (860–443–7427). As you might guess, this also-casual place is great for meaty ribs plus sunset views of the Sound and river. Plenty of other choices like chicken, pastas, salads, burgers, and much more. Full bar. Indoor and outdoor seating on upper and lower decks. Small dock for transient boaters looking for a lunch or dinner place. Open daily for lunch and dinner. $$

Illiano's Pizzeria 709 Broad Street Extension (860–437–1999). Like its sister ristorante in Old Lyme (163 Boston Post Road; 860–434–1110), this authentic pizzeria offers delicious thin-crust pizza seven days a week. It also makes Italian-American favorites like spaghetti, ravioli, manicotti, calzones, antipasti, and grinders. Open daily 10:30 A.M. to 10:30 P.M. $–$$

Riverside Grocery Deli Bait and Tackle 150 Shore Road (860–444–0681). If you need beach or boat ride treats, picnic goods, breakfast to go, grinders, homemade breads, or food (or hooks) for the little fishies, they've got it here. Just a block from the Pleasure Beach boat launch at Jordan Cove. Open daily from 8:00 A.M. to 8:00 P.M., except on Sunday and Monday when they close at 1:00 P.M. $

Village Stop Restaurant 97 Rope Ferry Road (860–443–1177). Located in historic Jordan Village, this little place is perfect for breakfast or lunch, eat in or take out. Daily breakfast favorites like Belgian waffles and special omelets; lunch specials; homemade desserts. Open Tuesday through Friday 5:30 A.M. to 2:00 P.M. and weekends 6:00 A.M. to 1:00 P.M. $

Places to Stay in Waterford

Camp View Motor Court 334 Rope Ferry Road (Route 156), off

I-95 exit 74 (860–442–1047). 20 cottages with kitchenettes and a beautiful view overlooking Long Island Sound and the Niantic River. Old-fashioned sort of cabins meticulously kept by the same owner for many years. It's not the Harkness mansion, but it's a clean place to rest your head. Playground and beach passes. May to November. $$

Blue Anchor Motel 563 Boston Post Road, off I-95 exit 75 (860–442–2072). 15 efficiencies, each with one double bed, small fridge, gas stove, basic kitchen furnishings, cable TV, private bath with shower. Close to the Niantic River. Friendly owner—always a plus. $$–$$$

Lamplighter Motel 211 Parkway North, off I-95 exit 81 (860–442–7227). 38 units, including 20 recently renovated efficiencies with kitchenettes, cable TV and phone; exercise equipment and outdoor pool. Pets welcome. Continental breakfast. Senior citizen rates. $$$

Oakdell Motel 983 Hartford Turnpike (Route 85), off I-95 exit 82 (860–442–9446 or 800–676–REST). Owned by the same family for nearly three decades, this immaculate motel seems more like a bed-and-breakfast than a roadside motel. The Oakdell has 22 semi-efficiencies; each room has fridge, microwave, private bath, cable TV, phone, and either one or two double beds. Outdoor pool and barbecue grills. Complimentary continental breakfast. Open year-round. Nightly and weekly rates. $$–$$$

Fairfield Suites by Marriott 401 Frontage Road, off I-95 exit 82 or 83 (860–439–0151). Brand-new hotel right off the highway near New London border. Each room has two queen-size or one king-size bed plus a pull-out couch, microwave, sink, refrigerator, and coffeemaker. Indoor pool and exercise room. Complimentary continental breakfast. Open year-round. $$$–$$$$

Public Boat Launches

Niantic River State Boat Launch Located approximately a quarter-mile northeast of the Route 156 bridge across the Niantic River. From the Waterford side of the bridge, take the first left-hand turn onto West Street; take another left at the stop sign, and then a quick right, which will lead you down to Mago Point Park. Parking for 100 cars is at the river edge straight ahead. Fee in summer. Access to both the Sound and the Niantic River and Bay.

Jordan Cove at Pleasure Beach Route 213, then south on Goshen Road and straight to Dock Road. Launch is straight ahead.

No fee. Very crowded on weekends. Parking for 45 cars.

For Further Information

Waterford Parks Department (860–444–5881) or **Waterford Beach Park** (860–437–4385). Information on nonresident use of the town beach, which is limited to Waterford residents or their guests from Memorial Day to Labor Day. Guests must be registered in advance on a guest list and pay $2 per day for use of the beach. Waterford Beach Park has a playground and picnic area, volleyball courts, restrooms, and showers. Nonresidents may use the beach in the off-season. The park is off Great Neck Road, adjacent to the O'Neill Theater.

New London

Many a New London boy turned his back on the land and took to the sea right from the wharves of this city. Like its sister city, Groton, across the Thames River, New London has a long maritime history that has influenced its development into a center of commerce and industry. Nowhere else on the Connecticut shoreline is there a city with an economy more closely connected to the sea. A quick tour of the places where New London touches the Sound and the river reveals ferries, lobster boats, shipyards, and yacht brokers, and all of the businesses that supply and support them—sail lofts and suppliers of navigation equipment, tackle shops and boat riggers, marinas and seafood shacks. In the air are the sounds of bell buoys and foghorns, of Jet Skis and powerboats and even the Coast Guard band. In good weather and bad the Thames is crowded with boat traffic from single scull to sunfish to submarine. There's no doubt that New London boys are still heading for the sea.

Settled in 1646 as Pequot Plantation by John Winthrop Jr., New London had agrarian beginnings like other Connecticut shoreline

New London's Historic Center

These important points of interest are near or within New London's Historic District:

1833 Robert Mills U.S. Customs House and Museum of American Maritime History 150 Bank Street (860–447–2501). On the banks of the Thames is the oldest customs house in the United States, now restored, with a museum on the American customs service and exhibits on maritime history and industry. Hours are limited; call for information. Free.

Nathan Hale Schoolhouse Foot of State Street (860–449–1110). One of the two Connecticut schools where Hale taught before losing his life in the American Revolution. Open Saturdays in summer.

Whale Oil Row Huntington Street. Restored row of 1832 Greek Revival houses owned by whaling tycoons.

Ye Townes Antientist Burial Ground Huntington Street. Oldest graveyard in New London County, featuring interesting headstones.

settlements, but its river also formed the largest and the deepest harbor on the Connecticut coast. By 1846 it had become the second largest whaling port in the world. Long a manufacturing and ship-building city, its eclectic assortment of attractions frequently allude to the history and importance of the city as a center of maritime activities both industrial and recreational.

The Best of New London

United States Coast Guard Academy

On land donated to the federal government by the people of New London, the beautiful 100-acre campus of the U.S. Coast Guard Academy overlooks the Thames River. Having grown from its beginnings in the 1790s as the Revenue Cutter Service in charge of enforcing customs and tariffs on maritime commerce, the Coast Guard now protects fisheries, ports, waterways, and people—responding to an average of 70,000 search and rescue calls each year. The Academy is the place where cadets are educated and trained. A museum here traces the history of this branch of our Armed Forces, and a visitors' center features a multimedia show on cadet life. Pick up a self-guided walking tour brochure at the visitors' center if you'd like to explore the campus. Tours of the tall-ship training vessel, the barque

USCG *Eagle*, are offered whenever it is in port (call 860–444–8595 to check its schedule). Dress parades and concerts by the Coast Guard Band are held on a seasonal schedule, usually on Fridays at 4:00 P.M. in the spring and fall.

15 Mohegan Avenue, off Route 31 (Public Affairs Office 860–444–8270). Campus open daily year-round 9:00 A.M. to sunset. Visitors Pavilion open May through October 10:00 A.M. to 5:00 P.M. Museum open year-round 8:00 A.M. to 4:00 P.M. on weekdays and 9:00 A.M. to 5:00 P.M. on weekends and holidays. The training vessel, when in port, is open for tours Friday through Sunday 1:00 to 5:00 P.M. Free.

Hempsted Houses

These two homes in the historic downtown area include one of the oldest documented houses in America; both are among the few New London structures to have survived the burning of the city in 1781 by British troops under the command of Benedict Arnold. Ten generations of the Hempsted family lived on this soil since the town's early history as a seaport, and the diaries of rope-maker Joshua Hempsted have contributed greatly both to the excellent interpretation of the house itself and to our knowledge of eighteenth-century colonial American life. The 1678 Joshua Hempsted House is one of the oldest frame buildings in New England. The 1759 Nathaniel Hempsted House is one of the most unusual historic homes in New England—it has two-foot-thick stone walls, a gambrel roof, and an exterior projecting beehive oven.

Hands-on activities are offered on special weekends once each month. On Labor Day weekend a special focus is put on women's work of the eighteenth century. A Hempsted Thanksgiving is celebrated on the Saturday after Thanksgiving. Costumed docents, open-hearth cooking, and food samples are part of the celebration. In addition, an excellent colonial life summer camp is offered for children ages 8 to about 12.

11 Hempstead Street (860–443–7949 or 860–247–8996). Open mid-May to mid-October on Thursday through Sunday; tours are given from noon to 4:00 P.M. Adults $4, children $1.

Monte Cristo Cottage

An aura of sadness seems to pervade the boyhood home of Pulitzer and Nobel Prize–winning playwright Eugene O'Neill. It's not that the house is not impeccably kept or that summer sunshine doesn't stream through the bare or lightly dressed windows

Connecticut College

The picturesque campus and wonderful liberal arts tradition at **Connecticut College** (270 Mohegan Avenue; 860–447–1911) draw students from every corner of the nation. Visitors are also drawn to the 750-acre **Connecticut College Arboretum** (enter on Williams Street; 860–439–5020) of native trees and shrubs arranged in naturalized plantings with ponds, benches, and walkways throughout the property. Admission is free from dawn to dusk daily throughout the year, and free tours are given on Saturdays and Sundays at 2:00 P.M. from April through October. The galleries of the college's **Cummings Art Center** (860–439–2740) offer student and faculty exhibitions, plus a performing arts series featuring international artists in music, dance, and theater from September through May. The beautiful **Harkness Chapel** (860–439–2450) offers religious services as well as such musical events as the June concerts of the **Connecticut Early Music Society Festival** (860–444–2419). Also on campus is the **Connecticut Storytelling Center** (860–439–2764), which invites the public to its Connecticut Storytelling Festival held annually in late April.

of this modest 1840s cottage. Decay and neglect are nowhere apparent, in fact, and yet the house has a disconcerting effect of ghostliness. Perhaps the visitor is simply struck by the astonishing re-creation of the room and views that O'Neill described so minutely in his stage settings for *Long Day's Journey into Night;* perhaps the tales of the family's life told in a video presentation and on the tours adds to some sense of pain or longing that seems to have plagued its former occupants. In any case, the cottage is fascinating, and its beautiful views of the harbor account for O'Neill's love for the sea and its sailing ships. Look for O'Neill's statue, sweetly portraying his boyhood, on a rock overlooking the harbor near Union Station and the ferry terminals, just off New London's old Main Street, now renamed Eugene O'Neill Drive.

325 Pequot Avenue (860–443–0051). Open Memorial Day to Labor Day, from Tuesday through Saturday 10:00 A.M. to 5:00 P.M. and Sunday 1:00 to 5:00 P.M. Adults $4, children under 12 free.

Shaw Mansion

Built for wealthy Captain Nathaniel Shaw in 1756 and used as a naval war office during the American Revolution, this house is owned and operated by the friendly and helpful New London Historical Society. Eighteenth-century furniture and artifacts, gardens, and portrait collection are what you will see on a self-guided tour. Guided tours focus on early New London history and the West Indies trade. Stories of the Shaws and their roles in the shipping trade and the Revolution are tailored to visitors of all ages.

11 Blinman Street (860–443–1209). Blinman Street is a small, one-way street separated from Bank Street by a grassy strip; look for firehouse, then gorgeous Georgian mansion. Open May through October, Wednesday through Friday from 1:00 to 4:00 P.M. and Saturday from 10:00 A.M. to 4:00 P.M. Adults $4, seniors $3, children $1; under 6 free.

Lyman Allyn Museum

The Lyman Allyn owns one of Connecticut's little-known but exceptional small art collections. Located in a pristine setting near Connecticut College and the U.S. Coast Guard Academy, this beautiful neoclassical museum contains 30,000 pieces of fine and decorative arts from America, Europe, Asia, and the South Pacific. From an Egyptian falcon mummy to Old Master drawings to contemporary American works, the museum presents a good overview of world art history, but the American collection is especially fine. The entire first floor is given over to the American works. Silver, glass, porcelain, furniture, and paintings are arranged in a chronological development to show the progression of the American style from the late 1600s onward through American Impressionism.

Admission is free every Sunday afternoon, and the first Sunday of each month features special activities, from live music performances to storytellings, poetry readings, or gallery tours. Art classes and other special events are offered from time to time throughout the year.

625 Williams Street (860–443–2545). Open year-round Tuesday through Saturday 10:00 A.M. to 5:00 P.M. and Sunday 1:00 to 5:00 P.M.; closed on major holidays. Adults $4, seniors and students $2, children 12 and under free.

Science Center of Eastern Connecticut

Emphasizing the life sciences and nature, this museum gives children a chance to see, touch, and feel the principles of science demonstrated in accessible and interactive exhibits, laboratories, and discovery stations. The invitation to learn is irresistible in nearly sixty stations related to discoveries about light, sound, microbiology, electricity, optics, animals, tools, and simple machines. A shop area includes an opportunity for children to build a wooden boat or a birdhouse; in another, children learn about chromatography by experimenting with water and filter paper. An observation beehive and a marine touch tank are among the animal exhibits. Other special features are a science theater offering daily programs, a photographic darkroom, a greenhouse, and access to the trails in the Connecticut College Arboretum, where the science center is located. A picnic on the lovely property, which includes trees and shrubs native to eastern North America, is a nice way to end a visit here.

33 Gallows Lane (860–442–0391; e-mail scec@conncoll.edu). Open year-round Tuesday through Saturday 10:00 A.M. to 6:00 P.M. and Sunday 1:00 to 5:00 P.M.; closed on major holidays. Adults $6, children under 12 $4.

Garde Arts Center

If you have never been to a real movie palace, the kind with gilded architecture and acoustics to spare, plush seats, and a giant movie screen revealed at the opening of sweeping velvet curtains, go to the 1926 Garde Theater, downtown in the historic district. A five-year, $19 million restoration/expansion is transforming this already grand lady into a state-of-the-art performing arts center on par with others in New Haven, Boston, and New York. The stunning results of the first phase are already in place in the form of a new grand entrance and circular marquee that usher audiences into three floors of new and newly restored Moroccan-style lobbies.

In addition to its noteworthy new and classic film series, the 1,500-seat theater presents nationally and internationally known live performance arts throughout the year. Subscriptions as well as single tickets are available to a Broadway series, a Family Theatre series, plus country music, dance, and comedy series and single-night special events. The Garde is also the home of the Eastern Connecticut Symphony Orchestra, so be sure to call for announcements of its four-concert classical and pops series.

325 State Street (information 860–444–6766; box office 860–444–7373 or 888–ONGARDE). The center's Web site is http://www.gardearts.org and the e-mail address is admin@gardearts.org.

Ocean Beach Park

For the kind of seaside fun wherein everybody gets wet, come to a place that offers not one but *three* ways to get soaked. Right on the

Sound, Ocean Beach Park is both old-fashioned public beach resort and newfangled party/conference/banquet facility. A half-mile long, very clean white sand beach is the focal point of the park. Owned and maintained by the City of New London, Ocean Beach Park also has Connecticut's only wide wooden boardwalk down the length of the beach. It leads past food concessions, a pinball and electronic game arcade, a kiddie playground, volleyball nets, and an eighteen-hole miniature golf course.

The park and the beach are open year-round, and off-season access is offered at no charge at all. The pool, water slide, and other entertainments are seasonal only, and they generally open on the Saturday before Memorial Day and close after Labor Day. A full staff of lifeguards and a first-aid station help make this a popular destination for families. Entertainment on the boardwalk on Friday, Saturday, and Sunday is provided for all park visitors. An immaculate Olympic-size swimming pool and a beautiful bathhouse with changing rooms, lockers, and showers are available for individual fees, currently $2 per adult on weekdays and $3 on weekends.

Once home to carnival-style kiddie rides, the park now has one remaining amusement-park-style water slide. A triple-run, three-speed tower of serpentine slides, this is a humdinger of a ride and, with the exception of the beach itself, is the most popular attraction here. A height requirement of 46 inches helps to keep the ride safe for all visitors. The three flumes begin about 50 feet up at the top of a challenging set of stairs, so depending on your speed and stamina, you'll get ten to fifteen runs down the flume of your choice in a half-hour time slot. Each person pays $5 for a half-hour or $15 for unlimited rides throughout a whole day.

1225 Ocean Avenue (860-447-3031 or 800-510-7263). Access to beach and park at no charge year-round, dawn to dusk. Entertainments and concessions open Memorial Day weekend through Labor Day weekend, 9:00 A.M. to 11:00 P.M. Admission collected through a parking fee of $5 on weekdays and $8 on weekends.

Boat Excursions and Charters

Chartered fishing trips: The following boats offer fishing charters for up to six passengers. Full and half-day trips can be arranged by most captains. In-shore as well as deep-sea trips are offered, usually from April or May through October. All trips are planned by reservation only. **A'Vanga:** Captain Byron Smith Jr. (860-848-0170), Burr's Yacht Haven. *Fish:* Captain Peter Fisher

(860–739–3611), Thamesport Landing. *Lady Margaret:* Captain Claude Adams (860–739–6837), Thamesport Landing. *Playin' Hooky:* Captain Robert Demagistris (800–322–2754), Thamesport Landing. *Wanderer:* Captain Claude Adams (860–739–2801), Thamesport Landing. *West Wind III:* Captain Cecil Brooks (860–526–9453), Burr's Yacht Haven. *White Lightning:* Captain Ted Harris (860–739–6906), Burr's Yacht Haven.

Thames River Cruises (860–444–7827). Journey through three centuries of maritime history onboard *Patriot,* a 50-foot Coast Guard-certified open tour boat with full canopy that departs City Pier at the foot of State Street for narrated tours past historic port of New London, Coast Guard Academy, submarine base and *Nautilus,* Fort Griswold, and more. June through September; call for daily departure times. Lighthouse cruises and River Rambles feature most of these plus other sites. Cruises are 45 or 75 minutes. Adults $10 or $14, seniors $9 or $13, children 4 to 13 $6 or $8, under 4 free.

New London Ledge Lighthouse Cruises (800–364–8472). From Avery Point Campus in Groton, take Project Oceanology's Enviro-Lab for a two-hour cruise of the Thames River, New London harbor, and a walking tour of the partly restored 1909 lighthouse. Reservations required. Adults $11, children under 12 $8; children under 6 cannot debark from boat at the lighthouse due to safety concerns.

Block Island Ferry (860–442–7891). Leaves from 2 Ferry Street (across from Union Station) once daily from the second Saturday in June to the second Sunday in September for round trips to Old Harbor, Block Island. The huge three-deck *Anna C* leaves New London at 9:00 A.M., arrives at Old Harbor at 11:00 A.M. (On Fridays only, a second trip departs New London at 7:15 P.M. and arrives in Old Harbor at 9:15 P.M., with no return trip the same evening.) Cars need reservations, passengers and bicycles do not. The fare is $13.50 one way for adults, $17.50 for round-trip return on the same day; children under 12 pay $9 one way, $11 for round-trip return on same day. Bicycles are $3.50 extra each way.

Fishers Island Ferry (recorded information 860–443–6851; reservations 860–442–0165; island office 516–788–7463). Four or more round-trips daily year-round, except Christmas Day, with as many as a dozen crossings on Fridays. No reservations necessary. One-way fare: adults $4, children under 12 $2, bicycles $5.

Cross Sound Ferry Services (860–443–5281). At 2 Ferry

Street (across from Union Station). Year-round high-speed vehicle and passenger-only service to and from Orient Point, Long Island. Vehicle ferries take 1.5 hours one way; passenger-only high-speed ferries (April through December) take 45 minutes. Call for vehicle reservations and ferry schedule, plus information on attractions in Orient Point and the North Fork, Long Island's picturesque farming and wine-making district. Visitors to Connecticut from Long Island will find easy connections to casinos, local attractions, taxis.

Viking Fleet (800–666–8285). This ferry and sightseeing service from New London to Montauk, Long Island, is Montauk-based, offering late May through early September passenger-only service from New London to Montauk once each Friday and Sunday evening. The adult one-way fare is $17; children 6–12 pay $12; bicycles are $6 extra. No reservations are necessary; payment is in cash on the boat. The ferry departs New London from the Montauk Ferry Dock near the New York City Ferry Terminal off Crystal Avenue. The Viking Fleet also offers passenger and vehicle service from Montauk to Martha's Vineyard and Block Island, plus special excursions such as casino cruises, whale-watching trips, fall foliage cruises, wine-tasting cruises to Long Island's North Shore, and a great variety of sportfishing trips.

Places to Eat in New London

Lighthouse Inn's Mansion Restaurant 6 Guthrie Place, off Lower Boulevard (860–443–8411). In a beautifully restored 1902 mansion offering lodgings to travelers for more than seventy years, this award-winning shoreline restaurant is perhaps New London's finest dining experience. Dinner is classically American with a focus on seafood but with fair attention paid to treats like roasted duck and tenderloin of beef. Don't pass up the tantalizing desserts. In a chandeliered dining room, the well-trained staff graciously serves breakfast daily from 7:00 A.M., lunch Thursday through Saturday from 11:45 A.M. to 2:30 P.M., dinner daily from 5:00 P.M., and an outstanding Sunday brunch ($11.95) year-round. At dinnertime, gentlemen must have a collar or jacket. $$$–$$$$

Timothy's 181 Bank Street (860–437–0526). Everyone's raving about this downtown establishment serving continental cuisine in the form of grilled poultry and seafood, tasty signature crab bisque, good pastas, great salads, and appetizer portions for small appetites. Ensemble entertains on Friday nights. Lunch Monday through Saturday; dinner daily. $$

Bangkok City 123 Captain's Walk (State Street) (860–442–6970). If you like Thai cuisine, come to this casual downtown eatery offering authentic scorchers as well as milder delicacies for tender Western palates. Delicious. Open for lunch and dinner daily. $–$$

Fred's Shanty Pequot Avenue, overlooking Thamesport Marina (860–447–1301). The quintessential seafood shack, immortalized in Mark Shasha's children's picture book *Night of the Moonjellies.* Read the book and go have a great time getting into the act. Boats, gulls, "long dogs," fries, great seafood, burgers, outdoor-only seating. Call for seasonal hours. $

Captain Scott's Lobster Dock Restaurant 80 Hamilton Street at T.A. Fisheries (860–439–1741). Excellent fish and chips, fresh lobster just moments from the boat, clams, chowder, much more. A New London casual classic, with picnic tables in the open air on Shaw's Cove. Open daily from April to October for lunch and dinner from 11:00 A.M. to 9:00 P.M. $–$$

Recovery Room 445 Ocean Avenue (860–443–2619). A cousin to the equally wonderful Pizzaworks in Mystic and Old Saybrook, this pizzeria was voted the best in New London County. Terrific menu and atmosphere for families as well as adults in the mood for thin-crust and other pies, plus salads, pastas, and sandwiches. Cocktails and beer and wine. Open year-round Monday through Friday for lunch, daily for dinner. $

Chuck's Steak House 250 Pequot Avenue (860–443–1323). If you have ever been to a Chuck's, you know you'll get great steaks, seafood, and chicken, and an excellent salad bar here. This one near Burr's Yacht Haven has a rustic indoor dining room and an outdoor patio overlooking the Thames and the marinas. Open for dinner only, Monday through Saturday at 4:00, Sunday at 2:00. $$

Places to Stay in New London

Lighthouse Inn 6 Guthrie Place, off Lower Boulevard off Pequot Avenue (888–443–8411). In business as an inn for seventy years, this grandly restored 1902 mansion overlooking Long Island Sound near the mouth of the Thames River offers ocean swimming at its private beach and the well-respected Mansion Restaurant open to the public for three meals each day. Mahogany staircases lead to 50 luxuriously decorated and spacious rooms. Continental breakfast. $$$$

Queen Anne Inn 265 Williams Street (860–447–2600 or

800–347–8818). This elegant Victorian inn right in the center of the city has 10 antiques-filled rooms with eight private baths, plus a tower suite. A third-floor bath with a Jacuzzi may be used by all guests. Many of the air-conditioned rooms have fireplaces and romantic touches like tall, four-poster canopied beds and lovely nautical artworks on the walls. Full gourmet breakfast and afternoon tea. Open year-round. $$$$

Holiday Inn Frontage Road (860–442–0631 or 800–HOLIDAY). 136 units including 24 efficiencies and deluxe rooms with extras like coffeemakers, hair dryers, whirlpool tubs. Outdoor pool, exercise room. Steakhouse restaurant serves breakfast and lunch; sports bar lounge serves lunch. Shuttles to casino. Senior rates. $$$

Radisson Hotel New London–Mystic 35 Governor Winthrop Boulevard (860–443–7000). 120 newly renovated deluxe rooms, including 3 suites with living area, microwave, fridge, and wet bar. Indoor pool and Jacuzzi. Winthrop's Grille restaurant, lounge. Complimentary transportation to Amtrak, ferries, casinos. Senior rates. $$$

Public Boat Launch

Thames River Access From I–95 exit 84, follow signs to Crystal Avenue and State Pier. Launch is directly under I–95 on the west side of the river. Parking for 50 cars; seasonal fee on weekends and holidays.

For Further Information

Trolley House Information Station in the public parking lot at the corner of Eugene O'Neill Drive and Golden Street (860–444–7264). Open 10:00 A.M. to 4:00 P.M. daily from June 15 to September 15 and on Friday through Sunday from May 1 through June 14 and September 16 through October 31. Maps, brochures, directions, information on lodging, attractions, restaurants. The station can also lend visitors an audiocassette and booklet for a self-guided driving tour of New London historic sites; ask for the Thames River Valley Heritage Tour prepared by the New London Historical Society.

Southeastern Connecticut Chamber of Commerce One Whale Oil Row, New London 06320 (860–443–8332).

Groton

With a good imagination, you can see that Groton must once have been a thoroughly beautiful place, with its wooded uplands sweeping down from the northern hills to the raggedy-edged quasi-peninsula formed by the Thames River to the west, Long Island Sound to the south, and the smaller Mystic River to the east. Raggedy because of its many coves and smaller estuaries near the Sound, the Groton area was a favored summer encampment of the Pequots, a savvy group who enjoyed the bounty of the sea as much for its savory nutritive value as for its economic value: Control of the shellfish beds and the shells used as trading wampum was among the many reasons that the Pequots were the most powerful tribe of the Algonkian people.

Unfortunately for nearly all concerned, the fierce Pequots had already made more than a few enemies by the time Dutchman Adriaen Block came on the scene in 1614. When the Dutch began trading with the Pequots for furs, some nasty confrontations between the Pequots, the other tribes, and the Europeans ensued. Far from benign, the Pequots took on the Dutch and English settlers and the natives alike, and the English took it upon themselves to rid the land of the warrior tribe that threatened their peace, safety, and prosperity. Soon the salty tides of the Sound were flooded with the bloodshed of hundreds, as the Pequot fort on the Mystic River was attacked at dawn in the spring of 1637 by an army under the command of Captain John Mason of the Connecticut Colony. The massacre of nearly the entire tribe of more than 600 Pequot men, women, and children cleared the way for the English development of the peninsula.

In 1646 John Winthrop of the Massachusetts Colony established a settlement on the western bank of the Thames and named it, astonishingly, Pequot Plantation. Groton developed simultaneously on the eastern bank. Soon the pretty vistas down the Thames River were forever changed as wharves, warehouses, and mills sprang up on both banks. Groton piers rang with the sounds of wooden boat building, and Groton seamen sailed to all corners of the globe in search of whale oil and seal furs.

National Submarine Memorial

In honor of the 3,600 American seamen who lost their lives in U.S. submarines in World War II, a memorial monument has been placed near the banks of the Thames River in Groton, the last place where many of the men touched dry land. A moving reminder of their sacrifice, the polished black granite wall of honor includes fifty-two plaques, for each lost sub, each one engraved with the names of its lost men. The V-shaped monument stands next to the conning tower of the USS *Flasher,* a World War II sub that had the most successful patrols of all subs employed during the war. Close to the Thames Street docks and marinas, the monument is at the corner of Bridge and Thames Streets and is accessible at no charge year-round.

In 1868, 112 acres at the eastern edge of the Thames became a federal navy yard, and in World War I, it was officially commissioned as a submarine base. Often called the Submarine Capital of the World, for much of the last century Groton has been most famed as the home of the Electric Boat Division of General Dynamics, the leading designer and manufacturer of nuclear submarines.

Less well known is Groton's marine science institute on the University of Connecticut's campus at Avery Point, and its huge complex of Pfizer pharmaceutical corporation facilities. Groton also is the site of two state-owned land and wildlife conservation areas—a tribute to the efforts of Groton citizens and the state of Connecticut to preserve and protect the open space that reminds visitors of Groton's beauty as a coastal town.

The Best of Groton

USS *Nautilus* Memorial and Submarine Force Museum

A visit to Groton has to include a visit to the USS *Nautilus,* the world's first nuclear submarine and now a National Historic Landmark. The USS *Nautilus* Memorial near the submarine base on Route 12 includes tours of the *Nautilus* and an award-winning museum that explores the history and technology of submarines.

Excellently presented in a state-of-the-art facility, the museum exhibits celebrate the achievements of the human mind in devising this technology. Visitors can stand in the re-created sub attack center and hear the sounds of battle. They can operate any of three working periscopes. They can watch films of submarine history, and they can explore four mini-subs outside and a variety of models inside. Many other outstanding exhibits explain the important uses of the submarine both in defense and underwater exploration.

Aboard the *Nautilus,* visitors explore the sonar and torpedo rooms and the navigation and control room, as well as the crew's living quarters, the galley, the captain's quarters, and much more. The impact of the huge size of the ship is somewhat lost due to the way it is moored to give visitors access, but, once inside, visitors will easily imagine life and work aboard this amazing vessel that explored beneath Arctic ice and the 20,000 leagues of the deep ocean.

Adjacent to the U.S. Naval Submarine Base on Crystal Lake Road off Route 12 (800–343–0079 or 860–449–3174). Open from May 15 to October 31, Wednesday through Monday 9:00 A.M. to 5:00 P.M. and Tuesday 1:00 to 5:00 P.M., and from November 1 to May 14, Wednesday through Monday 9:00 A.M. to 4:00 P.M. Closed the first full week of May and the last full week of October, plus Thanksgiving, Christmas, and New Year's Day. Handicapped access to the submarine is limited. Gift shop. Submarine Force research library open by appointment (860–694–3558). Free.

Fort Griswold Battlefield State Park and the Ebenezer Avery House

Revolutionary War buffs might want to visit this site of the 1781 massacre of American defenders under the command of William Ledyard by British troops under the command of Benedict Arnold. Originally, the square fort with 12–foot-high stone walls was surrounded by ditches on the high banks of the Thames River. When the British finally broke through the fortifications after several bloody assaults, Ledyard surrendered his sword to a Tory officer, who abruptly ran him through. The Patriot militiamen, who had also thrown down their arms, attacked the enemy with sheath knives and fists, but the British slaughtered dozens of them in a swift counterattack.

Today the site includes ramparts, battlements, and buildings dating from the Revolution as well as a 134-foot granite monument to the defenders. Climb the 166 stairs to the top of the obelisk for beautiful views of the river, the cities, and the countryside. When you descend, visit the museum that tells the full story of the bat-

Avery Point and Groton Long Point

Among the shore areas offering beautiful views of the Sound are Avery Point on the western side of the city and Groton Long Point toward the east. **Avery Point** is the place where the University of Connecticut has its marine science institute and where the *Enviro-Lab* boats depart for exploration of the Sound. The campus is largely open to the public. A gazebo and picnic tables overlook the water, and visitors are welcome to use the public areas for picnicking, biking, in-line skating, and walking. To find the campus, take Benham Road south 1.5 miles to the campus entrance off Shennecossett Road.

Groton Long Point, accessible from Groton Long Point Road (Route 215), is one of Connecticut's prettiest shore points. Largely residential, the area can be toured by car, but strictly limited parking makes the area much more easily accessible to walkers and bikers. Shore Avenue, South Shore Avenue, East and West Shore Avenues, and Sound Breeze Avenues are the main thoroughfares in this pristine enclave of sun-washed cottages. **East Beach, Main Beach**, and **South Beach** are open to all visitors, but cars must have stickers indicating their membership in the Groton Long Point Association. Day-trippers will have to walk in or bicycle in after leaving their cars elsewhere. Some people park at the **Esker Point Beach** just before Groton Long Point. From late May to September, you can stop for a casual meal at the **Point Spa Luncheonette** (860–572–1567) at the Casino, a 1920s gambling house that now houses the Groton Long Point post office and police station and community activity rooms. You might find a place or two to park out front if you're here just for a quick bite. If you feel the need to linger, call Jennifer at the **Shore Inn** (860–536–1180), a B&B right on the water at 54 East Shore Avenue.

tle. Other exhibits tell the history of early Groton and other aspects of southeastern Connecticut history. You may guide yourselves or ask to be accompanied by an interpretive guide (well worth it). Ask for the dates of the Revolutionary War reenactment in early September.

Also on the park grounds is the 1750 **Ebenezer Avery House**, which, in its original site on Thames Street, had been a repository for some of the wounded Patriots. Moved to the park in 1971, its kitchen and weaving room are furnished as they might have been in the eighteenth century. Tours are also offered there.

Monument Street and Park Avenue (860–445–1729). Battlefield and fort ruins open daily year-round 8:00 A.M. to sunset. Picnic areas and restrooms available. The Monument House Museum (860–449–6877) and the monument are open from Memorial Day to Labor Day 10:00 A.M. to 5:00 P.M. and from the weekend after Labor Day until Columbus Day on weekends only at the same hours. The Avery House (860–446–9257) is open only on weekends from Memorial Day to Labor Day 1:00 to 5:00 P.M. Free admission to all sites.

Bluff Point Coastal Reserve

Those who prefer to explore the shore on foot may do so at this 800-acre preserve. From the parking area on Depot Road, it might take up to a half-hour to walk the 1.5-mile main trail through upland forest to the rocky bluff for which the park is named. Below this headland lies a mile-long sand spit and a tidal salt marsh overlooking Mumford Cove, the Poquonnock River, and the Sound. Make your way through the colorful beach peas and roses in summer and early fall to enjoy saltwater fishing, shellfishing, beachcombing, swimming, snorkeling, and scuba diving at the narrow tombolo beach that curves to the west. No lifeguards are stationed here, and those who venture into the water do so at their own risk.

A wonderfully wild place from which to enjoy the sea, Bluff Point offers limited facilities for humans. Pit toilets are the only amenities, so pack in your own drinking water, first-aid supplies, and snacks or picnic if you are planning on making the full hike out to the beach. No campfires or cooking fires are allowed in any part of the park.

You can horseback ride, hike, and mountain bike on side trails throughout the park, but no maps of the area are provided for visitors. Signage is fairly clear, but be sure you pack in water if you're trekking off the main trail. Tick repellent or proper clothing is a must for protection against deer ticks. The trails are sometimes used for cross-country skiing in the wintertime.

Folks who like life *on* the water, not in, can bring powerboats, Jet Skis, or sea kayaks and such to launch from the sand ramp near the park entrance.

Depot Road off Route 1 (go to the very end of Depot Road under the railroad overpass to reach the parking lot). Open year-round 8:00 A.M. to sunset at no charge. For information, call the rangers at Fort Griswold (860–445–1729) or the Monument House Museum (860–449–6877).

Shore Points

Thames River Fireworks and Sailfest

If you can get to Groton and New London on the second weekend in July, your visit will coincide with the annual Sailfest, a three-day celebration of life on the water. Sailing regattas, musical entertainment, boat shows, craft shows, flea market, children's activities, a parade through historic New London, and much more are on the schedule that touches both cities on the Thames. Most activities center on New London's Bank and State Streets from noon on Friday, all day on Saturday, and from noon to 6:00 P.M. on Sunday.

The crowning event has to be the enormously popular and absolutely fantastic simulcast Grucci Brothers Fireworks Show. Sponsored by the Mashantucket Pequot Tribal Nation, the fireworks are launched from three barges in the middle of the Thames River. The second largest display in the United States (Macy's New York still beats 'em), this is a must-see show, but you have to like crowds. Groton's Fort Griswold State Park is the best viewing site; get there by 7:00 P.M. for the very best spots. Call for exact dates and further information (860–444–1879); if that number has changed, try the Southeastern Connecticut Chamber of Commerce (860–443–8332) or the Southeastern Connecticut Tourism District (800–863–6569).

Haley Farm State Park

This 204-acre state park is on a former farm site at the north of Palmer Cove not far from Groton Long Point and the village of Noank. Signage near the park entrance and parking area explains the history of the site, and ruins of farm buildings adjacent to the parking area provide an intriguing incentive to get out of the car or off the bicycle to explore here a while. Trails lead throughout the park, and recreational use through the year includes hiking, running, and cross-country skiing. Bikers are also welcome to use the park trails, but they are urged to offer the right-of-way to joggers and walkers.

Bird-watchers and other nature lovers will appreciate the large variety of plant and animal life at this pretty, quiet place. Facilities are limited to portable toilets, so pack in whatever you might need. No cooking fires are allowed on the property.

Haley Farm Lane off Brook Street, which is off Groton Long Point Road (Route 215). For information, call the ranger at Fort Griswold

(860–445–1729 or 860–449–6877). Open year-round 8:00 A.M. to sunset at no charge.

Boat Excursions and Charters

Project Oceanology

The lure of the sea may be irresistible in Groton. If so, head to the Institute of Marine Science at the Avery Point campus of the University of Connecticut where you can board the 55-foot *Enviro-Lab* for a two-and-a-half-hour cruise called Project Oceanology. *Enviro-Lab*'s instructors are marine scientists who accompany each group of about twenty-five passengers for an afternoon or morning of study. Passengers measure and record data about the geology and biology observed; learn the uses of nautical charts and navigation instruments; collect and test water, mud, and sand samples; and pull trawl nets and examine the plants and animals swept from the bottom. All the while, the crew and captain provide a wonderfully interesting narration about the islands, lighthouses, and watercraft that surround your area of exploration.

Wear sunscreen or a hat and sneakers, and bring a sweatshirt or windbreaker. Soft drinks are available for purchase at the Project Oceanology building, but there is no food concession and you should not go aboard hungry. You can picnic on the campus before or after a cruise if you bring your own makings.

Inquire also about the seal observation cruises in the wintertime; usually offered, weather permitting, in February and March, these cruises feature the harbor seals that inhabit the Sound in cold weather. Some folks may also be interested in the walking tour of the still-operating New London Ledge lighthouse in the middle of New London Harbor; call for details on this special cruise.

104 Shennecossett Road, at foot of Benham Road, Avery Point Campus of UConn (call 800–364–8472 between 9:00 A.M. and 4:00 P.M.). Public cruises from mid-June to Labor Day at 10:00 A.M. and 1:00 P.M. Adults $18, children under 12 $12. Reservations strongly recommended; Visa or MasterCard required to hold reservation.

Captain Bob's See Submarines by Boat Cruises Thames Harbour Inn and Marina, 193 Thames Street (860–434–5681). *Captain Bob II* expeditions cruise upriver and down for fairly close-up views of the submarine base and the world's first nuclear-powered submarine, the USS *Nautilus,* plus the U.S. Coast Guard Academy and its tall ship, the bark *Eagle,* the high-speed ferries, and the Electric Boat facilities. Cruises depart hourly Tuesday through Friday 11:00 A.M. to 3:00 P.M. and Saturday and Sunday 11:00 A.M. to 6:00 P.M. Adults $9, seniors $8, children 5 to 15 $3, children under 5 free. Free parking at the dock. Romantic evening cruises and fishing trips also available, by charter only.

Hel-Cat II Hel-Cat Dock, 181 Thames Street (860–535–2066 or 860–445–5991). Captain Brad Glas offers fishing trips for striped bass and bluefish in summer (daily from June through October) and for cod, pollock, mackerel, blackfish, sea bass, and more in winter and spring (weekends and holidays from January through May) on 114–foot party boat. No reservations required. Leaves Groton at 9:00 A.M., returns 3:00 P.M. Adults $27; children 12 and under, half-fare. Rental tackle $5; bait provided; help and instruction from deck technicians. Nonfishing adults pay half-fare; nonfishing children pay $5. On-board restaurant and restrooms. Night fishing and evening charters for private parties also available.

Places to Eat in Groton

The Fisherman 937 Groton Long Point Road (860–536–1717). Very popular for its views and its classic American seafood dishes, this establishment at the entrance to Groton Long Point Road between Palmer Cove and the Sound serves fresh fruits of the sea, steaks, poultry, and pasta in the main dining room. Lighter fare, including fish platters, sandwiches, chowders, and salads, is served in the lounge. Be sure to share a piece of the house signature dessert: chocolate peanut butter pie. Outdoor seating in season. Open year-round daily for lunch and dinner from 11:30 A.M. $–$$

Diana Restaurant 970 Poquonnock Road (Route 1) (860–449–8468). The focus in this warmly welcoming establishment is Lebanese cuisine with a delicious selection of grilled dishes with a Mediterranean flavor. The seafood is particularly exquisite—intriguingly and delicately seasoned and garnished. Open daily for lunch (except Sunday) and dinner (every day). $$

G. Willikers 156 Kings Highway (860–445–8043). Located at the Clarion Inn, this establishment's enormous American menu ranges from simple sides to steaks, poultry, and seafood, lots of great sandwiches, salads, burgers, a raw bar, and more. Full bar and lounge. Convenient for day-tripping families as well as adults on their own. Open daily year-round for breakfast, lunch, and dinner until 10:00 P.M. $–$$

Paul's Pasta Shop 223 Thames Street (860–445–5276).

Specializing in freshly made-in-house pastas and pasta companions, this marvelous pasta shop with full-service restaurant offers a lunch and dinner menu of cold and hot pasta specials with seafood, meat, poultry, and vegetarian toppings, plus garlic bread, several salads, a fresh housemade soup daily, and a great selection of desserts. Wine and beer. Open daily 11:00 A.M. to 9:00 P.M. $

Angelo's Pizzeria 90 Plaza Court (860–445–1400). Gourmet Italian brick-oven pizza and full Italian dinners. Wonderfully creative thin-crust specialty pies, plus traditional toppings. Classics like eggplant Parmesan and baked lasagna. Beer and wine. Open daily for lunch and dinner. $–$$

Places to Stay in Groton

Best Western/Olympic Inn 360 Route 12 (860–445–8000 or 800–528–1234). 140 rooms 3 suites); restaurant, lounge, health club, sauna. $$$$

Bluff Point B&B 26 Fort Hill Road (860–445–1314). On Route 1 not far from Bluff Point State Park, this restored colonial-style home offers 3 comfortable rooms with private baths and a common room with a TV. Continental breakfast; no smoking. No handicapped access or facilities for young children. $$$

Groton Inn and Suites 99 Gold Star Highway (Route 184) (860–445–9784 or 800–452–2191). 115 units, with 10 efficiencies and 25 suites; in-room refrigerators, TV; restaurant, lounge. Senior rates. $$–$$$$

Shore Inn 54 East Shore Avenue (860–536–1180). Seasonal B&B in Groton Long Point; 5 immaculate but casually comfortable guest rooms, each with private bath, in beautiful setting directly on the water. Continental breakfast with homemade treats and fresh fruits. Passes to three other beaches in walking distance; bring a fishing pole. $$$

Thames Harbour Inn and Marina 193 Thames Street (860–445–8111). 26 efficiencies; overnight and seasonal boat dockage on the Thames River. Fishing. Senior rates. $$$

The Sojourner Inn 605 Gold Star Highway (Route 184) (860–445–1986 or 800–MY–SUITE). 45 rooms of varied sizes, all with kitchenettes, some with Jacuzzi and suite-like floor plans; pull-out couches for extra guests. Laundry room, valet dry cleaning, passes to community exercise center. Continental breakfast. Kids under 12 stay free; senior rates. $$–$$$$

Quality Inn 404 Bridge Street (860–445–8141 or

800–221–2222). 106 units with restaurant, lounge, exercise room, outdoor pool. Continental breakfast. Senior rates. $$$

Morgan Inn and Suites 133 Route 184 (800–280–0054). 56 rooms (45 suites); outdoor pool. Continental breakfast. Senior rates. $$$$

Clarion Inn 156 Kings Highway (203–446–0660 or 800–443–0611). 69 rooms, 36 with kitchenettes; 5 suites; nonsmoking rooms available. Health center, sauna, Jacuzzi, game room, indoor pool, laundry room, barbecue and picnic area. G. Willikers restaurant and lounge. Salon with hair styling, facials, tanning, massage. $$$

Public Boat Launches

Bluff Point State Park Route 1 to Depot Road; go to end of Depot Road under the railroad overpass. Sand ramp with direct access to Long Island Sound, just inside park entrance.

Bayberry Lane Long Island Sound access off I–95 exit 87 to Route 349 (also called Clarence Sharp Highway), which becomes Shennecossett Road. Follow this road south to left on Bayberry Lane. Parking for 65 cars. Seasonal fee weekends and holidays.

Mystic River Long Island Sound and river access for cartop/carry-in boats only. I–95 to Allyn Street exit or River Road north from downtown Mystic. Parking for 8 cars; no fee.

Thames River Long Island Sound and river access from Bridge Street to right on Fairview Avenue; Ken Streeter launch is on left under the bridge. Parking for 25 cars; no fee.

 # Noank

One of Connecticut's most picturesque shoreline enclaves, 300-year-old Noank rivals Stonington for its qualities as an authentic New England seaside village. Quiet, narrow streets, historic buildings, lobster boats, and small shops and markets create the aura of a step back in time, while the cottages, marinas, pleasure boats, and barefoot children add to the beach-town atmosphere.

On a peninsula that juts out into Fishers Island Sound at the mouth of the Mystic River, Noank was once a summer encampment area of the Pequots, who controlled the extensive shellfishing beds of the nearby estuaries. Later settled by English farmers who held a lottery in 1712 to draw their plots of land, Noank soon evolved into a shipbuilding, whaling, fishing, and maritime trade center. Today its harbor and coves are dotted with marinas and lobster pots, and the faces of its sun-kissed citizens are dotted with freckles. Perfect in summer, Noank is also lovely in winter and a veritable paradise on a warm afternoon in early fall.

The Best of Noank

Latham-Chester Store Museum

Once the home of a marine hardware store owned first by the Lathams and then by the Chesters, this restored structure near the foot of Main Street and close to the town landing is opened in the summertime for an annual exhibition by local artists. Oil and watercolor paintings and photographs are among the works that are displayed. Call ahead to see what's on the current schedule.

108 Main Street (860–536–7026). Hours are usually limited to Wednesday, Saturday, and Sunday afternoons in the summertime (typically 1:00 to 4:00 P.M.) or at other times for special events; call ahead. Free.

Noank Historical Society

Maritime exhibits and local memorabilia are the focus at this social and marine history museum housed in the beach-stone-sheathed Grace Episcopal Church, built in 1902 to serve Noank's summer visitors. Among the many artifacts are hand-hewn tools and nautical gear. Exhibits focus on fishing methods and the Noank fishing industry, methods of building wooden boats, and the history of the Noank shipyards. Ask curator and Noank native Ken Hodgson about the adventures of Captain Dan Chester and the clipper ship *Dauntless,* the Noank single-room schoolhouse, and the Central Park obelisk that journeyed across the Atlantic in a specially outfitted Noank clipper ship.

On the Water

Recreational sailing and fishing are the primary water activities in Noank, but swimmers also can explore the quiet waters of protected Fishers Island Sound. **Esker Point Beach** (860–572–9702), near the elbow of Groton Long Point Road (Route 215) and Marsh Road, surely lies at one of the prettiest points on the Connecticut coast, with beautiful views of such islands as little Mouse Island just offshore and Fishers Island farther out in the Sound. A fine wading beach for children because of its shallow swimming area, Esker Point is actually not all that terrific for older swimmers because the water rarely reaches more than waist high. Still, for a day in the sun by the shore, Esker Point offers lots of sand, restrooms, a snack concession (in season, Thursday through Sunday only), and a picnic area with hibachi-style grills so you can linger through a couple of meals to catch the sunset. Parking here costs $1 per vehicle. On Thursday evenings, free concerts suitable for all ages are held at the beach at 6:30; parking for the concerts is $3.

Walkers may also want to check out the tiny beach at the **Town Dock** at the foot of Main Street. Slightly larger than a few good-sized beach blankets, it can also be a nice place to take a quick dip, or relax on benches while you soak up the view. The **Noank Play Area** in the park on Main Street and Ward Avenue has a children's playground and a picnic area perfect for taking a break from a village stroll. **Spicer Park** on Spicer Avenue (go back across the railroad bridge on Mosher Avenue to Route 215 and then a block to Spicer Avenue) overlooks pretty Beebe Cove and has grills and picnic areas open to all visitors. Beebe Cove is well known with bird-watchers who say it is a fine spot for sighting nesting shorebirds and seabirds.

Sylvan Street (860–536–7026) or call Ken Hodgson (860–536–3827). Open July 4 through October 12 on Wednesday, Saturday, and Sunday from 2:00 to 5:00 P.M. or by appointment. Free; donations gratefully accepted.

Boat Excursions and Charters

Coastline Yacht Club Eldridge Yard, Marsh Road (860–536–2689 or 800–749–7245). Twenty-two vessels for bareboat or skippered charters on classic motor or sailing vessels. Food and beverage services. Boat-and-breakfast accommodations available, with evening cruise, overnight lodging on board back at the dock, and continental breakfast brought aboard in the morning.

Chartered Fishing Trips: All of the following hold up to six passengers, and have captains licensed by the U.S. Coast Guard and registered by the State of Connecticut. ***Trophy Hunter Sportfishing:*** Captain Ron Helbig (860–536–4460), Noank Village Boatyard. Half- and full-day charters for inshore bass and bluefish or offshore tuna, shark, marlin. See the whales while you fish. Experts and novices welcome; crew offers help, instruction. ***Mataura*** **and** ***Mataura Lite:*** Captain Tom McLaughlin (860–536–6970 or 800–605–6265), Riverview Avenue Dock. Saltwater fly-fishing for blues, bass, and bonita or deep-sea fishing for tuna and shark. Half- and full-day charters for up to six passengers. ***Anna R.:*** Captain Franklin Rathbun (860–536–0529), Rathbun's Dock. ***Duffy D.:*** Captain Jack Dougherty (413–569–6780), Spicer's Noank Marina. ***First Light:*** Captain Bob Romeo (860–632–8455), Noank Shipyard. ***Magic:*** Captain Art Goodwin (860–429–9276), Spicer's Noank Marina. ***Reelin':*** Captain Ernest Celotto (860–536–0642), Noank Village Boatyard.

Places to Eat in Noank

Carson's Store Main Street (860–536–0059). Pull a stool across black-and-white floor tiles to the Formica counter of this market-cum-luncheonette and order freshly made to order American favorites like egg sandwiches and french toast or a frosty malt or milkshake. Established in 1907 for the purposes of providing "Ice Cream, Coffees, Sundries, and Conversation," Carson's is also the place to buy a copy of *National Fisherman* or penny candy, postcards, or a souvenir sweatshirt. The charm and friendly service are free. Open year-round daily; summer hours are 6:00 A.M. to 7:00 P.M. $

Noank Village Bakery 19 Pearl Street (860–536–2229). Once the home of the Noank post office, this bakery/cafe is open from 7:00 A.M. to 1:00 P.M. Tuesday through Friday for breakfast. Come early to eat here or buy beach and picnic food. Choose pastries or griddle favorites like pancakes with fresh fruit; great breakfast and lunch sandwiches and daily-special salads and soups make terrific take-out fare. $

Abbott's Lobster in the Rough 117 Pearl Street (860–536–7719). Fifty-plus years of extraordinary seaside ambiance with views of fishermen, bobbing sailboats, and the offshore islands. Eat out in the breeze and sun on picnic tables, under the striped tent, or inside the casual dining room. Lobsters, steamers, clams and oysters, steamed-

A Village Stroll

Noank's streets are lined with an intriguing collection of nineteenth- and early twentieth-century houses and churches. Although signs of modernization are evident on some homes, old-fashioned details are far more apparent on beautifully restored and original structures ranging from neocolonial to Greek Revival to Victorian and other styles. Stroll wherever you can throughout town. Be sure to soak up the views from **Snake Hill**, which you'll reach from Palmer Court off Pearl Street. On a clear day, the vista is breathtaking, but even on hazy days you'll see far and wide across the water to Stonington, Watch Hill, Fishers Island, and more. On a walk through the mile-wide village, stop also to admire the 1843 **Noank Baptist Church** on the hilltop of Church Street. Wander as far as you can down to Morgan Point. Parts of this pretty area are private, including the beautiful black-capped stone lighthouse at its end, but walkers can look for the Coastal Public Access sign that shows where you can go to reach West Cove.

Before you head back to the present time period, take a memento of this lovely Brigadoon with you. Browsers and serious buyers alike may want to peruse the **Pratt Wright Galleries** (48 Main Street; 860–536–9243). Fine American and European landscapes and seascapes are among the beautiful works for sale here. Around the corner at the **Stone Ledge Art Gallery** (59 High Street; 860–536–7813), you may find the works of local artists, plus prints and posters of regional subjects. If you are here in lobster season, stop for some fresh beasts at the picturesque and much-photographed **Ford's Lobster House** (860–536–2842) on Riverview Avenue. One of Connecticut's last wooden lobster boats brings you the Sound's finest crustaceans. You'll have to steam them yourself, but you won't forget Noank for a long time after you scrape the last morsel from each claw.

in-the-husk corn on the cob, seafood sandwiches, barbecued chicken, and more, topped off with strawberry shortcake. Bring your own bottle. Open May through Labor Day, noon to 9:00 P.M. daily, then weekends only (including Fridays) through Columbus Day from noon to 7:00 P.M. $–$$

The Seahorse 65 Marsh Road (860–536–1670). A local favorite tucked near Spicer's Marina, this seafood restaurant doesn't have the same views as Abbott's, but it doesn't have the crowds, either. Exuding the true flavor of Noank, it serves fresh catch of the day from scallops to lobster, plus lots of other classic shore dinner choices. Sandwiches, salads, chowder, and options for meat-lovers.

Open for lunch and dinner daily from 11:00 A.M. to 10:00 P.M. $$

Costello's Clam Company Pearl Street (860–572–2779). Right on the dock at the Noank Shipyard, this casual, all-outside-seating establishment operated by Abbott's is the place to come for mostly fried seafood, a twin lobster special (two one-pounders for $13.99), steamed shrimp and clams, chicken sandwiches, raw bar, chowder, and such for lunch and dinner daily from noon to 9:00 P.M., from late May through Labor Day. $–$$

Universal Food Store 17 Pearl Street (860–536–3767). In business the better part of a century, this is a great, old-fashioned place to stop for picnic foods, fresh produce, salads, grinders, calzones, strombolis, deli meats, breads, beverages, fresh pizza, and lasagna. Open year-round on Friday and Saturday from 8:00 A.M. to 8:00 P.M. and until 7:00 P.M. the rest of the week. $

Place to Stay in Noank

The Palmer Inn 25 Church Street (860–572–9000). The only hostelry in Noank, the Palmer Inn is a fully restored bed-and-breakfast beauty dating from 1907. Built by shipwrights for shipbuilder Robert Palmer Jr., the magnificent white house with tall columns and two-story portico is secluded from the street by the tall hedges. The 6 antiques-filled guest rooms have private baths and either double or queen-size beds. Nonsmoking; no in-room phones or TVs. Two-night minimum on weekends; no pets; children must be 16 or older. Complimentary continental breakfast of homemade treats. A block from the water and in walking distance of galleries and restaurant. Open year-round. $$$$

Public Boat Launch

Mystic River Access to river and Fishers Island Sound: from I-95 exit 89, go south on Allyn Street, then take first left on Sandy Hollow Road. At end, take left on High Street and take next right on Bindloss Road. At its end, take left on River Road. Launch is on the west bank of the Mystic River, just north of I-95. Cartop/carry-in boats only. Parking for 8 cars. No fee.

For Further Information

Town Parks and Recreation Department (860-441-6777).

Mystic

Rich in history that harks back to the earliest days of the Connecticut Colony, Mystic is a community that has witnessed the first of the painful compromises between settler and native, the glory days of whaling and shipbuilding, the rise of industrialization and the decline of agriculture. Throughout nearly three centuries, Mystic has remained a vital community comprised of diverse citizens engaged in the simple craft of building an American tradition.

For many years in this century, Mystic has been a tourist destination, most notably because of Mystic Seaport, arguably the nation's most outstanding maritime history museum. Now home to other notable attractions, Mystic is a destination for more tourists than ever before in its existence. Even its wonderful downtown, until somewhat recently unknown to out-of-towners, is now a thriving center enjoyed by tourists as well as townies.

The Best of Mystic

Mystic Seaport Museum

The first stop in Mystic for most visitors, the seaport's seventeen acres of historic buildings and re-creations represent a nineteenth-century New England whaling and shipbuilding village. An incredible array of educational and entertainment activities are offered here throughout the year. From rope-making to printing to oystering, from sailor to chandler to merchant, the arts, crafts, and occupations of an early American seaport are celebrated.

Among the major exhibits are the *Charles W. Morgan*, the last surviving wooden American whaling ship; the 1882 training vessel *Joseph Conrad*; and the *L. A. Dutton*, a 1921 fishing schooner. New to the museum experience is the work-in-progress hand-hewn replication of the *Amistad* (see the New Haven chapter for the story of this vessel). The $2.8-million project of re-creating the 77-foot schooner will be finished in the year 2000, and the ship will set sail on a world journey designed to educate others about the enduring lessons of the *Amistad* incident.

Horse and buggy rides, planetarium shows, sea chantey sing-alongs, chowder festivals, lantern-light holiday dramas, tall ship tours, hands-on activities of all sorts, and an outstanding calendar of special events are parts of the key to the Seaport's success. Summer camps, living history workshops, lectures for children and adults, boat excursions, concerts, and much more are among the opportunities for families and individuals. After your adventures, shop in the Seaport's excellent five-part Museum Shop for a memento of your trip. The Galley restaurant provides very casual fare for on-site dining.

75 Greenmanville Avenue (Route 27) off I-95 exit 90 (860-572-5315). The Seaport is open year-round, daily except for Christmas Day. In summer, the schedule is 9:00 A.M. to 8:00 P.M.; from October to April, 10:00 A.M. to 4:00 P.M.; spring and early autumn hours, 9:00 A.M. to 5:00 P.M. Adults $16; children 6 through 12 $8; 5 and under free.

Mystic Marinelife Aquarium

The redesigned and expanded Mystic Aquarium is busy establishing itself as the premier aquarium of the Northeast. The aquarium's 6,000 marine mammals have been moved into twenty-four new or newly renovated exhibits representing the trio of "islands" of marinelife found across the globe: the estuaries, the coral reefs, and the upwelling zones. From a New England tidal marsh to a brand-new 30,000-gallon coral reef re-creation to the Roger Tory Peterson penguin paradise, indoor and outdoor exhibits focus on the myriad and fascinating mammals, fish, and invertebrates of the sunlit seas, with a focus on the vital importance of all the essential elements of a healthy ocean ecosystem. The outdoor seal and penguin exhibits are exceptional representations of the animals' natural habitats. The first has been designed to reflect the habitats of northern fur seals and Steller's sea lions of the North Pacific Pribilof Islands. The latter allows visitors to see both above and below water in the African black-footed penguin rookery. The newly renovated skylit marine theater, World of the Dolphin, allows staff marine biologists to demonstrate the dramatic talents and capabilities of Atlantic bottlenose dolphins.

From the deep, dark ocean to the sunny California coast, visitors now make an entertaining and educational journey across the planet, gaining throughout an understanding of the interrelatedness of all life. Conserving Our Oceans exhibits highlight those species facing particular pollution and habitat destruction issues.

A viewing window into the veterinary care lab gives visitors a close-up look at the work of aquarium scientists. The aquarium has also entered a relationship with underwater explorer Robert Ballard in creating an Institute for Exploration, which introduces visitors to undersea technology, oceanographic exploration, and marine archaeology.

The aquarium has a new cafe and an excellent gift shop/bookstore, which shoppers may browse without an admission ticket. Workshops, classes, and special events are held throughout the year.

55 Coogan Boulevard, off I-95 exit 90 (860–572–5955). Open daily (except New Year's Day, Thanksgiving, and Christmas); admissions from 9:00 A.M. to 5:00 P.M. (visitors may remain until 6:00), and in summer, admissions until 6:00 P.M. (visitors may remain until 7:00). Adults $13, seniors $12, children 3 to 12 $8, 2 and under free.

Downtown Mystic

A few years back only the locals knew the secrets of the "real" historic center of Mystic. Now the whole downtown area rocks and rolls with the tourist crowd that has discovered the inner core of the village. If your appetite for the sea has simply been whetted by the sights upriver, head downtown to Route 1 via Route 27 and the famed counterweighted bascule drawbridge that leads you to picturesque Mystic center. Linger awhile on the bridge itself (park the car somewhere else first) and watch the jellyfish and other flotsam on their way to beautiful Fishers Island Sound. Stay to see the hourly raising of the bridge and the passage of the yachts and sailboats as they cruise up or down river. Then stroll the boutiques, the art galleries, the bookstores, the candy shops, the restaurants.

This wonderful village encapsulates a unique blend of old and new. Discover your own favorite places, but be sure to linger a while at the Mystic River Park, the incredible Mystic Army Navy Store, the excellent **Mystic Art Association Museum and Gallery** (9 Water Street; 860–536–7601), the fanciful as well as practical Emporium, the Mystic Drawbridge Ice Cream Company, and the incomparable Sea Swirl seafood shack. You'll find them all easily in the 1-mile historic district. If you can, come in mid-August for the famed **Outdoor Art Festival** (860–572–5098), a two-day juried show of 300-plus artists who bring their wares from all parts of the nation to the sidewalks, parks, and riverbanks of downtown Mystic. The most beautiful of all

Lanternlight Tours at the Seaport

During the month of December (call 860–572–5315 for the exact schedule) the seaport offers lanternlight tours that reenact the scenarios that may have enlivened a similar town of the eighteenth century at holiday time long ago. Costumed reenactors set the scenes in a dozen or more sites throughout the village while you and your family eavesdrop on the goings-on as your host or hostess leads you by lamplight through the darkened streets. You'll enter parlors and taverns and shops, and even go down to the crew's quarters on the whaler *Charles W. Morgan.* The wind may wail, rain may lash at your cheeks, or perhaps snow will fall lightly on your path, but all seem merely enhancements to the special effect of these marvelous portrayals. Reservations are a must.

annual events that can be enjoyed south of the Seaport and downtown is the **Antique and Classic Boats Rendezvous** (860–572–5315) in late July. Sponsored by the Seaport, this festive and colorful reunion of restored wooden power and sailboats built before the 1950s features a Sunday parade downriver of all the boats and their authentically costumed crews.

West and East Main Street (Route 1), Water Street, Bank Street, Pearl Street, and other nearby streets

Olde Mistick Village

A mere shopping center built as a re-creation of a circa-1720 New England village, this complex's pretty paths, reproduction freestanding shops, and ponds, fences, stone walls, and waterwheels make for a very pleasant shopping experience. Franklin's General Store, Elizabeth and Harriet's Fine Handcrafts, and Wind and Wood are personal favorites among the sixty-plus restaurants, tea shops, jewelry stores, clothing and toy shops, gourmet coffee and chocolate shops, and other establishments here.

Olde Mistick Village is especially pretty in summer when its ponds are busy with waterfowl, its gazebo is the site of free concerts, and its flowers and trees are in bloom. During December the village and its pretty white New England church replica are aglow with holiday light displays, and various complimentary festivities and promotions in individual shops lure cheerful holiday shoppers along the luminaria-lined pathways.

At the junction of Route 27 and Coogan Boulevard (860–536–4941),

Other Mystical Attractions

Mystic County Fair Carousel and Fun Center Greenmanville Avenue (Route 27) (860–572–9949). Need to satisfy the urge to ride a carousel? This family entertainment center (read noisy, busy pay-as-you-play amusement arcade) in the same yellow building as the Carousel Museum has a full-size operational carousel and antique band organ. Take a whirl! Open daily year-round.

Denison Homestead Museum Pequotsepos Road (860–536–9248). If the Seaport fails to satisfy a history craving, this unusual 1717 house might do the trick. Still owned by descendants of the Denison family and furnished with original Denison belongings, its rooms represent periods from the 1720s to the 1940s. Across the street from the Denison Pequotsepos Nature Center, it is open from May through October; call for the current hours. Adults $4, seniors and students $3, children $1.

Portersville Academy 74 High Street (860–536–4779). This Greek Revival two-story schoolhouse with belfry, separate entrances for boys and girls, and a one-room school on the second floor is furnished as it had been in 1840. The first floor, which resembles a courtroom, served as a district voting hall and now is used for changing exhibitions on topics of local historical interest. Open mid-May through mid-October on Tuesday 10:00 A.M. to noon, Thursday noon to 3:00 P.M., and on the first and third Saturdays of the month from 11:00 A.M. to 3:00 P.M.; call for off-season hours.

Williams Beach Park at Mystic Community Center off Mason's Island Road (860–536–3575). Saltwater beach with playground, picnic and snack bar pavilions, grills, sports fields, and more, open at no charge to visitors. Fitness center with Nautilus equipment and more (day-use passes $13 per person over the age of 14). Indoor pool (day-use passes $8 adult, $3 child). Beach open June to Labor Day; no lifeguards.

immediately adjacent to the Mystic Marinelife Aquarium. Open year-round Monday through Saturday from 10:00 A.M. to 6:00 P.M. and Sunday from noon to 5:00 P.M. Summer and holidays hours are often extended.

The Carousel Museum of New England

Like its sister museum in Bristol, Connecticut, this museum is a joyful collection of the gallant and prancing steeds that graced the beautiful carousels of the nineteenth and early twentieth centuries. Some retain their aged appearance, others are remarkably restored to their original splendor, and still others can be seen in parts or in process as both the construction and restoration of these fine artworks are displayed for visitors. A re-creation of an antique carousel carving shop is among the displays, and a real carving shop is also behind the scenes. Carving classes are offered here for interested carousel enthusiasts and other artisans.

193 Greenmanville Avenue, just north of I-95 (860–536–7862). Open April through November, Monday through Saturday from 10:00 A.M. to 6:00 P.M. and Sunday from noon to 6:00, and December through March, Thursday through Saturday from 10:00 A.M. to 5:00 P.M. and Sunday from noon to 5:00 P.M. Adults $4, children 4–14 $2.50.

Denison Pequotsepos Nature Center

If you need a break from marine and historical themes, visit this 125-acre preserve with 7 miles of trails through woods and meadows and past ponds. Wildflower and fern gardens are among the areas created to encourage homeowners to create their own similar backyard habitats. Here you may see otter, mink, and other mammals native to southeastern Connecticut, plus 150 species of birds, including bluebirds and scarlet tanagers.

A trailside natural history museum includes indoor native wildlife exhibits and outdoor flight enclosures for non-releasable raptors. You'll have a look at a great horned owl and other live birds of prey. The Trading Post gift shop sells field guides, children's books, birding supplies, great natural science materials for children, and locally made items like painted walking sticks and hinged birdhouses with peek-in windows. A full schedule of guided walks, summer camps for children ages 3 to 16, birding activities, and field trips can be obtained at the museum.

The nature center also owns the Peace Sanctuary on River Road on the western bank of the Mystic. Atop rocky ledges, this wooded, thirty-acre preserve offers trails overlooking the river. Ask for directions when you visit the main center. Open at no charge from dawn to dusk, it is well named and especially lovely to explore during the early morning and close to dusk when the birds are most active and visible.

109 Pequotsepos Road (follow Coogan Boulevard to its eastern end, take right on Jerry Browne Road, then right on Pequotsepos) (860–536–1216). Open year-round Monday through Saturday from 9:00 A.M. to 5:00 P.M. and Sunday from 1:00 to 5:00 P.M. Adults $4, *children 6–12 $2, 5 and under free. Trails open dawn to dusk; leave a donation in the box. Cross-country skiers welcome, weather permitting.*

Boat Excursions and Charters

Mystic Whaler Cruises

If you have the time and the money, these just may be the cream of the crop in terms of boat excursions along the entire Connecticut coastline. The cruise options are varied to suit nearly any desire, the schooner is an awe-inspiring 110-foot beauty carrying 3,000 square feet of sail, and the crew cheerfully invites both landlubbers and skilled show-offs to hoist the sails, plot the course, or take a turn at the wheel. If you can spring for an overnight sea trek, you can choose from five accommodations options, including the tiny Sloop, the Great Room that gives a taste of life below decks for the common sailor, and the Clipper cabins that provide luxuries like skylights, private showers, and double beds.

Three-hour lobster dinner cruises include steamed lobster and fresh clam chowder served on deck under sail. Six-hour day sails include a hearty barbecue lunch fresh off the on-board grill served while cruising Fishers Island Sound; if the wind is right, it includes a swim on a sheltered cove before returning to Mystic. Overnight sails of one, two, three, and five days include such ports of call as Mystic herself, Block Island, Shelter Island, Sag Harbor, Newport, Cuttyhunk, and Martha's Vineyard. Full-moon cruises, pirate-treasure adventure cruises, lighthouse cruises, and art cruises that encourage you to bring along your art supplies and camera are just some of the maritime mini-vacations that Captain John Eginton plans to tempt you aboard. You may have the adventure of a lifetime.

P.O. Box 189, Mystic 06355 (860–536–4218 or 800–697–8420). Sails May 1 to November 1; cruises range from $60 to $620 per person. Children 10 and older welcome on overnight voyages at full fare; children 5 to 10 welcome on day sails and evening cruises at half-fare. Reservations required. Cruises depart from 7 Holmes Street in Mystic.

Voyager Cruises

The *Argia,* a replica nineteenth-century gaff-rigged schooner, takes passengers on two- or three-hour morning, afternoon, or evening sails in scenic Fishers Island Sound. Skippered by Captain Frank Fulchiero, this beautiful 81-foot white bird glides gracefully across the Sound's sheltered waters, providing a gentle ride that cannot fail to relax and refresh weary day-trippers.

Sunset cruises offered at twilight (6:00 to 8:00 P.M.) daily are the most romantic of the *Argia* options. Families may especially enjoy the Sound Experience cruises, although interested visitors of all ages are more than welcome. Offered only on the Tuesday afternoon cruises from 2:00 to 5:00 P.M., these special educational sails feature an onboard naturalist from the Marinelife Aquarium who answers questions and provides information about creatures drawn up from the sea in Captain Frank's trawl nets.

73 Steamboat Wharf (860–536–0416). Daily (weather permitting) from mid-April to mid-October at 10:00 A.M., 2:00 P.M., and 6:00 P.M. Adults $32 Monday through Friday afternoon, $34 Friday evening through Sunday; children under 18 are $22 for all sails; under 2 are free. Seniors get a $5 discount off the adult fare. Reservations recommended.

Sabino Mystic River Cruises

The *Sabino* is the last coal-fired passenger steamboat in operation. Built in 1908 in East Boothbay, Maine, for passenger service on the Damariscotta River, she is now a working exhibit of the Seaport Museum. Board as her steam whistle calls passengers to her double decks for a cruise downriver. Watch her crew shovel anthracite coal into the glowing maw of her steam plant, then shift your gaze to the beautiful historic homes that grace the banks of the peaceful Mystic River. For the evening cruise, bring a picnic dinner aboard or ask about their boxed dinner and beverage service. Bring a sweatshirt or jacket and settle in for the hour-and-a-half journey down the river and into Fishers Island Sound.

From the Sabino Dock at Mystic Seaport; use south parking lot across from Seaport main entrance (860–572–5315). Call for rates and reservations after 10:00 A.M. Daily half-hour cruises leaving on the hour, from 11:00 A.M. to 4:00 P.M. from the third week in May to Columbus Day; extra cruises in midsummer. Adults $5, plus Seaport admission; children 6–12 $3, plus admission; children under 6 free. Evening cruises at 5:00 P.M. in early and late part of the season, 7:00 P.M. in midsummer. Adults $8.50, children $7, no Seaport admission necessary.

Sylvina W. Beal 120 School Street, West Mystic (860–536–8422 or 800–333–6978). Departs from the West Mystic Wooden Boat Yard; reservations required. This authentic 1911 knockabout schooner operated by the Mystic Nautical Heritage Society goes out on weekend, three-day, and five-day windjammer cruises from Mystic to Block Island, Long Island, Newport, and the Vineyard from late May through November 1. Up to eighteen passengers pay $285 to $500 for the varying cruises; meals are included. Chartered day sails for groups of up to thirty can also be arranged.

Brilliant Mystic Seaport, 75 Greenmanville Road (860–572–5315). No experience is necessary to join the crew of this 61-foot schooner and try your hand at navigation, sail handling, and even onboard cooking (no easy feat!). Weekend programs are offered in spring and fall for adults; multiday summer programs are open to youth.

Breck Marshall Mystic Seaport (860–572–5315). Half-hour sails aboard 24-foot gaff-rigged wooden sailboat. Mid-May through mid-October.

Resolute Mystic Seaport (860–572–5315). Antique wooden motor launch that was once the tender for the America's Cup defender of the same name. Half-hour trips throughout the day, mid-May through mid-October.

Karen Ann Captain Jeff Eckert, Mystic Harbor Marina, Mystic (860–345–2570). Chartered fishing trips for stripers, bass, others.

Shaffer's Boat Livery 106 Mason's Island Road (860–536–8713). Rentals of 16-foot fiberglass skiffs with 6-horsepower engines for exploring and fishing in Mystic River, Fishers Island Sound, Noank, Stonington. Full selection of bait and tackle available. Ramp.

Sterling Yacht Charters 44 Water Street (860–572–1111). Traditional or contemporary yachts of nearly any size for private or corporate parties or cruises.

Places to Eat in Mystic

The Mooring 20 Coogan Boulevard in the Mystic Hilton (860–572–0731). One of the finest restaurants in Mystic is this nautically dressed establishment with a sophisticated ambiance and a sure-handed focus on seafood and steak. Among the Continental and American dinners are its famed seafood pie, poultry and pasta specials, traditional veal and beef dishes, and inventive choices like duck strudel. Soundings Lounge. Breakfast and lunch also available. Open year-round daily for breakfast from 6:30 A.M., lunch from 11:30 A.M., and dinner from 5:30 P.M. $$$

The Flood Tide Junction Route 1 and Route 27 (860–536–8140). For an exceptionally gracious dining experience on the picturesque grounds of the Inn at Mystic overlooking the harbor and the town, come to the Flood Tide for American cuisine with Continental overtones. Roast duckling, chateaubriand, rack of lamb Dijonaise, excellent pastas, and fresh seafood. Piano player at dinner nightly and on Sunday afternoons. Impressive and reasonably priced buffet breakfasts and luncheons and beautiful Sunday brunches. Patio seating in summer. Open daily year-round for breakfast from 7:00 A.M., lunch from 11:30 A.M., dinner from 5:30 P.M., and Sunday brunch 11:00 A.M. to 2:30 P.M. $$$$

Captain Daniel Packer Inne 32 Water Street (860–536–3555). In the eighteenth-century National Historic Register home of a Mystic whaling captain is this charming bi-level restaurant overlooking the Mystic River. The first-story pub is a cozy affair with a large fireplace that makes for a delightful winter afternoon here. Upstairs are two dining rooms and five more fireplaces. The fare is basically American with a few Asian touches. The house signature dish is its steak Black Jack, a beautifully seared sirloin splashed with Jack Daniels. Duck, veal, and poultry share the spotlight. The pub menu features full dinners and lighter fare for lunch. Live jazz, blues, and pop in the pub on weeknights. Open year-round Monday through Saturday for lunch 11:00 A.M. to 4:00 P.M. and dinner 5:00 to 10:00 P.M. and on Sunday from 2:00 A.M. to 10:00 P.M. $$$–$$$

Seamen's Inne Greenmanville Avenue, just outside the north entrance to the Seaport (860–536–9649). With a special Connecticut Yankee ambiance, this tavern-like restaurant is a great place for regional American seafood cuisine like shrimp Creole, Maryland crab cakes, and New England seafood pot pie in a pastry-sealed crock. At dinnertime, lobster and prime rib probably outsell all of these, however. At lunch, soups, salads, stews, sandwiches, and seafood rolls are de rigueur. The Samuel Adams Pub offers beer and ale on tap and entertainment nightly. Come back for the Dixieland Sunday brunch for southern-style fare. Open daily for lunch, dinner, Sunday brunch. Lunch $; dinner $$–$$$

Go Fish Corner of Coogan Boulevard and Route 27 in Olde Mistick Village shopping center (860–536–2662). Touted as the best new restaurant in New London County and one of the best seafood establishments in the state, Go Fish is a wonderfully imaginative, contemporary place immersed in images of the deep ocean. It offers an enormous sushi bar, a wine bar, and a coffee bar—as if the delicious, perfectly prepared seafood were not enough. Must-tries are the excellent seafood bisque and the superb bouill-abaisse. Open for lunch Monday through Saturday 11:30 A.M. to 2:30 P.M., dinner Monday through Saturday from 4:30 P.M., and Sunday dinner from 11:30 A.M. to 9:30 P.M. $$–$$$:

Under Wraps 7 Water Street (860–536–4042). A fun and won-derful menu with an Asian and Caribbean twist. Lots of deliciously ethnic combinations like this: Moroccan curried vegetables, raisins, cukes, island salsa, and couscous in a low-fat whole wheat tortilla; or perhaps grilled chicken or shrimp with tomatoes, pep-pers, spinach, cukes, pesto, parmesan, and couscous in a spinach tortilla—ooh, baby! Frozen smoothies cool the stimulated palate. Eat-in or take-out, open daily from 11:00 A.M to 9:00 P.M. $

Mystic Pizza 56 West Main Street (860–536–3737). Who can resist? It's convenient, it's good, the menu has lots more than pizza, and it's famous, so be there, just for fun. Open for lunch and dinner daily year-round. $

Places to Stay in Mystic

The Inn at Mystic Junction Routes 1 and 27 (860–536–9604 or 800–237–2415). Beautiful resort complex overlooking the town and the sea. Has 5 suites in the inn, which is on the National Register of Historic Places; 47 rooms, suites, and efficiencies in the cream-of-the-crop motor inn; 5 fireplace rooms with whirlpool in the gatehouse; and ultra-luxe rooms with private balconies over-looking the harbor in the East Wing. Indoor and outdoor pools, exceptional Flood Tide restaurant, tennis, boating, exercise room, formal gardens. $$$$

Harbour Inne and Cottage 15 Edgemont Street (860–572–9253). At the edge of the Mystic River, this small inn has 4 charmingly decorated and air-conditioned guest rooms, each with private bath and kitchen privileges. Common room with piano and fireplace; waterfront gazebo and picnic tables. Private three-room cottage has a bedroom with two double beds and a fire-place, a fully equipped kitchen, a living room with a pull-out couch, and a furnished deck with a hot tub spa. Pets are welcome. $$$–$$$$

Steamboat Inn 73 Steamboat Wharf (860–536–8300). This inti-mate establishment is right at the docks on the Mystic River and offers luxurious privacy just steps from all the activity at the heart of downtown. Each of the 10 elegant rooms has a private bath and whirlpool; second-level rooms have fireplaces, dock-level rooms have small kitchens with refrigerators and coffeemakers. Fully air-conditioned. Continental-plus breakfast and afternoon sherry or tea in the Common Room. $$$–$$$$

Whaler's Inn 20 East Main Street (860–536–1506 or 800–243–2588). Beautiful white clapboard historic inn with 45 comfortable and recently redecorated rooms right down by the bascule bridge. Homey ambiance; children stay free. Great restaurant called **Bravo Bravo** (860–536–3228) with indoor dining room and outside terrace. Also the home of the C.C. Bagel Company. $$$–$$$$

Red Brook Inn 2750 Gold Star Highway, Old Mystic (860–572–0349). This seven-acre country setting features the 1740s Haley Tavern and the 1770s Crary Homestead. Among the special luxuries of nearly a dozen antiques-filled rooms are queen-size beds, whirlpool baths, and fireplaces. Large common areas from cozy parlors to game room and terrace. Full country-style breakfast and afternoon refreshments; special packages. $$$$

House of 1833 72 North Stonington Road (860–536–6325 or 800–367–1833). If you crave something close to splendor, come to this Greek Revival mansion. From the base of its tall columns to the top of its unusual cupola, the house has been impeccably restored and gorgeously decorated. It offers beautiful guest rooms with working fireplaces, luxe private baths, and some private porches. Plenty of common space, tennis court, swimming pool, and bicycles. Gourmet breakfasts. $$$$

Pequot Hotel B&B 711 Cow Hill Road (860–572–0390). This inn was once an 1840s stagecoach stop; today it offers 23 wooded acres of solitude with 3 meticulously kept country-style guest rooms and suites. Among the varied luxuries are queen-size beds, fireplaces, and whirlpool baths. The two-bedroom suite with connecting bath works great for families. Your hostess provides a full country breakfast each morning. Nonsmoking. $$$$

Mystic Hilton 20 Coogan Boulevard (800–HILTONS). This imposing brick hotel perched on a hill near the aquarium and outlets has 184 rooms, some suites, an indoor pool, a fitness room, and an outstanding restaurant, The Mooring. Lots of special treatment for children. $$$$

Seaport Motor Inn Route 27 (860–536–2621). Practically a hotel with 118 rooms on two levels, outdoor pool, nice grounds, lounge, and restaurant; reasonable rates considering the competition. $$–$$$

Best Western/Sovereign Hotel 9 Whitehall Avenue (800–363–1622). 150 units, restaurant, lounge, sauna, indoor pool. Senior rates. $$$

Comfort Inn Mystic 48 Whitehall Avenue (860–572–8531 or 800–572–3993). 120 units, health club, continental breakfast. Special packages available; complimentary shuttles. $$$

Days Inn Mystic 55 Whitehall Avenue (860–572–0574 or 800–572–3993). 122 units, restaurant, playground, outdoor pool. Inquire about special packages; complimentary shuttles. $$$

Residence Inn by Marriott 41 Whitehall Avenue (860–536–5150). 80 suites with fully equipped kitchens, indoor pool, sport court, continental breakfast. $$$$ (Inquire about accommodations at its lovely **Whitehall Mansion,** 42 Whitehall Avenue, 860–572–7280—a recently restored historic home that has been made into an inn with 5 guest rooms with period furnishings, fireplaces, and modern baths with Jacuzzi tubs; complimentary wine, continental breakfast.)

Kittiwake Boat and Breakfast 1 Washington Street (203–686–1616). Stay aboard an immaculate 57-foot Chris-Craft yacht on the Mystic River. Choose either the captain's cabin or the guest stateroom. Private bath. Air-conditioned (or heated if you need it). Your husband-and-wife hosts leave you some privacy in the evening when you arrive and make you a full breakfast in the morning. One- or two-night stays from May through late October. $$$$

Seaport Campgrounds Route 184, Old Mystic (860–536–4044). Out in the country away from the crowds is this spacious family campground for tenters and RVs. Hookups for the motorized campers; separate open and wooded sites for the tents. Swimming pool, fishing pond, rec center, laundry, restrooms and showers, playground, miniature golf, grocery store, wood, ice, dumping station, more. Open mid-March through late November. $

Public Boat Launch

Mystic River Access to river and Fishers Island Sound for carry-in/cartop boats only. Take River Road on west bank of Mystic River to parking area just north of I–95 overpass. No fee.

For Further Information

Mystic River Historical Society 74 High Street, West Mystic (860–536–4779). The historical society has put together a wonderful small book of walking tours of historic sites. *Curbstones, Clapboards, and Cupolas* is available for $3 at the society's building on High Street, open Tuesday 9:00 A.M. to noon and on Wednesday and Thursday from noon to 3:00 P.M.; book also sold at Mystic Public Library (860–536–7721) and Bank Square Bookstore (860–536–3795).

Mystic Chamber of Commerce 16 Cottrell Street (860–572–9578). Maps, brochures, and other helpful information. Boaters as well as shore explorers may want to ask for a copy of the *Mystic Waterfront Directory,* which provides a complete list of marinas, charter boats, liveries, and cruise operators in the Mystic area. Open year-round Monday through Friday 9:00 A.M. to 5:00 P.M., plus outdoor computerized visitor information center available 24 hours daily.

Mystic and Shoreline Information Center Building 1D, Old Mistick Village, Coogan Boulevard off Route 27, Mystic (860–536–1641). Open in summer season Monday through Saturday 9:00 A.M. to 6:00 P.M. and Sunday 10:00 A.M. to 6:00 P.M.; in the off-season from September through April, the center closes one hour earlier.

Tourist Information Depot of Mystic Route 27, opposite the I–95 exit 90 southbound off-ramp (860–536–3505). Open 7:00 A.M. to 9:00 P.M. daily year-round. Stop here for discount coupons for area lodging and dining and discounted admissions to some local attractions.

SNET Visitor Information Center off exit 92 southbound on I-95 (860–599–2056). Open daily from Memorial Day to Columbus Day 8:00 A.M. to 6:00 P.M., and daily the rest of the year 8:30 A.M to 4:30 P.M.

Bed and Breakfasts of the Mystic Coast (860–892–5006). Reservations service for nearly thirty B&Bs in New London County and Westerly, Rhode Island.

Visit Mystic Web site http://www.visitmystic.com.

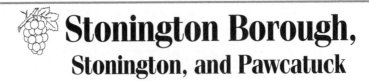

Stonington Borough,
Stonington, and Pawcatuck

Bounded by the Mystic River on the west and the Pawcatuck River on the east is Connecticut's easternmost coastal town of Stonington. It includes a large part of what most folks think is the separate town of Mystic (but is not), a self-governing village called Stonington Borough, an area simply called Stonington, *and* the village of Pawcatuck. This guidebook deals with the section of Mystic in another chapter, as an entity separate from its actual existence as parts of both Groton and Stonington. The collected parts of Stonington plus some lodgings in the town of North Stonington are the focus of this chapter's exploration of the eastern corner of the Connecticut shore.

Stonington Borough is the most beautiful and evocative of all Connecticut shore towns. Very quaint and very New England, it exists as if in a time warp. In Stonington Borough, it's easy to imagine the days of sea captains and West Indies trading ships.

Originally a farming community settled in 1649 by families from Plymouth Colony, Stonington was both a major whaling and sealing port and a shipbuilding town throughout the first three quarters of the nineteenth century. In the last quarter of the century, the graceful wooden clipper ships were replaced by steamships, and the look of Stonington Harbor changed as the maritime industry decreased and the tourist industry grew. When the railroad built bridges over the rivers and began interstate rail lines linking the cities, bustling Stonington changed again. For a while, the local fishing fleet had the whole port to itself, but soon pleasure boaters and yachters began to share this pretty harbor.

Today, Connecticut's only remaining commercial fleet docks in Stonington along with the recreational boaters, and Stonington can still appear stuck in time if you overlook the expensive yachts with high-tech equipment. In the cozy village laid out neatly in 1752, the eighteenth- and nineteenth-century houses cuddled nearly gable to gable offer a glimpse backward to a time when every citizen was well-acquainted with his or her neighbors, and merchants catered to a clientele whose needs and preferences were well known and discreetly met.

Outside of Stonington Borough is the remaining town of Stonington, a little less evocative but nonetheless picturesque. East of the main town is the village of Pawcatuck, nearly in Rhode Island. Inland is the separate town of North Stonington, off the shore path but linked in spirit to the quiet way of life that city visitors may yearn for nostalgically. Come in all seasons to savor the peaceful pleasures of coastal country life.

The Best of Stonington Borough

Once you have crossed the Route 1A bridge to the borough, park anywhere and just stroll. The whole of Stonington is not that small, actually, but its borough is a great place for walking. Weave your way down narrow Water Street, stopping at the shops and galleries as you wander. Stop at **Cannon Square** to see the marker that commemorates the success of the Stonington militia in repelling

Shore Points
The Battle of Stonington

In 1814 the residents of Stonington were heavily invested in their bustling village. As Patriots, they had successfully thwarted the attack of the British on their harbor during the Revolution, and they had settled down right tidily to their lives as *American* shipbuilders, sailors, farmers, merchants, and tradesmen. When the Brits showed up again in August of 1814 and blockaded Long Island Sound, the Stonington townsfolk were not about to take any guff. With five ships in the harbor carrying a total of 160 guns, British Captain Thomas Hardy had sent a note ashore to the Americans, warning them that they had one hour to leave town before the village would be bombarded. The feisty Stonington folk stayed exactly where they were and planned to defend their beloved homes with the town's three cannons. A three-day volley between ship and shore began, and in the end, with their own paltry supply of munitions boosted by backup shipments of cannonballs from New London, the Stonington defenders drove out the British and returned to their farming, shipbuilding, and whaling. At Cannon Square, a granite monument topped with British cannonballs commemorates the victory, and one of the cannons used in the Battle of Stonington still faces the sea—just in case.

DuBois Beach

Even gross hyperbole inadequately describes the beauty of tiny DuBois Beach at Stonington Point. The amenities are few, the sand is pebbly, the space is limited, the privacy is practically nil, and yet it remains the most exquisite spot on the Connecticut shore.

At the foot of Water Street, the beach parking area is open year-round and day-trippers in cars can have a tool around and perhaps a brief walk at no charge. To park and stay at the beach, a fee of $2 on weekdays and $3 on weekends is charged per person; families pay $5 or $6, respectively. The beach is lifeguarded daily in July and August and on weekends at other times in the swimming season. For more information, call the Stonington Community Center (860–535–2476).

the British attack on Connecticut during the War of 1812, then rest a while at a cafe or coffeehouse. Enjoy the model railroad that re-creates the setting of the Stonington Line Railroad and the Town Dock as they appeared in the mid-1800s; the display is in the **Anguilla Gallery** (72 Water Street) and is open to the public from 10:00 A.M to 5:00 P.M. daily year-round.

Shoppers may want to peruse hand-painted French pottery at **Quimper Faience** (141 Water Street; 860–535–1712; open Monday through Saturday 9:00 A.M. to 5:00 P.M.) or the used collection of volumes at **Battersea Books** (106 Water Street; 860–535–1622; open Wednesday through Sunday 11:00 A.M. to 5:00 P.M. or by appointment). Antiques collectors may want to search shops like Ronald Noe's **Grand and Water Antiques** (860–535–2624); **Neil Bruce Eustace Antiques** (on Water Street; 860–535–2249); or, a bit farther afield, the **Stonington Antique Center** (71 Cutler Street; 860–535–8373). If you are here in summer, stop to smell the roses—literally. The borough overflows with flower beds and window boxes.

Old Lighthouse Museum

Inside the stone lighthouse at the foot of the village are six rooms displaying whaling and fishing equipment, swords and cannonballs and other instruments of defense, nineteenth-century portraits, and much more. One exhibit focuses on the wonderful treasures brought back to Stonington by the captains of the China trade route. Another shows a collection of antique shoes found in the walls of old houses to protect them from evil spirits. The antique dollhouse, decoys, toys, and model ships are often especially interesting to children.

You can learn about the history of Stonington and its role in the War of 1812. You can discover the history of the lighthouse itself—the first one in Connecticut, commissioned in 1823 by the U. S. government and rebuilt in 1840. Learn the details of the railroad that once transferred passengers from luxury liners to river steamboats, and climb the stone staircase of the lighthouse tower for a view of the harbor.

7 Water Street (860–535–1440). Open daily in July and August from 11:00 A.M. to 5:00 P.M.; open in May, June, September, and October from Tuesday through Sunday at the same hours. Adults $4, children 6–12 $2. Combination tickets to this and the Palmer House are $6 and $3, respectively.

Captain Nathaniel B. Palmer House

Home of the discoverer of Antarctica and his equally adventurous brother, this mid-nineteenth-century mansion at the far north end of the village has sixteen rooms filled with the clever architectural design work of the crafty captain himself. Better known for their success in the China trade and Nat's discovery of the southernmost

The Blessing of the Fleet

Perhaps the quaintest and most touching annual event in Connecticut is the blessing ceremony that offers spiritual protection to the fishermen who ply these waters for the seaborne bounty that provides to them a living and to us a feast. Held usually on the last weekend in July, the two-day event begins with a traditional lobster/clambake under a tent at the town dock at the end of Pearl and Front Streets. Portuguese sweetbreads and sausages, chowders, corn on the cob, and all kinds of fish build everyone's stamina for an evening of dancing on the dock until midnight. The next morning the Fisherman's Mass is offered at 10:00 A.M. at St. Mary's Roman Catholic Church on Broad Street in the village, and then the street parade gets underway by 1:00 P.M., encircling the town before returning to the dock. A dockside ceremony at about 3:00 P.M. precedes the bishop's boarding of the decorated fleet's lead vessel, which moves into the harbor to bless each of the remaining boats as they pass in their own parade. Following the blessing, the vessels pass the breakwater and go out on the Sound, where the families of deceased fishermen toss into the sea floral tributes formed like broken anchors. Call for further information (860–535–3150).

continent in 1820 in the sloop *Hero* while on a sealing expedition, Nathaniel Palmer and his brother Alexander filled their elegant home with a variety of innovations and contraptions that intrigue young and old visitors. Lively stories told by the docents tell of the many adventures of clipper ship designer Nat and daring Alexander; the tours take one hour. Be sure to climb to the top of the home's octagonal cupola to have a look at the glorious view of Stonington Harbor that allowed the residents to identify the sailing ships that approached the harbor after long sea journeys.

40 Palmer Street at North Water Street (860–535–8445). Open May through October, Wednesday through Monday 10:00 A.M. to 4:00 P.M. (last tour at 3:00), and by appointment. Adults $4, children 6–12 $2. Combo tickets ($6 and $3) available for this and the lighthouse museum.

The Best of Stonington

Once controlled by the Pequots, who were decimated in a horrific scene in 1637, the area now called Stonington was once a part of the Massachusetts Colony and was called Southerton. When it came under the control of the Connecticut Colony in 1662, it was renamed Mystic, an Anglicization of a native word meaning "large tidal river." After a year of trying to farm the New England soil, however, the townsfolk rechristened their settlement Stonington. Today a few of the town's attractions disprove the assumption that Stonington farmland might be a cursed plot of countryside.

Stonington Vineyards

The climate of coastal Connecticut has proven to produce some wonderful wines from the vineyards that benefit from the shoreline's mild but crisp winters and sunny summers. Stonington Vineyards is among the state's most successful growers, and the 58–acre setting is the perfect destination for a summer or fall day. Though the twenty-minute guided winery tours are scheduled at 2:00 P.M. only, visitors who arrive early in the day are welcome to enjoy a stroll through the vineyards themselves and may even spread a picnic blanket.

Visitors who take the guided tour will see the wine-making cellars and learn how the vintner makes 15,000 gallons of wine annually. A tasting room ensures that all guests may sample the six premium wines that have been aged to a balanced finish in French oak

Clyde's Cider Mill

To visit Clyde's on a crisp day in early fall when the apples are at their peak and the cider is at its sweetest, swing north out of Stonington Borough on Flanders Road and take a left on the Pequot Trail (Route 234) and head toward the village called Old Mystic. Take a right on North Stonington Road (Route 201) and find Clyde's Cider Mill (860–536–3354) at number 129, not far up the road. Watch this huge 1881 mill press the amber juices from the apples that fill barrel after barrel to the brim.

The largest and oldest operating steam-powered cider press in New England, the mill produces both sweet cider and hard cider. Although pressings are usually done on a regular but unscheduled basis throughout the week, a crowd typically gathers on Saturday and Sunday afternoons when pressings are scheduled for 1:00 and 3:00 P.M. The mill is open daily from the last weekend in September until the day before Thanksgiving: from 9:00 A.M to 6:00 P.M. until Halloween and until 5:00 P.M. the remainder of the season. Clyde's always has an aura of festivity as spectators also shop for fresh apples, jams, honey, maple syrup, pumpkins, gourds, freshly ground cornmeal, and more.

barrels. Both chardonnay and pinot noir grapes are used to create both crisply dry and subtly sweet fruity wines perfect for all cuisines. If you are so inclined, browse the gift shop and buy a bottle or two.

523 Taugwonk Road (860-535–1222). Open daily year-round 11:00 A.M. to 5:00 P.M., except on major holidays. Guided winery tours at 2:00 P.M. or by appointment for groups of ten or more. Free.

Adam's Garden of Eden

More than five acres of themed gardens are the focus of this nursery and garden shop. Herbs are the specialty here, but all kinds of annuals, perennials, everlastings, dig-your-own mums, pumpkins, Christmas trees, and water plants are among the traditional plants and unique horticultural treasures gardeners may find. Famed for the flower arrangements and topiaries they ship to special events from New York to Boston, Adam's began as a small dig-your-own-mum farm. Now it is an island of color and fragrance in the Stonington countryside.

A pond with a waterfall and a Victorian-style gazebo are among the features that punctuate the gardens and pathways. While it remains true that Adam's is a retail operation with a shop over-flowing with floral and gardening merchandise, it is also true that the setting draws thousands of visitors who come just to share the beauty. Weddings and receptions are not uncommon here, and free annual events such as the Garlic Fest in midsummer bring crowds of happy revelers. A fall festival celebrating pumpkin season means free hayrides to the pick-your-own pumpkin fields and freshly pressed cider for all visitors. In December, return to cut your own Christmas tree or buy a decorated wreath or Christmas topiary.

360 North Anguilla Road (860–599–4241). To find the gardens, take Route 2 west to the rotary at Route 184; travel west on Route 184 to the first left; the gardens are on the left three quarters of a mile from that turn. Open daily except Thanksgiving and Christmas.

The Best of Pawcatuck

The easternmost village in the lower part of the county just before you cross the Rhode Island border on I-95, Pawcatuck is another speck of a place with some fun attractions. Two miles wide and about four miles from north to south, its location on the Pawcatuck River and its access to shipping created a small center of manufacturing and a good-sized downtown near the junction of Route 1 and Route 2. Choose from the simple pleasures of Pawcatuck's recreational attractions, then stop downtown for a bite to eat or a stroll through the shops. Just a blink away is Rhode Island, the beautiful area of Watch Hill and Napatree Beach, and Atlantic playgrounds like Misquamicut.

Maple Breeze Park

For the pure fun of it, you must come to Maple Breeze Park. Just bring a bathing suit and prepare to get wet. Two 350-foot water slides are tons of fun for anyone roughly taller than 40 inches. All riders must ride separately. You can also ride motorized bumper boats (you have to be at least 48 inches tall to ride alone, but smaller children can ride along with taller siblings or parents) or play eighteen holes of very classic miniature golf.

Next to the mini-golf course are motorized kiddie karts for little tykes and across the street are go-karts reached through a tunnel that goes under the road. Each driver gets four laps around a

The Pequot Trail and More

From Route 1 in Pawcatuck drive west (the sign may say north) on the Pequot Trail (Route 234), the designated scenic highway that was once the supposed warpath of the Pequots. The road meets Route 184 at the village of Old Mystic near the banks of the Mystic River, and it is especially lovely to drive this way as the sun begins to set as you travel west. For a truly Sunday-drive sort of trek, take Route 184 eastward about six or seven miles (again, ironically, the signs might say north) to Route 49 in North Stonington, and take a left to head north on Route 49 for a scenic ride past forests and farms along another designated highway that actually extends 19.5 miles to Sterling in Windham County. The farms and fields along these roads are spectacular in all seasons.

quarter-mile track. Small children can ride with anyone over 16.

Admission to the park is free, and use of the rides and games is administered through the purchase of tokens. Bumper boats cost $3 per person for a four-minute ride; the go-karts cost $3 for a three-minute ride. Mini-golf is $4.50 per person; the water slide is $6.50 for a forty-minute turn. A snack bar and an ice cream stand with twenty-four tempting flavors are also on the premises.

Off I-95 exit 92 at 350 Liberty Street (Route 2) (860–599–1232). Open in May and June on weekends only from 10:00 A.M. to 10:00 P.M. and daily from approximately July 1 through Labor Day at the same hours, weather permitting. Call to confirm hours early in the season or in questionable weather.

Davis Farm Horsedrawn Hayrides

Davis Farm is one of southeastern Connecticut's famed farms held by the same family for more than three hundred years. While the farm produces and sells its own sweet corn, sweet cider, and other organically grown vegetables, it has also diversified into the agri-tourism business. In the fall and early winter only, six magnificent pedigreed Belgian horses pull visitors along more than 2 miles of trails through the farm's fields and woods. Call for the current rates per person, per family, and per group, and ask for the seasonal schedule.

Haunted hayrides begin after dark in October, on weekends only the first two weeks and daily thereafter through Halloween. Oriented to children, the rides are spooky but not terrifying or gory. From the day after Thanksgiving through December, an enchanted Christmas hayride treks past 150 lighted and decorated Christmas trees and other seasonal scenes on the way to Santa's cabin in the woods. Private daytime carriage rides can be arranged at other times of the year.

576 Green Haven Road (860–599–5859). Rides: ages 13 and up $7.50, 4 through 12 $5, 3 and under free; $100 for private rides for groups of approximately 15 passengers. Reservations required for all rides.

Barn Island State Wildlife Management Area

Take Green Haven Road south from the traffic light on Route 1 where a sign says "Barn Island State-owned Boat Launching Area." A nearly immediate left on Palmer Neck Road takes you past Wequetecock Cove and down to the shore, where the state manages an undeveloped wildlife area. Situated on Little Narragansett Bay between the cove and the Pawcatuck River, this pretty refuge has trails and unpaved roads across the tidal marshes and uplands of oak forest. A parking lot off Palmer Neck Road provides space for the vehicles of all visitors.

If you have a boat, launch it at the state boat ramp here and cruise the quiet inlets. Saltwater canoeing and sea kayaking is especially pleasant in this peaceful place. You can also fish here, usually without too many boaters to disturb your serenity. A great variety of waterfowl winter in the bay, and hunting is also allowed in season with permits. Those who prefer live birds will appreciate the many songbirds and shorebirds.

Palmer Neck Road (off Green Haven Road off Route 1). For information call area supervisor John Lincoln (860–445–1729).

Cottrell Brewing Company

Old Yankee Ale is the specialty of this microbrewery, one of several Connecticut coastal enterprises aiming to brew distinctive beers with a regional flair. Discover the secrets of the process on a brewery tour, then sample some of the wares.

100 Mechanic Street (860–599–8213). Tours on Saturday at 3:00 P.M or by appointment. Take Route 1 east toward Rhode Island. Take the last right in Connecticut onto Mechanic Street; brewery is slightly less than a half-mile down on the left; follow signs to the back of the building.

Places to Eat in Stonington Borough, Stonington, and Pawcatuck

The Yellow House Coffee and Tea Room 149 Water Street, Stonington Borough (860–535–4986). Wonderful coffees and biscotti in a sunny space splashed with cheerful colors. Tasty sandwiches, excellent soups, and other casual fare perfect for shoppers, day-trippers, and children. Open daily from 6:30 A.M. (to 6:00 P.M. on weekdays; to 10:00 P.M. on weekends) for breakfast and lunch served all day long, plus afternoon tea from 3:00 to 5:00 P.M. $

Noah's 113 Water Street, Stonington Borough (860–535–3925). Three solid meals a day are served at this warm and casual place with a down-home flair. Twirling ceiling fans and a tin ceiling add to the old-fashioned, casual ambiance. Good cookin', served with a smile, keeps the place busy all day. House-made pasta, excellent soups, and great seafood. The scrod melts in your mouth. Open Tuesday through Sunday for breakfast and lunch from 7:00 A.M. until 2:30 P.M. and for dinner from 6:00 to 9:00 P.M. $–$$

Water Street Cafe 142 Water Street, Stonington (860–525–2122). This sweet survivor of a disastrous fire simply took up digs elsewhere and went on. The cafe serves a more relaxed menu than the fine dining it had offered earlier but is just as fresh and inventive as before, with some French and Asian influences as well as regional American overtones. Open for dinner daily and for lunch also, except for Tuesday and Wednesday. $$

One South, a Cafe 201 North Main Street, Stonington Borough (860–535–0418). In one of the village's charming old homes, this casual but sophisticated restaurant serves regional and international cuisine made from the finest seasonal ingredients available. Hearty scratch-made soups, creative appetizers, fresh salads, seafood (including their famed grilled mussels), steaks, pasta, and poultry leave just a little room for excellent house-made desserts. Open daily for lunch from 11:30 A.M. (except Sunday) and for dinner from 5:00 P.M. $$–$$$

Quiambaug House 29 Old Stonington Road, Stonington (860–572–8543). Out of the village just off Route 1 between Stonington and Mystic, this rambling structure set back near the salt marsh reveals one wonderful surprise after the other, from its charming lobby to the casually elegant yet homey decor in its large dining room, and the pub-style, family-friendly club room. The renowned Ainslie Turner and her husband, Jerry, have raised this old roadside eatery to new heights with a seasonal menu based on a standard of excellence unmatched in the region. Open daily for luncheon and dinner. Jazz on Sunday from 2:00 to 6:00 P.M. $–$$$

Festivals Family Restaurant 163 South Broad Street (Route 1), Pawcatuck (860–599–0880). Across from the high school, dine on chicken, surf and turf, veal, pastas, pizza, seafood, grinders, sandwiches, and a delicious "rainbow" salad. Open daily for lunch and dinner year-round. $–$$

Nutmeg Crossing Restaurant 1 West Broad Street, Pawcatuck (860–599–3840). On the bridge overlooking the Pawcatuck River in downtown Pawcatuck, this casual, family-style restaurant serves breakfast, lunch, and dinner seven days a week year-round. Wine and beer list; extensive menu of American cuisine. $–$$

Randall's Ordinary Route 2, North Stonington (860–599–4540). Gourmet open-hearth cooking with a waitstaff dressed in eighteenth-century attire is the intriguing attraction at this rustically restored colonial country inn just a third of a mile north of I-95. Open daily for a la carte breakfast and lunch and a prix fixe dinner ($30), the inn serves authentic fare at every meal. At dinner, guests receive cheese and crackers and hearth-baked breads, soup, a choice of three entrees (a seafood dish, a red meat, or a poultry), and dessert and a beverage. Guests may also stay overnight. $$–$$$$

Places to Stay in Stonington Borough, Stonington, and Pawcatuck

Cove Ledge Motel on Route 1 on Pawcatuck side of Stonington (860–599–4130). Right near the hub of a marina, this waterfront 16–unit motel is picturesque and convenient, with fishing and boat launching easily available. Four efficiency units, outdoor pool, playground, continental breakfast. Guest boat docking. Open May through October. $$$

Sea Breeze Motel 812 Stonington Road (Route 1), Stonington (860–535–2843). On a little arm of the sea, 30 units offer the basic necessities, plus air-conditioning and TV. $$$

Stonington Motel 901 Stonington Road (Route 1), Stonington (860–599–2330). 12 air-conditioned units with in-room fridges and TVs. $$

Lasbury's Guest House 24 Orchard Street, Stonington Borough (860–535–2681). This 3-room cottage is tucked away in the secluded backyard of a private home on a quiet residential street, the only place in the whole borough offering guest accommodations. The smallest of the three has a private bath; the larger rooms share a bath. Antique furnishings, in-room fridges and TVs; no cooking facilities, but complimentary continental breakfast. $$$

Randall's Ordinary on Route 2, North Stonington (860–599–4540). In addition to its famous open-hearth-cooked meals, the eighteenth-century inn and tavern on twenty-seven acres has 3 guest rooms with queen-size canopied beds, private baths, and fireplaces in the main inn; 9 rooms with queen-size or double beds and private baths in the adjacent 1819 dairy barn restoration; and a unique silo suite with a fireplace and a winding staircase to a Jacuzzi. The room rate includes breakfast for two guests or a la carte breakfast for any extra guests in the same room or suite. Inquire about the dinner and lodging package for two. $$$–$$$$

Antiques and Accommodations 32 Main Street, North Stonington (860–535–1736). To-die-for antiques and gracious decor in the 1860 main house with 3 lavish guest rooms, one with a fireplace, all with private baths. An equally charming 1820 Garden Cottage has an upper suite with two bedrooms and two baths plus a library and fireplace in a common room; downstairs is a suite with three bedrooms, a complete kitchen, a living room, a private bath, and a fireplace. Furnished throughout with antiques and queen-size canopied beds, this beautiful country inn offers a four-course candlelit breakfast to all guests. The perfect place for a couple's romantic getaway, this B&B is also warmly welcoming to families if you think the children can feel comfortable with and respectful of the furnishings. $$$$

Arbor House at Kruger's Old Maine Farm 75 Chester Maine Road, North Stonington (860–535–4221). Have your kids join their kids at this country-style B&B with ice skating and cross-country skiing in winter and catch-and-release fishing on the pond on summer, plus lots of fun chores to pitch in on as the folks here care for their pigs, goats, chickens, cats, ducks, and sheep. Pluck fresh eggs all year-round and fresh apples right off the trees in the orchard in autumn. Tour the hard-cider winery and sample Mystic Soda to quench your thirst. At night, cozy up in the second-floor guest rooms or the third-floor, two-bedroom suite with adjoining sitting room and private bath if you are taking the whole floor; other options also make this cheerful place perfect for families. Full breakfast. $$$–$$$$

High Acres B&B 222 Northwest Corner Road, Stonington

(860–887–4355). Way out in the country is this 1743 farmhouse with an 1840s addition. Farmland rolls in all around this homestead; horse pastures, equestrian trails, and stables are right on the property. The 5 guest rooms have private baths, queen- and king-size beds, down comforters. Full breakfast. $$$$

Highland Orchards Resort Park 118 Pendleton Hill Road (Route 49), North Stonington (860–599–5101 or 800–624–0829). Family camping resort located on eighty-five acres of a former colonial farm. Offers 270 wooded and open RV and tent sites; swimming pool, fishing pond, miniature golf, playground, basketball, shuffleboard, game room, restrooms, free showers, laundry room, dump station, hookups, firewood, ice, groceries, camp supplies. Open year-round. Nightly and weekly rates; reservations recommended. $

Public Boat Launch

Barn Island Wildlife Management Area Ramp off Palmer Neck Road for Long Island Sound access; take Route 1 to Green Haven Road, go south on Green Haven to Palmer Neck, 1.5 miles to end. Parking for 65 cars. Seasonal fee. Very popular on weekends.

For Further Information

Stonington Community Center (860–535–2476). This organization operates the public DuBois Beach, a community senior center, and four tennis courts also open to the visiting public.

Stonington Historical Society (860–535–1131). Sponsors occasional walking tours and special events.

State Welcome Center I–95 southbound, entering Connecticut at North Stonington from Rhode Island. Open daily year-round; restrooms; staff in summer. Maps, state tourism guides, brochures.

General Index

Special Indexes

About the Author

A lifelong resident of the Connecticut shore, with the exception of a three-year sabbatical on the California coast, Doe Boyle works as a freelance writer and editor in a shoreline house that has been cooled by the breezes from Long Island Sound for more than 250 years. Beach peas and saltspray roses rugosa bloom in her gardens; four daughters have blossomed beside them. Author of Globe Pequot's *Fun with the Family in Connecticut* and eleven children's picturebooks published by Soundprints in association with the National Wildlife Federation and the Smithsonian Institution, Boyle is also a master teaching artist of the Connecticut Commission on the Arts. When not busy sampling boat rides and clam chowders, Boyle is often engaged in classes with Connecticut's young writers.